P9-BBU-820

Start Here!™

Learn Microsoft®
Kinect API

Rob Miles

Published with the authorization of Microsoft Corporation by:
O'Reilly Media, Inc.
1005 Gravenstein Highway North
Sebastopol, California 95472

ISBN: 978-0-735-66396-1

1 2 3 4 5 6 7 8 9 LSI 7 6 5 4 3 2

Printed and bound in the United States of America.

Microsoft Press books are available through booksellers and distributors worldwide. If you need support related to this book, email Microsoft Press Book Support at *mspinput@microsoft.com*. Please tell us what you think of this book at *http://www.microsoft.com/learning/booksurvey*.

Microsoft and the trademarks listed at *http://www.microsoft.com/about/legal/en/us/IntellectualProperty/ Trademarks/EN-US.aspx* are trademarks of the Microsoft group of companies. All other marks are property of their respective owners.

The example companies, organizations, products, domain names, email addresses, logos, people, places, and events depicted herein are fictitious. No association with any real company, organization, product, domain name, email address, logo, person, place, or event is intended or should be inferred.

This book expresses the author's views and opinions. The information contained in this book is provided without any express, statutory, or implied warranties. Neither the author, O'Reilly Media, Inc., Microsoft Corporation, nor its resellers, or distributors will be held liable for any damages caused or alleged to be caused either directly or indirectly by this book.

Acquisitions and Developmental Editor: Russell Jones

Production Editor: Kristen Borg

Editorial Production: Tiffany Rupp, S4Carlisle Publishing Services

Technical Reviewer: Peter Robinson

Copyeditor: Heath Lynn Silberfeld

Indexer: WordCo Indexing Services, Inc.

Cover Design: Jake Rae

Cover Composition: Karen Montgomery

Illustrator: S4Carlisle Publishing Services

To Gus

Contents at a Glance

Contents

What do you think of this book? We want to hear from you!

Microsoft is interested in hearing your feedback so we can continually improve our books and learning resources for you. To participate in a brief online survey, please visit:

microsoft.com/learning/booksurvey

Chapter 12 Taking Kinect Further   229

What do you think of this book? We want to hear from you!

Microsoft is interested in hearing your feedback so we can continually improve our
books and learning resources for you. To participate in a brief online survey, please visit:

microsoft.com/learning/booksurvey

Introduction

The Kinect sensor provides a genuinely new way for a computer to make some sense of the world around it. The fusion of a camera, a directional microphone system, and a depth sensor into a single, mass-market device provides an opportunity for software developers to advance the field of computer interaction in all kinds of exciting ways.

It is now possible to create programs that use the Kinect sensor to create a computer interface with the ability to recognize users and understand their intentions using a "natural" user interface consisting of gestures and spoken commands. In addition, the device's capabilities have a huge range of possible applications, from burglar alarms to robot controllers.

Start Here! Learn the Kinect™ API gives you an overview of how the Kinect sensor works and how the Kinect for Windows SDK exposes each of the data sources. The book introduces each of the sensors in the context of solving a well-defined problem. The full source code is provided for each example program. You will also find plenty of ideas for further development of both the sample programs and your own applications.

In addition to an overview of the Kinect for Windows SDK, this book explores the fundamentals of the signals being processed: how video, audio, depth, and 3D skeleton information can be represented in a program. Also included is coverage of specific programming issues that are highly relevant to the creation of programs that deal with large streams of data from sensors, including memory allocation, creating unmanaged code to improve performance, and threading. If you want to learn more about these aspects of program development, you will find good coverage and sample code that works. Although this book doesn't cover every Kinect for Windows SDK, it provides a solid starting point for experimentation and further development.

Who Should Read This Book

This book is intended to be read by C# developers who have a Kinect sensor, either from an Xbox 360 or a Kinect for Windows device, and want to find out how to use the Kinect for Windows SDK to create programs that can process video, sound, and depth views and perform skeleton tracking. If you have an idea for a product based on the Kinect sensor, you can use this book to get a solid grounding in the technology—and you might even be able to use some of the sample code as the basis of your first steps along the road to a working solution.

Assumptions

This book expects that you have a reasonable understanding of .NET development using the C# programming language. You should be familiar with the Visual Studio 2010 development environment and object-oriented programming development.

All the examples are provided in the C# language. It will be helpful (although not required) if you have some experience with Windows Presentation Foundation (WPF) development. In addition, some examples make use of the XNA game development framework. The key development principles important to the development of Kinect software are explained in some detail, so you can use the text to broaden your programming knowledge.

Who Should *Not* Read This Book

If you have never programmed before, you will not find sufficient background on the C# language to be able to understand the examples. If you want to learn how to use the language, you might consider reading John Mueller's *Start Here!™ Learn Microsoft® Visual C#® 2010* (Microsoft Press, 2011) and/or John Sharp's *Microsoft® Visual C#® 2010 Step by Step* (Microsoft Press, 2011).

The text of this book provides coverage of the managed code Application Programmer Interface (API) supported by the Kinect for Windows SDK. So if you are a C++ developer who wishes to learn how to interact with the Kinect sensor from unmanaged C++ programs, you will find that the code samples supplied will not provide this information.

Organization of This Book

This book is divided into four sections, each of which builds on the previous section to give you an overview of the Kinect sensor, the Kinect for Windows SDK, and how to create programs that make use of the data. Part I, "Getting Started," provides an overview of how the sensor works and how you can get a Kinect sensor connected to and working with your computer. Part II, "Using the Kinect Sensor in Programs," covers the fundamentals of sensor initialization and then introduces each of the data sources, video, depth, and sound. Part III, "Creating Advanced User Interfaces," shows how the Kinect SDK performs body tracking and how a program can use this information. It also shows how data from the sensors can be combined to produce augmented-reality applications. Finally, Part IV, "Kinect in the Real World," shows how you can use the

Kinect to interact with external devices. This section provides additional programming insight and identifies future directions for exploring this fascinating new sensor.

Conventions and Features in This Book

This book presents information using conventions designed to make the information readable and easy to follow:

- Boxed elements with labels such as "Note" provide additional information or alternative methods for completing a step successfully.

- A plus sign (+) between two key names means that you must press those keys at the same time. For example, "Press Alt+Tab" means that you hold down the Alt key while you press the Tab key.

- A vertical bar between two or more menu items (e.g. File | Close), means that you should select the first menu or menu item, then the next, and so on.

System Requirements

You will need the following hardware and software to complete the practice exercises in this book:

- Windows 7, 32- or 64-bit version

- Visual Studio 2010, any edition (multiple downloads may be required if using Express Edition products)

- The Kinect for Windows SDK

- Computer that has a 1 GHz or faster processor (2 GHz recommended)

- 1 GB (32 bit) or 2 GB (64 bit) RAM

- 3.5 GB of available hard disk space

- 5,400 RPM hard disk drive

- DirectX 9 capable video card running at 1024 x 768 or higher-resolution display

- DVD-ROM drive (if installing Visual Studio 2010 from DVD)

- Internet connection to download software or chapter examples

Depending on your Windows configuration, you might require local administrator rights to install or configure Visual Studio 2010 and SQL Server 2008 products.

Code Samples

Most of the chapters in this book include exercises that let you interactively try out new material learned in the main text. All the sample projects can be downloaded from the following page:

http://go.microsoft.com/FWLink/?Linkid=252996

Follow the instructions to download the *KinectStartHereCompanionContent.zip* file.

Installing the Code Samples

Follow these steps to install the code samples on your computer so that you can use them with the exercises in this book:

1. Unzip the *KinectStartHereCompanionContent.zip* file that you downloaded from the book's website to a directory on your hard drive. It's best to create a directory near the root of your drive, such as C:\KinectExamples.

2. If prompted, review the displayed end user license agreement. If you accept the terms, select the accept option, and then click Next.

> **Note** If the license agreement doesn't appear, you can access it from the same webpage from which you downloaded the *KinectStartHere CompanionContent.zip* file.

Using the Code Samples

The folder created by the Setup.exe program contains a subfolder for each chapter. In turn, these subfolders contain a number of subfolders, one for each example. The examples have the folder names provided in this book's text. Each contains the complete Visual Studio project and all the source code and resources required to build them. (To reduce the size of the download file, the examples do not contain the executable programs themselves; you will have to compile the example programs using Visual Studio run them.)

Note Some of the folder paths created by Visual Studio 2010 can be quite "deep"—that is, a folder may contain a subfolder and so on for a number of levels. Installing the sample code in a folder that is already deep in the folder hierarchy on your disk may lead to problems when you try to build the program, because some file systems in use on Windows PC systems have a restriction on the maximum length of a path to a file. If you encounter problems running the example programs, you may be able to solve the problem by moving the examples folder closer to the root of the drive you are using.

Acknowledgments

I'd like to thank the following people: Russell Jones for being such a patient and constructive editor, Peter Robinson for sterling duty on the technical editing front, and Tiffany Timmerman and Kristen Borg for breathing on the text and making it so much nicer to read. Finally, I'd like to thank the Kinect team for making such a fascinating product that is such fun to play with!

Errata and Book Support

We've made every effort to ensure the accuracy of this book and its companion content. Any errors that have been reported since this book was published are listed on our Microsoft Press site at oreilly.com:

http://go.microsoft.com/FWLink/?Linkid=252997

If you find an error that is not already listed, you can report it to us through the same page.

If you need additional support, please email Microsoft Press Book Support at mspinput@microsoft.com.

Please note that product support for Microsoft software is not offered through the addresses above.

We Want to Hear from You

At Microsoft Press, your satisfaction is our top priority, and your feedback our most valuable asset. Please tell us what you think of this book at:

http://www.microsoft.com/learning/booksurvey

The survey is short, and we read every one of your comments and ideas. Thanks in advance for your input!

Stay in Touch

Let's keep the conversation going! We're on Twitter:

http://twitter.com/MicrosoftPress

Getting Started

In this section you will learn what happens inside the Kinect sensor and how it collects data that lets it see and hear the environment around it. You'll also find out how the signals that it collects are sent over to your computer or Xbox 360. Finally, you will install the Kinect SDK and work with the software to build your first programs that use data from the sensor.

Chapter 1

An Introduction to Kinect

After completing this chapter, you will:

- Understand how the Kinect sensor generates data about the world around it

- Identify the key components of the Kinect sensor and how they work

- Appreciate how the sensors and the Kinect provide useful signals to a connected computer or console

The Kinect Sensor

UNTIL RECENTLY COMPUTERS HAD A very restricted view of the world around them, and users had very limited ways of communicating with computers. Over the years, computers have acquired cameras and audio inputs, but these have been used mostly for *unrecognized* input; computers can store and play such content, but it has been very difficult to make computers *understand* input in these forms.

For example, when people hear a sound, they can make judgments about the distance and direction of the sound source relative to their own position. Until recently, computers had more trouble making such judgments. Audio information from a number of microphones does provide considerable information about the distance and direction of the audio source, but determining this information is difficult for programs to do. Similarly, a video picture provides an image of the environment for the computer to analyze, but a computer has to work very hard to extract information about the objects in pictures or video because an image shows a flat, two-dimensional representation of a three-dimensional world.

Kinect changes all this. The Kinect sensor bar contains two cameras, a special infrared light source, and four microphones. It also contains a stack of *signal processing hardware* that is able to make sense of all the data that the cameras, infrared light, and microphones can generate. By combining the output from these sensors, a program can track and recognize objects in front of it, determine the direction of sound signals, and isolate them from background noise.

Getting Inside a Kinect Sensor

To get an idea of how the Kinect sensor works, you could take one apart and look inside. (Don't do that. There are many reasons why taking your Kinect apart is a bad idea: it's hard to do, you will invalidate your warranty, and you might not be able to restore it to working condition. But perhaps the best reason not to take it apart is that I've already done it for you!)

Figure 1-1 shows a Kinect sensor when it is "fully dressed."

FIGURE 1-1 A Kinect sensor.

Figure 1-2 shows a Kinect with the cover removed. You can see the two cameras in the middle and the special light source on the left. The four microphones are arranged along the bottom of the sensor bar. Together, these devices provide the "view" the Kinect has of the world in front of it.

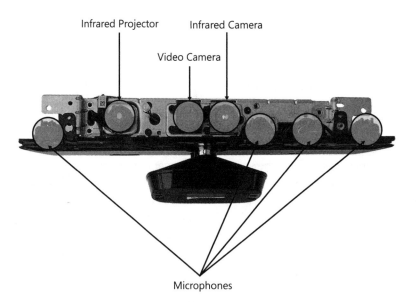

FIGURE 1-2 A Kinect sensor unwrapped.

Figure 1-3 shows all the hardware inside the Kinect that makes sense of the information being supplied from all the various devices.

FIGURE 1-3 The Kinect sensor data processing hardware.

To make everything fit into the slim bar form, the designers had to stack the circuit boards on top of each other. Some of these components produce quite a bit of heat, so a tiny fan that can be seen on the far right of Figure 1-3 sucks air along the circuits to keep them cool. The base contains an electric motor and gear assembly that lets the Kinect adjust its angle of view vertically.

Now that you have seen inside the device, you can consider how each component helps the Kinect do what it does, starting with the "3D" camera.

The Depth Sensor

Kinect has the unique ability to "see" in 3D. Unlike most other computer vision systems, the Kinect system is able to build a "depth map" of the area in front of it. This map is produced entirely within the sensor bar and then transmitted down the USB cable to the host in the same way as a typical camera image would be transferred—except that rather than color information for each pixel in an image, the sensor transmits distance values.

You might think that the depth sensor uses some kind of radar or ultrasonic sound transmitter to measure how far things are from the sensor bar, but actually it doesn't. This would be difficult to do over a short distance. Instead, the sensor uses a clever technique consisting of an infrared projector and a camera that can see the tiny dots that the projector produces.

Figure 1-4 shows the arrangement of the infrared projector and sensor.

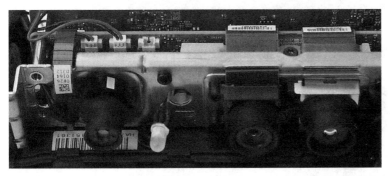

FIGURE 1-4 The Kinect infrared projector and camera.

The projector is the left-hand item in the Figure 1-4. It looks somewhat like a camera, but in fact it is a tiny infrared projector. The infrared camera is on the right side of Figure 1-4. In between the projector and the camera is an LED that displays the Kinect device status, and a camera that captures a standard 2D view of the scene. To explain how the Kinect sensor works, I'll start by showing an ordinary scene in my house. Figure 1-5 shows my sofa as a person (okay, a camera) might see it in a room.

FIGURE 1-5 My sofa.

In contrast, Figure 1-6 shows how the Kinect infrared sensor sees the same view.

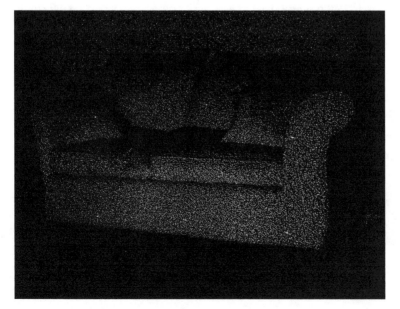

FIGURE 1-6 The sofa as the Kinect infrared sensor sees it.

The Kinect infrared sensor sees the sofa as a large number of tiny dots. The Kinect sensor constantly projects these dots over the area in its view. If you want to view the dots yourself, it's actually very easy; all you need is a video camera or camcorder that has a night vision mode. A camera in night vision mode is sensitive to the infrared light spectrum that the Kinect distance sensor uses.

Figure 1-6, for example, was taken in complete darkness, with the sofa lit only by the Kinect. The infrared sensor in the Kinect is fitted with a filter that keeps out ordinary light, which is how it can see just the infrared dots, even in a brightly lit room. The dots are arranged in a pseudo-random pattern that is hardwired into the sensor. You can see some of the pattern in Figure 1-7.

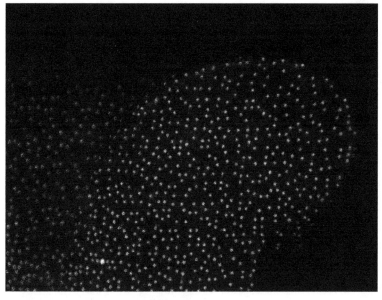

FIGURE 1-7 The dot pattern on the sofa arm.

A pseudo-random sequence is one that appears to be random, but it is actually mechanically generated and easy to repeat. What's important to remember here is that the Kinect sensor "knows" what the pattern looks like and how it is drawn. It can then compare the image from the camera with the pattern it knows it is displaying, and can use the difference between the two to calculate the distance of each point from the sensor.

To understand how the Kinect does this, you can perform a simple experiment involving a darkened room, a piece of paper, a flashlight, and a helpful friend. You need to adjust the flashlight beam so it's tightly focused and makes a small spot. Now, get your friend to stand about 5 feet (1.5 meters) away from you, slightly to your right. Ask your friend to hold the paper to the front of you, holding the torch in your left hand, shine the torch dot onto the piece of paper. Now ask your friend to move forward toward you. As the person comes closer, you will see that the dot on the paper moves a little to the left because it now hits the paper before it has traveled quite as far to the right.

Figure 1-8 shows how this works. If you know the place you are aiming the dot, you can work out how far away your friend is by the position of the dot on the paper. The impressive thing about the Kinect sensor is that it performs that calculation for thousands of dots, many times a second. The infrared camera in the Kinect allows it to "see" where the dot appears in the image. Because the software knows the pattern that the infrared transmitter is drawing, the hardware inside the Kinect does all the calculations that are required to produce the "depth image" of the scene that is sent to the computer or Xbox.

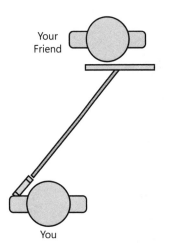

FIGURE 1-8 Showing how the Kinect distance sensor works.

This technique is interesting because it is completely different from the way that humans see distance. Each human eye gets a slightly different view of a scene, which means that the closer an object is to a human, the greater the difference between the images seen by each eye. The brain identifies the objects in the scene, determines how much difference there is between the image from each eye, and then assigns a distance value to each object.

In contrast, the Kinect sensor shines a tightly focused spot of light on points in the scene and then works out how far away that point is from the sensor by analyzing the spot's reflection. The Kinect itself doesn't identify any objects in a scene; that task is performed by software in an Xbox or computer, as you'll see later.

The Kinect Microphones

The Kinect sensor also contains four microphones arranged along the bottom of the bar. You can see them in Figure 1-2: two on the left and right ends, and two more on the right side of the unit. The Kinect uses these microphones to help determine from where in a room a particular voice is coming. This works because sound takes time to travel through air. Sound travels much more slowly than light, which is why you often hear a thunderclap long after seeing the corresponding bolt of lightning.

When you speak to the Kinect sensor, your voice will arrive at each microphone at different times, because each microphone is a slightly different distance away from the sound source. Software can then extract your voice waveform from the sound signal produced by each microphone and—using the timing information—calculate where the sound source is in the room. If several people are in a room with the Kinect, it can even work out which person is talking by calculating the direction from which their voice is coming, and can then "direct" the microphone array to listen to that area of the room. It can then remove "unwanted" sounds from that signal to make it easier to understand the speech content.

From a control point of view, when a program knows where the speech is coming from (perhaps by using the distance sensor), it can direct the microphone array in that direction, essentially creating a software version of the directional microphones that are physically pointed at actors to record their voices when filming motion pictures.

Recognizing People with Kinect

One very popular use for the Kinect sensor is recognizing and tracking people standing in front of it. The Kinect sensor itself does not recognize people; it simply sends the depth image to the host device, such as an Xbox or computer. Software running on the host device contains logic to decode the information and recognize elements in the image with characteristic human shapes. The software has been "trained" with a wide variety of body shapes. It uses the alignment of the various body parts, along with the way that they move, to identify and track them.

Figure 1-9 shows the output produced by the body-tracking software as a "stick figure" with lines joining the various elements.

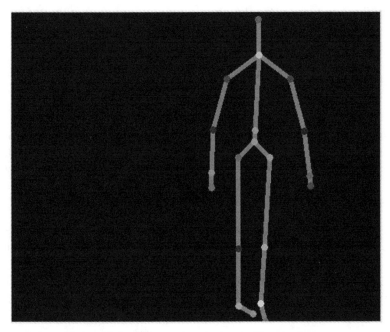

FIGURE 1-9 Skeleton information retrieved using the Kinect software.

The Kinect software can also recognize the height and proportions of a particular person. For example, this feature lets Xbox Live users "train" their Xbox so it recognizes them when they walk into a room.

Programming the Kinect

The software described in the previous sections, and which you'll see more of in this book, is called the *Kinect for Windows Software Development Kit* (SDK). Installing the SDK lets you write programs that use the power of the Kinect at different levels. You can obtain direct access to the low-level video and depth signals and create applications that use that low-level data, or you can make use of the powerful library features built into the SDK that make it easy for a program to identify and track users.

You can download the Kinect for Windows SDK for free. The SDK provides a set of libraries that you can add to your own programs and games so they can use the sensor. The SDK also contains all the drivers that you need to link a Kinect to your computer.

You can use the Kinect SDK from a *managed code* programming language (such as C# or Visual Basic.NET) or from unmanaged C++. The SDK provides a set of objects that expose properties and methods you can use in your programs. The following chapters explore how you can write programs that use these objects to create some novel and fun programs that support completely new ways of interacting with a computer.

The next chapter describes how to install the SDK on your computer and get it connected and talking to the Kinect.

Kinect for Xbox and Kinect for Windows

You can write programs that use either the Kinect for Xbox sensor or the Kinect for Windows sensor. The Kinect for Xbox sensor has been set up to allow it to be most effective when tracking the figures of game players. This means that it can track objects that are up to 12 feet (4.0 meters) away from the sensor but cannot track any objects that are closer than 24 inches (80 cm). The Kinect for Windows sensor has been set up to allow it to track a single user of a computer, and it has much better short-range performance as it is able to track objects as close to the sensor as 12 inches (40 cm).

The Kinect for Windows SDK was, as the name implies, primarily created for use with the Kinect for Windows sensor, but it will also work with an Xbox 360 Kinect sensor. Microsoft engineers will provide support into the future for Xbox Kinect from this SDK, but for best results, particularly if you want to track objects very close to the sensor bar, you should invest in a Kinect for Windows sensor device. The Kinect for Windows device can even track individual finger movements and gestures of the computer user.

The bottom line is that if you have an Xbox 360 with a Kinect device attached to it, you can use that sensor to have some fun learning how to create programs that can see, measure distance, and hear users. However, if you want to get serious about providing a product of your own that is based on the Kinect sensor, you should target the Kinect for Windows device. If you want complete details of how this all works, read the detailed End User License here:

http://www.microsoft.com/en-us/kinectforwindows/develop/sdk-eula.aspx

Summary

This chapter gave you a look inside the Kinect sensor so you could see (without having to take your own Kinect apart) how complex it is. You saw that the Kinect contains two cameras (one infrared camera and one video camera) and a special infrared transmitter that produces a grid of dots that measure the distance of objects from the Kinect and to compose a "depth map" of the image. You also learned that the Kinect sensor contains four microphones that can be used to remove background noise from an audio signal and to listen to sound from particular parts of a room.

You also saw that the Kinect sensor sends this data to a host device (Xbox or computer), which then processes the data in various ways, including recognizing the position, movement, and even the identity of people in front of the Kinect.

You also found out that two Kinect sensor bars are available, both of which can be used with the Kinect for Windows Software Development Kit (SDK). The Kinect for Xbox device has a good long-range performance for tracking game players, and the Kinect for Windows device has been optimized for shorter-range tracking so that a single computer user can use it to interact with a system that is nearby.

Chapter 2

Getting Started with Kinect

After completing this chapter, you will:

■ Identify any prerequisites to work with Kinect on your computer

■ Have installed the Kinect for Windows SDK on your computer

■ Have connected the Kinect sensor bar and tested it on your machine

Kinect for Windows SDK Prerequisites

THE KINECT FOR WINDOWS SDK fits alongside an installation of Visual Studio 2010 on your Windows computer. It works on Windows 7. In this section we will look at the things you need to have to get the best out of your Kinect sensor.

Kinect Device

It should come as no surprise that you will need a Kinect device and its power supply along with a USB port so you can plug it into your computer. You can use either of two Kinect sensor bars with the Kinect for Windows SDK. You can use a Kinect sensor from an Xbox console, or you can use a Kinect for Windows sensor that has been optimized for computer use. The examples in this book will work with either sensor bar.

It is best if the Kinect is given exclusive use of a USB connection—that is, if you have a USB hub with your webcam, printer, and external hard disk plugged into it, you should not add the Kinect to the hub as well. The Kinect sensor can produce a lot of data, and it works best if it has exclusive use of its own USB connection.

Note You should plug the Kinect sensor into your computer *after* you have installed the Kinect for Windows SDK. When the SDK is installed, it also adds the USB drivers needed for Kinect; these are not provided as part of a standard Windows 7 installation.

Visual Studio

Before you install the Kinect for Windows SDK, you must make sure that you have Visual Studio 2010 installed on your machine. The SDK can be used with either C++, C#, or Visual Basic .NET. This text will focus on the use of C# to create managed applications that use the sensor, but the fundamentals of the way the libraries present data to your programs are the same. You can use any version of Visual Studio 2010, including those that are available for free from the Visual Studio Express website:

http://www.microsoft.com/express

DirectX Studio

Some of the C++ examples that are supplied with the Kinect SDK make use of the DirectX graphics SDK. If you want to compile and run these programs, you will need to have the DirectX SDK installed. You can download the SDK from here:

http://msdn.microsoft.com/en-us/directx

There is no need to install this SDK if you only plan to use the Kinect SDK from C# and Visual Basic .NET.

Installing the Kinect for Windows SDK

The Kinect for Windows SDK is a free download. The SDK also contains the USB drivers for the various elements inside the Kinect sensor itself. You can find the Kinect for Windows SDK at the Kinect for Windows website:

http://kinectforwindows.org

This site also contains links to detailed descriptions of the Kinect and other useful resources.

Note Although the SDK is provided free of charge, this does not mean that it is free for commercial purposes. Using the Kinect SDK for personal experimentation is not a commercial purpose. It is also not a commercial purpose to use the Kinect SDK in the process of teaching or academic research, even if you are regularly employed as a teacher or professor or if you intend to apply for research grants through such research. However, if you intend to sell a product based on the Kinect device, you should read the License Agreement.

Installing the Kinect SDK

You should make sure that any older Kinect drivers that are not part of the Kinect system are removed from your system before you install the Kinect SDK. You should also make sure that Visual Studio 2010 is installed on your Windows computer (but not actually open) when you perform the install. If you have any problems you should check out the "Troubleshooting Your Kinect Installation" section at the end of this chapter. To install the Kinect SDK on your PC follow this sequence:

1. You can perform the installation of the Kinect SDK directly from the download webpage:

    http://www.microsoft.com/en-us/kinectforwindows/develop

2. To do this you should click on the Download link to select the appropriate version for your system.

3. Your browser will ask you if you want to run or save the install file. You should select the Run option, as shown above. Click Run to start the installer, which will display the Welcome Screen as shown below.

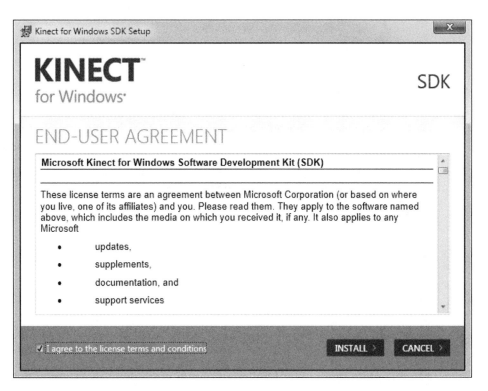

4. When the Install program starts, you will first see the Welcome Screen as shown previously. Select the tick box to accept the terms of the licensing conditions, and then click Install to begin installation.

5. Because this is a software installation on your computer, you may see a User Account Control dialog box confirming that you are going to allow the installer to make changes to the computer. Click Yes to continue.

6. The installation will now begin. During the installation it might be necessary to install some Visual C++ runtime components, as shown above. Just confirm the installation of each element in turn. Eventually you will see the completion dialog box, as shown below.

7. Once the installation has completed, you can create programs that use the Kinect for Windows SDK. You can also run programs that have been built using the Kinect SDK.

If you want to send your programs to Windows computer owners who will not be developing Kinect applications, the recipients must install the runtime version of Kinect for Windows. This contains the Kinect libraries and USB drivers, but it cannot be used to create new Kinect for Windows applications. The runtime version can be downloaded from the following website:

*http://download.microsoft.com/download/E/E/2/EE2D29A1-2D5C-463C-B7F1-40E4170F5E2C/
KinectRuntime-v1.0-Setup.exe*

Connecting the Kinect Sensor Bar

After you have installed the Kinect SDK, you can connect the sensor bar to your computer. The Kinect sensor bar works with any Windows computer that has a USB connection.

> **Note** Although you may not be using the Kinect sensor for playing games, you should still be mindful of how the sensor should be positioned and used. If you are using the sensor to detect movement and gestures, allow plenty of space around the device for operators to interact with the sensor. The sensor itself is not able to register depth information of objects that are closer than about 24 inches (800 mm), so make sure that it has a bit of breathing room in front of it.

Powering the Kinect Sensor

The Kinect sensor bar uses more power than is available from a standard USB connection. It needs about 1.5 amps of current, whereas a standard USB port on a computer is only able to supply 0.5 amp. A Kinect sensor bar can get the extra power in either of two ways. The newer, small Xbox 360 consoles have a specially modified USB connection on the back that can provide extra current. Owners of the older, larger Xbox 360s must use the Kinect power supply that is connected between the sensor bar and the console. The Kinect power supply allows use of the Kinect sensor bar with any device that has a standard USB connection.

The plug on the end of the wire coming from the Kinect sensor bar looks a bit like a USB plug, but in fact it is special and has one corner cut off so that it will not fit directly into a USB port in a desktop computer or laptop. If you force the Kinect plug into a standard USB socket, you will break the socket and do expensive damage to your system. Instead, use the Kinect power supply that is connected between the Kinect plug and the USB connection on your computer. The cable from the power supply includes a USB plug that can be fitted safely into a computer.

Once you have positioned your sensor bar and connected it to a power source, you are ready to connect it to your computer.

Installing the Kinect Sensor USB Drivers

The very first time that you plug the Kinect sensor bar into your Windows computer, it will automatically install all the USB drivers that are required. To ensure that you get the latest version of the drivers, your Windows computer will contact Windows Update during the install. It is therefore a good idea to connect the sensor bar for the first time when your computer has a working Internet connection.

Figure 2-1 shows the results of a successful Kinect installation. If the drivers do not install successfully, this may be because you have older drivers on your machine that need to be removed. Take a look in the "Troubleshooting Your Kinect Installation" section at the end of this chapter for details of how to search for and remove these drivers.

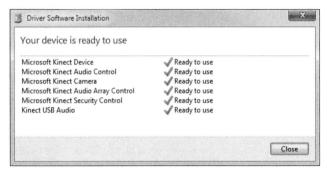

FIGURE 2-1 A successful driver installation.

Testing the Kinect Sensor Bar

The Kinect for Windows SDK is provided with some sample applications that you can use to demonstrate that the Kinect sensor is working correctly. Later in this book, we will take a look inside these applications to find out how they work.

The Kinect SDK Sample Browser

This sample allows you to demonstrate that the video and infrared cameras are working properly. It also gives a very good demonstration of the body-tracking abilities of the Kinect system. The program is supplied as part of the SDK and will be copied onto your computer when you install the

Kinect for Windows SDK on it. You can find the program on the Windows Start Menu in All Programs | Microsoft Kinect SDK v1.0 | Kinect SDK Sample Browser (Figure 2-2).

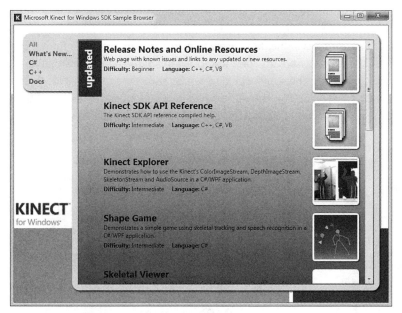

FIGURE 2-2 The Kinect SDK Sample Browser.

When you run the program, it displays a number of options that allow you to view documentation and run a number of sample programs, including the Kinect Explorer program (Figure 2-3).

FIGURE 2-3 Selecting the Kinect Explorer program.

If you click on the Kinect Explorer program, you get the option to read the documentation, install the sample code on your machine, and run the program.

Figure 2-4 shows the main screen displayed by Kinect Explorer. On the left is the image from the video camera, with the bones of any tracked skeletons displayed on top of it. On the right is the image from the "depth" camera. Points in the depth view that are different distances from the sensor are given different colors. The viewer also adds color to those parts of the depth view that have been identified as being part of a person in the scene. The display also shows the rate at which the display is being updated in frames per second (FPS). The sensors generate 30 frames per second. If the computer running Kinect Explorer is not fast enough to process and display each frame, this number will be lower.

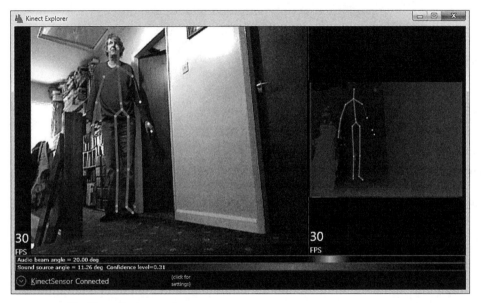

FIGURE 2-4 The Kinect Explorer main screen.

By clicking the down arrow at the bottom right of the screen, you can open the Settings menu, which allows you to configure the sensors in the Kinect device.

Figure 2-5 shows the options display. You can change the resolution of the color and depth cameras and also select the type of skeleton tracking that the program uses. You can also use the slider at the right side of the options to adjust the elevation angle of the sensor. This controls the motor in the base of the Kinect sensor and allows for adjustment of the angle of the sensor to get the best view of the scene.

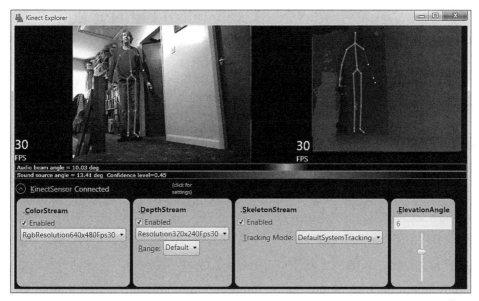

FIGURE 2-5 Kinect Explorer with option screen.

The Kinect Explorer program also shows how Kinect uses the four microphones in the sensor bar to locate sound. It displays the angle from the sensor to any sound source that it detects as well as the angle of the audio beam that it has directed at the sound. If you make a noise in front of the sensor, you will see that the display changes to display where in front of the sensor the sound came from. In the display in Figure 2-5, the indicator underneath the right-hand "30 FPS" shows the direction in which the microphone is being aimed, with the broader area underneath giving the broad area from where the sound is coming.

Kinect Explorer provides a very good introduction to the capabilities of the sensor. You will discover how each part of the Kinect sensor works and how to use it from your programs in the coming chapters of this book.

Troubleshooting Your Kinect Installation

Most of my installations of the Kinect for Windows SDK and the sensor bar have had no problems. However, you might find the following troubleshooting tips useful.

Remove Old SDK Installations

Ensure that you have removed all the previous Kinect Beta SDKs. These can be removed using the Control Panel at Control Panel\Programs\Programs and Features.

Ensure That Visual Studio 2010 Is Installed but Not Running During Installation

During the Kinect SDK installation the installer will add some environment settings that are picked up by Visual Studio 2010. For this to complete successfully, it is important that Visual Studio is not running on the computer when the Kinect SDK is installed.

Ensure That There Are No Windows Updates in Progress

The installation process will modify some system files that might be in use during a Windows Update. Before you start the Kinect SDK installation, you should check in the Control Panel at Control Panel | System and Security | Windows Update to make sure that no updates are in progress. You also should check to see if any updates are waiting to perform a reboot.

Ensure That the Kinect Is Powered Correctly

If Kinect fails to install all the USB drivers when it is plugged into the Windows computer for the first time, it may be because the sensor bar is not receiving any power. Make sure that the Kinect power supply is plugged in and that the green light on the power connector is lit.

If the Kinect is showing a steady red light, this may mean that the power supply is not correctly connected. When the Kinect is working correctly, the indicator light on the front of the sensor bar should flash green.

Remove Any Old USB Drivers

Make sure that any older Kinect drivers that are not part of the Kinect system are removed from your system before you install the Kinect SDK. If you have any problems with the Kinect device not being properly recognized because you have used other drivers, you can do the following:

1. Ensure that the Kinect sensor is not connected to your computer.

2. Open up a new command prompt running as an Administrator user. The best way to do this is to click the Start button, type **CMD** into the search box that appears, and then hold down CTRL+SHIFT and press Enter. If you get this right you will be rewarded with a User Account Control dialog box asking for permission to allow the Command Processor to make changes to this computer. Click OK.

3. Next, you need to set an environment variable to tell the Device Manager that you want to see all the hardware devices registered for this computer, not just the ones that are active at the moment. In the Command box, give the following command:

```
SET DEVMGR_SHOW_NONPRESENT_DEVICES=1
```

Note If you type this command incorrectly, you won't see an error of any kind, but the process won't work correctly as the Device Manager will not show you non-present devices.

4. Now you can give the command to start the Device Manager:

```
devmgmt.msc
```

5. Next, open the View menu and select Show Hidden Devices. This is actually quite fun, as now you will see every device that has ever been connected to your computer.

Note Your computer installation will look slightly different from this one.

6. If you use your machine like I use mine, you will see 50 or so different disk drives: one for every memory key that has been plugged in over the years. Look through the device tree for items with the word *Kinect* in the name, or the name of the package you are removing. Look in the "Human Interface Devices," "Sound, Video and Game Controllers," and "Universal Serial Bus Controllers" parts. To remove a driver, right-click on it in the list and then select Uninstall from the properties menu for that driver, as shown above. If the dialog that appears has a checkbox marked "Remove Driver Software Files," then you should select this so that the driver files are no longer on the machine.

Note You must be careful to remove drivers only for the Kinect sensor bar. If you are not sure which drivers are being loaded, you could plug the Kinect sensor in before you remove the driver and note what happens in the Device Manager when you do this. Drivers that become active at this point should be removed.

7. Once you have removed all the drivers, exit Device Manager and close the command prompt. Now you can plug in the sensor bar and the latest versions of the drivers should be loaded.

Summary

In this chapter you have seen how to get a Kinect sensor bar working with a Windows 7 computer and had a quick glimpse of its capabilities. In the next chapter you will write some code of your own to use the signals that the sensor bar produces.

Chapter 3

Writing Software for Kinect

After completing this chapter, you will:

- Understand how the Kinect libraries are added to programs that use the Kinect sensor

- Know how to create a Kinect runtime instance and connect to services that it provides

- Have created your first fully working Kinect application: a video camera display that uses the camera in the Kinect sensor

Making a Kinect Video Camera

YOU ARE GOING TO START by making a Windows application that gets the video stream from the Kinect camera and displays it on your PC. This will allow you to find out how to add the Kinect software to a project and then get information from the Kinect sensor bar.

Creating a New Visual Studio Project for Kinect

Installing the Kinect SDK does not add any extra features to the copy of Visual Studio 2010 on your computer. Instead, a library of classes is copied to your Windows PC. These classes contain the program code that communicates via the USB drivers to the Kinect sensor bar. When you want to create your program that uses the Kinect sensor, you must add this library file to your project. You are going to create a Visual Studio project and then add the Kinect resource to this project. You will need to do this each time you create a new Kinect program.

Creating a new Kinect Program

You are going to create a Windows Presentation Foundation (WPF) application and then add the Kinect classes so that the program can use the Kinect sensor bar. This text assumes that you are familiar with WPF programs. If you have not written WPF programs before, you will find it useful to read *Microsoft Visual C# 2010 Step by Step* by John Sharp (Microsoft Press, ISBN 0735626707), which provides a good introduction to C# and WPF.

1. The first thing you do is create a new Visual Studio Solution. Start Visual Studio and choose File | New | Project from the menu. This will open the New Project dialog box, as shown below. Find your way to the Visual C# Windows project list, and select WPF Application as shown below. Give your project the name KinectCam, and then click OK to create it.

2. Your program will use the Kinect SDK assemblies to control the Kinect sensor. Now you are going to add the Kinect SDK assemblies to your KinectCam project. Find the Solution Explorer in Visual Studio, and right-click the References item. This will cause the context menu to appear. Select Add Reference from this menu, as shown below.

3. The Add Reference dialog will now appear. The Kinect libraries were copied onto your system when you installed the Kinect SDK, and you will now have to find them. Select the Browse tab in the dialog box and navigate to the library assembly, as shown below, and click OK. If you have done a standard installation of the SDK you should be able to find the files in the following location or something similar, depending on the version of the Kinect SDK on your computer:

C:\Program Files\Microsoft SDKs\Kinect\v1.0\Assemblies\Microsoft.Kinect.dll

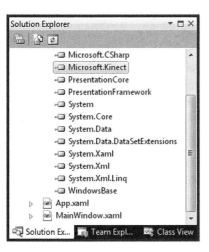

4. Once you have added the Kinect assemblies to the project, you should see them appear in the Solution Explorer for the project, as shown below.

5. Now that the project contains the library files, you can now add a using statement to the very top of your program. This makes it easier to use the Kinect classes in your programs. Rather than having to refer to the Kinect classes by their fully qualified name (e.g., Microsoft. Kinect.KinectSensor), once the using directive has been added, a program can just refer to KinectSensor and the C# compiler will automatically search the namespace for the class.

```
using Microsoft.Kinect;
```

Once you have added these elements to your program, your code can make use of the Kinect classes.

> **Note** The program you have created contains a reference to the Kinect libraries on the machine it is loaded on. It will not work on a system that doesn't have the Kinect SDK or the Kinect Runtimes installed on it.

You must follow this process to create any project that needs to use the Kinect sensor bar. This includes applications built for Windows Console, Windows Forms, WPF, or XNA games.

At this point you have a project that should run. You can press the F5 key to start the program, but all it will do is draw an empty form. Next you need to start the Kinect sensor running and get some video images from it.

Getting the Kinect Sensor Working

At this point the project has Kinect libraries installed but is not using Kinect to do anything. The program will build and run, but it does not make use of any of the Kinect features. In fact it doesn't do anything. The next thing to do is get control of Kinect.

Using the KinectSensor Class to Control the Kinect Sensor

To interact with Kinect, your program needs to obtain an instance of the *KinectSensor* class. This class is part of the Kinect SDK and will manage the connection to the sensor bar. You can think of the *KinectSensor* instance as a kind of "engine room" for the Kinect. Your program will send commands to the *KinectSensor* class in just the same way as a Starship captain would ask for "warp factor nine." The *KinectSensor* instance will either perform the task or send some kind of error response. You will add the error handling later.

1. You declare *KinectSensor* reference as a member of the *MainWindow* class in the application. Your program can then use this variable every time it wants to use the runtime instance to get the Kinect to perform a task. You can call the variable *myKinect*. The Kinect SDK can actually control multiple Kinect sensor bars so that a program can "see" several areas at once.

This program is going to use just one sensor bar. To declare *myKinect*, you first need to open the program source file that controls the main window in our program. Find the entry for the file *MainWindow.xaml.cs* in Visual Studio Solution Explorer, then double-click it to open the file.

2. You declare *myKinect* as a member of the *MainWindow* class in the application. The program can then use this variable every time it wants to control the Kinect. Add the declaration of the variable *myKinect* at the top of the program file, as shown below. This makes it possible for any of the methods in the *MainWindow* class to use the sensor.

```
public partial class MainWindow : Window
{
    KinectSensor myKinect;

    // rest of MainWindow here
}
```

3. Next, you need to add some C# code to set the variable *myKinect* to refer to an instance of the *KinectSensor* class that will be used to control the Kinect. The variable must be set up when the program starts running. The best place to do this would be in a *Window_Loaded* event handler method in *MainWindow*. This method will be called when the main window is loaded at the start of the program. You can get the Visual Studio designer to create this method and connect it to the *Window_Loaded* event.

4. To create the event handler, you should use the Solution Explorer in Visual Studio to open the *MainWindows.xaml* file in the *KinectCam* project. Next you must ensure that the Properties window is visible. It is normally in the bottom-left corner of the Visual Studio Windows. If you can't see it, select Properties window from the View menu in Visual Studio. Then follow the sequence shown above. Click on Window in the XAML file to select it. Then select the Events tab in the properties display for the window. Finally, create a handler for the *Loaded* event by double-clicking, as shown on the next page.

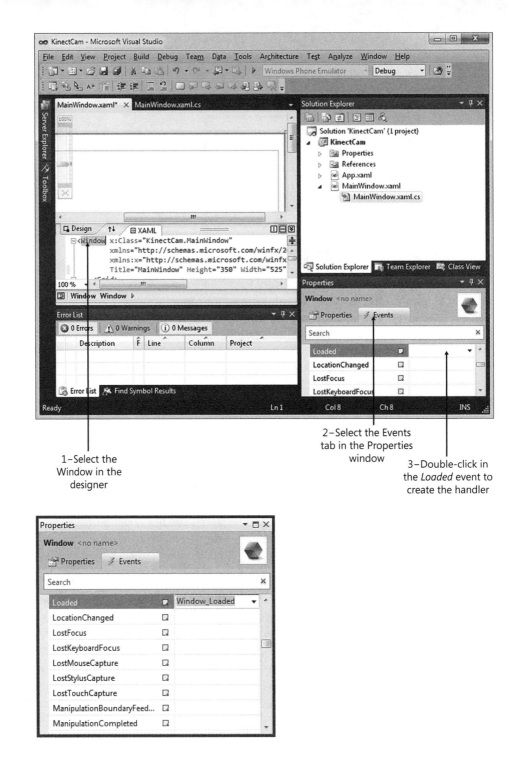

1–Select the Window in the designer

2–Select the Events tab in the Properties window

3–Double-click in the *Loaded* event to create the handler

5. If everything has worked properly, you should find that you have a *Window_Loaded* method defined in the events properties, as shown above. Visual Studio should also have moved to the *MainWindow.xaml.cs* file and be showing you the empty method:

```
private void Window_Loaded(object sender, RoutedEventArgs e)
{

}
```

6. This method will run when the program is started. At the moment it does nothing. You have to make it set the value of *myKinect* to refer to the *KinectSensor* class that the program will be using. You have already seen that the *KinectSensor* class is part of the Kinect SDK. It manages the connections to the Kinect sensor devices that can be connected to the computer. You want to make *myKinect* refer to the first (and only) sensor plugged into your machine. If you become rich enough to buy another sensor, or pair up with someone who has another sensor bar, you can change this code to allow multiple sensor bars to be connected. The Kinect sensors installed on a machine are provided by the *KinectSensor* class as a collection. You can get a hold of the first Kinect in the list by asking for the one at subscript zero in the list. The subscript is the value that tells C# which element of the array to use. In C# arrays and collections, start counting at zero so the element at the beginning of an array or item in a collection has the subscript zero. You should add the statement below to the *Window_Loaded* method.

```
myKinect = KinectSensor.KinectSensors[0];
```

7. Now that the program has an object that can be used to control a Kinect sensor, it can start giving the sensor orders. The first thing it must do is initialize the sensor and tell the sensor what kind of data to produce. We can ask the sensor for several different kinds of data. Your first program is just going to use the color video signal, so it must call the *Enable* method as follows. This version of the *Enable* method has no parameters and asks the Kinect sensor to generate video frames that are 640 pixels wide and 480 pixels high at the rate of 30 frames a second. You can add a parameter to the *Enable* method if you want different resolutions.

```
myKinect.ColorStream.Enable();
```

8. When the program starts running it will configure the Kinect to generate a stream of color images. The next thing the program must do is to tell the sensor what to do when it has captured some new video data to be displayed. The program will use an event handler to do this. Effectively it will say to *myKinect*, "When you get a new frame to display, call this method, which will draw it on the screen." You can get Visual Studio to generate the event handler method for you. Start by typing the following into the *Window_Loaded* method just underneath the call of *Initialize*:

```
myKinect. ColorFrameReady +=
```

9. Visual Studio will offer to create a connection to the event handler for you by popping up a helpful dialog. Press Tab to insert the suggested code.

```
myKinect.ColorFrameReady +=
            new EventHandler<ColorImageFrameReadyEventArgs>(myKinect_ColorFrameReady);   (Press TAB to insert)
```

10. Visual Studio will now offer to create the event handler for you by popping up another helpful dialog. Press Tab again to insert the suggested code.

```
myKinect.ColorFrameReady +=new EventHandler<ColorImageFrameReadyEventArgs>(myKinect_ColorFrameReady);
            Press TAB to generate handler 'myKinect_ColorFrameReady' in this class
```

11. The final thing you need to do is actually switch on the Kinect sensor. You do this by adding a final method call.

```
myKinect.Start();
```

You should now have two new methods in the *MainWindow* class. One runs when the program starts, configures the Kinect, and starts capturing video. The other will be run by the Kinect drivers whenever they have a new video frame to display. The *MainWindow* class in the program file *MainWindow.xaml.cs* should look a bit like this (I have added some comments to make the code clearer):

```
public partial class MainWindow : Window
{
    KinectSensor myKinect;

    public MainWindow()
    {
        InitializeComponent();
    }

    private void Window_Loaded(object sender, RoutedEventArgs e)
    {
        // Get the first Kinect on the computer
        myKinect = KinectSensor.KinectSensors[0];

        // Enable the color video stream
        myKinect.ColorStream.Enable();

        // Connect up the video event handler
        myKinect.ColorFrameReady += new EventHandler<ColorImageFrameReadyEventArgs>
                            (myKinect_ColorFrameReady);

        // Start the sensor
        myKinect.Start();

    }
```

```
void myKinect_ColorFrameReady(object sender, ColorImageFrameReadyEventArgs e)
{
    throw new NotImplementedException();
}
}
```

> **Note** The format of the preceding code sample might not exactly match the program code that you will see in the Visual Studio editor, but the content should be the same.

You do not have a working camera quite yet. When you attempt to run the program, it will fail because you have not yet added the code that runs when the Kinect sensor produces a new video frame. At that moment, the *myKinect_ColorFrameReady* method will throw an exception when it is called to process a new color frame. However, you are making good progress.

Displaying a Video Frame

You have now done nearly all the work to produce a video camera display. Your program establishes a connection to the sensor bar and then asks it to start producing video. Next, you have to add the code that takes the video frame and displays it on the screen. There are two stages to this. The first stage is to create an image display element in the WPF window on the screen, and the second stage is to create the code that will take the video data from the Kinect data stream and put it on the image on the screen.

Creating a WPF Image Display Element for the Kinect Camera

The program that you have built uses WPF to manage the display the user sees. WPF is a very powerful mechanism for creating extremely impressive-looking screen displays. Fortunately it is also quite easy to understand. Underneath every WPF window on the screen is a file of text that describes what the window should look like. This description includes details such as the size of the window, its background color, and any elements that are displayed in the window. This text file is formatted using eXtensible Application Markup Language (XAML).

When you are editing your program, Visual Studio will show you a preview of a window you are working on and also allows you to edit the XAML text that describes what the window looks like. At the moment the XAML describing the main window of your *KinectCam* program looks like this:

```
<Window x:Class="KinectCam.MainWindow"
        xmlns="http://schemas.microsoft.com/winfx/2006/xaml/presentation"
        xmlns:x="http://schemas.microsoft.com/winfx/2006/xaml"
        Title="MainWindow" Height="350" Width="525" Loaded="Window_Loaded">
    <Grid>

    </Grid>
</Window>
```

At the top of the description is some reference to the namespaces that hold definitions of the XAML that is being used. Underneath that can be seen some properties of the window itself. These include the title of the window, along with its width and height. If you change these values, the appearance of the window will change to match them.

You can also see the piece of XAML that links the *Loaded* event produced by the window to the *Window_Loaded* method in your program. This is how the WPF Window manager knows that when *MainWindow* is first loaded it must call this method.

At the bottom of the description is the place where WPF display elements are placed. These elements describe things to be drawn on the screen. WPF provides elements that will automatically arrange the layout of a window. A new window contains a grid that can be used to lay display elements out in a grid pattern on the window. For the first display you are going to dispense with the grid and replace it with an *Image* display element that will show the picture captured by the camera. Later on you will use the *Grid* to design a display that contains multiple display elements, but for now you don't need it.

Adding an Image Display Element to the WPF Window

You are going to add the display element by editing the XAML file that describes the MainWindow in your application.

1. Use Solution Explorer in Visual Studio to find and open the *MainWindow.XAML* file. This should have the content you can see in the preceding example. In the file, replace the *Grid* element with an Image.

   ```
   <Image Name="kinectVideo" />
   ```

2. You have created an *Image* element and given it the name *kinectVideo*. The program can use this name to refer to the image in the window on the screen.

The result of your efforts should be a *MainWindow.XAML* file that contains just a single *Image* element in the window.

```
<Window x:Class="KinectCam.MainWindow"
        xmlns="http://schemas.microsoft.com/winfx/2006/xaml/presentation"
        xmlns:x="http://schemas.microsoft.com/winfx/2006/xaml"
        Title="MainWindow" Height="350" Width="525" Loaded="Window_Loaded">
<Image Name="kinectVideo" />
</Window>
```

Now that you have your image on the screen, the next thing to do is make the final link in your program and add the code that displays the camera picture in the image.

Displaying the Kinect Camera Picture

You now have a Kinect sensor generating pictures and an Image display element that can show them. The next thing to do is to take the picture from the Kinect sensor and put it onto the image. You will do this by adding some code to the method that Visual Studio created for you previously. This is the method that was bound to the *ColorFrameReady* event that the *KinectSensor* generates. At the moment the method doesn't do much; it just throws an exception if it is ever called.

```
void myKinect_ColorFrameReady(object sender, ColorImageFrameReadyEventArgs e)
{
    throw new NotImplementedException();
}
```

You are going to add code into the method that will take the image from the Kinect sensor and then display it in the image element on the screen. Then, when the program runs it will display a succession of frames from the video camera.

Obtaining the Kinect Color Camera Video Data

The Kinect color video camera provides a lump of data that contains the pixel data. Later on you will find out more about how the data is arranged. The video data is supplied as part of a *ColorImageFrame* object that is passed into the event hander by means of the *ColorImageFrameReadyEventArgs* parameter. The code you are going to write must get the image out of this parameter and then use it to create a *Bitmap* to be displayed on the screen.

1. Use Solution Explorer in Visual Studio to find and open the *MainWindow.XAML.cs* file. Then find your way to the *myKinect_ColorFrameReady* method in the file. (It should look like the preceding example.) Delete the statement that throws an exception. This was added by Visual Studio 2010 when it created the *Empty* method for you.

2. Next get the color image frame out of the parameters supplied to the event handler. The *ColorImageFrameReadyEventArgs* type contains an *OpenColorImageFrame* method that will give your program the video frame produced by the camera. Add these statements to *myKinect_VideoFrameReady* to get the frame.

    ```
    using (ColorImageFrame colorFrame = e.OpenColorImageFrame())
    {
    ```

3. The *using* keyword identifies a block of code that will make use of a particular variable. It is saying to the C# runtime system, "The program only wants to use the *colorFrame* value inside the block of code that follows." This is important because the Kinect sensor will be creating 30 new frames every second, and it is important that each is destroyed when it is no longer required. By making the *colorFrame* value in this way, the program can make sure that it is removed as soon as the program has finished using it. However, the first thing the program must do with this value is make sure it is valid. If, for some reason, the event handler is slow to

respond to the *video frame–ready* event, the image data might no longer be available. In this case the call to open the frame will return a *null* result. The program must test to make sure that it has a genuine frame to work on.

```
if (colorFrame == null) return;
```

4. If the program gets beyond the test, it must have a proper frame of data. It must now create a buffer to hold all the video data that has been received from the camera. The video data is provided in the form of a large number of byte values in an array. The *ColorImageFrame* class provides a property called *PixelDataLength* that contains the number of bytes of video data in the frame. The program can use this to determine the size of the buffer to be created. Enter the following line of text to create the buffer:

```
byte[] colorData = new byte[colorFrame.PixelDataLength];
```

5. The preceding statement creates an array of bytes that hold the image data, now the program must extract the color data from the frame and put it in the array.

```
colorFrame.CopyPixelDataTo(colorData);
```

6. The *CopyPixelDataTo* method asks a *ColorImageFrame* instance to copy data from the frame into the supplied buffer array. At this point the program has an array of data that contains the image information. The next thing to do is make a WPF bitmap for this data.

```
kinectVideo.Source = BitmapSource.Create(
            colorFrame.Width, colorFrame.Height, // image dimensions
            96, 96,  // resolution - 96 dpi for video frames
            PixelFormats.Bgr32, // video format
            null,                   // palette - none
            colorData,              // video data
            colorFrame.Width * colorFrame.BytesPerPixel // stride
         );
```

7. The *Create* method is given a set of information about the type of bitmap to be created, along with a block of raw data that gives the picture information. It constructs a *BitmapSource* that is then set as the *Source* of the *kinectVideo* image in the WPF window on the screen. The comments in the preceding code give the meaning of each parameter accepted by the *Create* method. Just copy the values in the example. The final thing you need to do is close off the *using* block with the appropriate close bracket:

```
}
```

When you have finished these additions, you should have a method that looks like this:

```
void myKinect_ColorFrameReady(object sender, ColorImageFrameReadyEventArgs e)
```

```
{
    using (ColorImageFrame colorFrame = e.OpenColorImageFrame())
    {
        if (colorFrame == null) return;

        byte[] colorData = new byte[colorFrame.PixelDataLength];

        colorFrame.CopyPixelDataTo(colorData);

        kinectVideo.Source = BitmapSource.Create(
                            colorFrame.Width, colorFrame.Height, // image dimensions
                            96, 96,  // resolution - 96 dpi for video frames
                            PixelFormats.Bgr32, // video format
                            null,              // palette - none
                            colorData,         // video data
                            colorFrame.Width * colorFrame.BytesPerPixel // stride
                            );
    }
}
```

At this point all the links in the chain should be complete, and you have a program that should use the video camera in the Kinect sensor.

Testing the Kinect Camera

You should now have a program that will display the Kinect camera output on the screen of your computer (Figure 3-1). Before you run the program, you should make sure that your machine has the Kinect SDK installed, the Kinect sensor bar is connected, and the USB drivers for it have loaded successfully. You can then run the program and should see the view from the Kinect camera.

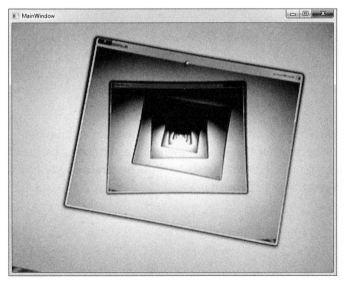

FIGURE 3-1 Kinect camera view of the Kinect program.

The first thing I did was to point the Kinect at the screen so that it was looking at the image it produces. You can get some quite interesting video feedback effects if you do this.

> **Sample Code: Simple Kinect Camera** The sample project in the "01 Simple Kinect Camera" directory in the resources for this chapter holds a working Kinect camera application (see the "Code Samples" section in the Introduction). The program uses the Kinect assembly from the standard Kinect SDK installation. If you have installed the Kinect SDK in a different place, you will need to modify the location of the resource.

Adding Error Handling

The software that you have created does not have any error handling. If any part of the program fails, it does not give a helpful error description; instead it stops with an exception in Visual Studio 2010, or worse, gets stuck. To make a proper application, you need to add some extra code to make the program a bit more user-friendly.

Detecting the Presence of a Kinect

To begin, it would be nice if the program displayed an error if the Kinect was not plugged in. Fortunately, this is very easy to set up. The program can find out how many items are in the *KinectSensors* collection provided by the *KinectSensor* class and display an error and exit if there is no Kinect present.

```
if (KinectSensor.KinectSensors.Count == 0)
{
    MessageBox.Show("No Kinects detected", "Camera Viewer");
    Application.Current.Shutdown();
}
```

This code checks to see if any Kinects are present, and if none is found it displays a message box and then shuts down the program. You could make the program even friendlier by making this into a loop construction that contains a message inviting the user to plug the Kinect sensor into the computer and try again.

> **Note** In the testing that I have performed with the Kinect SDK, the program does not actually fail if it tries to use a Kinect sensor that is not present. Instead it simply gets stuck when the *Window_Loaded* method fails. Fortunately, you can use the preceding test to detect whether a Kinect is present, so your applications should never try to use a Kinect sensor if one is not present.

Handling Setup Errors

The next possible error occurs when the program tries to perform an operation with the Kinect sensor that does not succeed. It is much less likely that this will happen. I can only think of two situations that would cause this problem: either another program is running and already using the Kinect, or your computer is running very short of memory and is unable to provide the space required by the Kinect SDK.

However, just because an error is not very likely doesn't mean that your program should not handle it. You can handle these errors by using exception handlers in your code. A method will throw an exception if it can't do what is required. Programs can catch exceptions and deal with them. If a program doesn't catch an exception, it stops running. You can add exception handlers and sensible messages by enclosing the Kinect method calls in the try-catch construction:

```
try
{
    myKinect = KinectSensor.KinectSensors[0];

    myKinect.ColorStream.Enable();

    myKinect.Start();
}
catch
{
    MessageBox.Show("Kinect initialise failed", "Camera Viewer");
    Application.Current.Shutdown();
}
```

If the Initialize method throws an exception, the block of code in the catch part of the construction will run. This will display a suitable message and then shut down the application.

> **Sample Code: Kinect Camera with Error Handling** The sample project in the "02 KinectCam with Error Handling" directory in the resources for this chapter (see the "Code Samples" section in the Introduction) holds a Kinect camera program that performs the preceding error handing example. If you run this program with the Kinect sensor disconnected, it will display an error message.

Summary

In this chapter, you have seen how to create a brand-new Windows application that uses the camera in the Kinect sensor bar to display an image on your Windows PC screen.

In the next chapter, you are going investigate how video signals are put together and how we can get some amazing video effects by playing with them.

PART II

Using the Kinect Sensor

Now that you know how the sensor bar works and how to write a program that uses it, you can put it to work. In this part you are going to explore each of the raw sensor facilities and discover how to use them from software. One great feature of Microsoft Kinect is that you can do lots of things with the information provided by the sensor bar. In Chapters 4, 5, 6, and 7, you are going to explore some ideas and pointers about the many fun things you can do with it, from operating it as a simple video camera to creating some amazing video effects.

Chapter 4

Your First Kinect Application—Video Snapshots

After completing this chapter, you will:

- Understand how video frames are presented by the sensor and how a program can work with video data

- Discover how to improve the memory use of image processing programs that use Kinect

- Find out how to speed up an image processing program by using pointers rather than arrays to access the video data

- Know how to save images to the hard disk of the computer

- Be able to apply noise reduction techniques in image processing, and how to use them to make some amazing image effects

- Find out how to improve the performance of the sensor on lower-specification computers

Image Storage in Computers

IN THE PREVIOUS CHAPTER YOU created a program that captured video data from the Kinect sensor. Now you are going to find out how this image data is stored and structured, and how a program can use it to perform some rather nice tricks.

Getting the Kinect Image Data onto the Screen

In Chapter 3 you learned that the video camera in the Kinect produces an event each time it has a new image available. To display the video image, you added a method that creates a new bitmap from the Kinect video data and displays the bitmap in the image on the screen. The method is connected to the *ColorFrameReady* event and runs each time a new image is available.

```
void myKinect_ColorFrameReady(object sender, ColorImageFrameReadyEventArgs e)
{
    using (ColorImageFrame colorFrame = e.OpenColorImageFrame())
    {
        if (colorFrame == null) return;

        byte[] colorData = new byte[colorFrame.PixelDataLength];

        colorFrame.CopyPixelDataTo(colorData);

        kinectVideo.Source = BitmapSource.Create(
                        colorFrame.Width, colorFrame.Height, // image dimensions
                        96, 96,  // resolution - 96 dpi for video frames
                        PixelFormats.Bgr32, // video format
                        null,               // palette - none
                        colorData,          // video data
                        colorFrame.Width * colorFrame.BytesPerPixel // stride
                        );
    }
}
```

Each time the method runs, the value of *e* is loaded with information about the event. This parameter *e* is of the type *ColorImageFrameReadyEventArgs*. The most important information about this parameter value is that it contains a method that can be used to get the latest image frame information. It is rather like a letter arriving that contains the message "You have won a big prize. Call this telephone number to find out what the prize is." However, in the case of the color image sensor, the prize is an image frame, and rather than making a telephone call, your program should instead call the method *OpenColorImageFrame* to get the image frame.

```
ColorImageFrame colorFrame = e.OpenColorImageFrame();
```

The *ColorImageFrame* type is used to describe a particular frame of video data. It contains lots of useful information, including a timestamp that tells the program when the image was captured, a frame number, and the dimensions of the frame in pixels. It also contains the actual raw image data that a program can extract and store in an array of bytes. To use the color data, a program must first create an array that can hold it.

```
byte[] colorData = new byte[colorFrame.PixelDataLength];
```

The preceding statement creates new array that can hold the color data from the image sensor. The *ColorImageFrame* provides a property called *PixelDataLength* that provides the number of bytes in the image that is being delivered. This is used to set the size of the byte array that is created. Once the program has a buffer array that can hold the color data, it can get the color image data from the frame that has been received.

```
colorFrame.CopyPixelDataTo(colorData);
```

The preceding statement uses the *CopyPixelDataTo* method, which instructs the newly received frame to copy the pixel data that it contains into the *colorData* array. The next thing the method does is make a new bitmap value and put this color data on the screen.

```
kinectVideo.Source = BitmapSource.Create(
                colorFrame.Width, colorFrame.Height, // image dimensions
                96, 96,  // resolution - 96 dpi for video frames
                PixelFormats.Bgr32, // video format
                null,               // palette - none
                colorData,          // video data
                colorFrame.Width * colorFrame.BytesPerPixel // stride
                );
```

The variable *kinectVideo* denotes the image element on the screen, and we set the source of this element to a brand-new *BitmapSource* that is created from the image data supplied by the Kinect. This means that that every new image the Kinect sensor delivers is displayed on the screen. However, how the program does this is perhaps not particularly efficient.

Figure 4-1 depicts the display from Task Manager showing what happened in my computer when I ran an early version of the Kinect Viewer program that was created in Chapter 3. The Physical Memory usage graph is very interesting. The memory use increases for a while and then suddenly drops, only to increase again. The reason for this is the way the program works. Every time it gets a new image from the Kinect sensor, the program makes a brand-new *BitmapSource* to go with it. Because this is happening many times per second, the result is that the program consumes more and more memory. When the use of memory gets too high, a garbage collection is triggered by the .NET Framework. The garbage to be collected is all the old bitmaps that were created, displayed for a fraction of a second, and then replaced by another one. If you look at the CPU loading graph you can see pulses of computer activity each time the memory goes down. This is where the computer has to work through memory, finding unused items and handing them back to Windows.

The little graph in Figure 4-1 tells you a lot about the way that bad programs can make the life of a computer (and the computer user) unpleasant. This program is a bad one, creating and discarding lumps of data at such a great rate that it can produce around a gigabyte (1,000 megabytes) of waste memory every few seconds. It is very impressive that the computer can keep displaying a good-quality display even while it is dealing with a program that is behaving so badly.

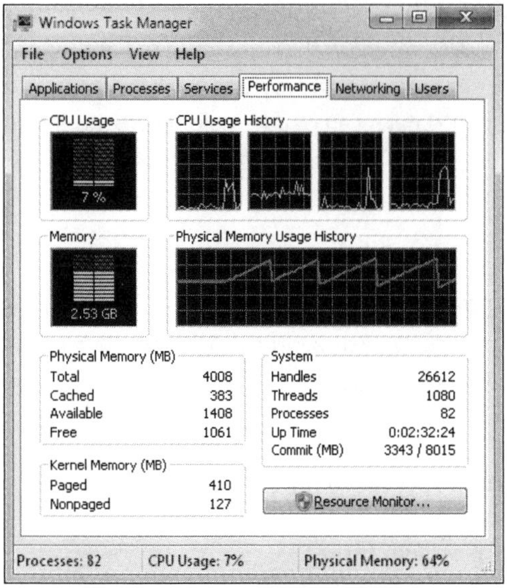

FIGURE 4-1 Kinect viewer memory usage.

The best way to solve this problem is to replace the *BitmapSource* with a different kind of bitmap that can be updated with new image data. A *BitMapSource* is intended to be used when a program displays an image that will not change as the program runs. The imaging classes in Windows Presentation Foundation also provide a *WriteableBitmap* that can be written to with updated video data. Rather than making a new bitmap for each image, the program now just has to update the video data in the bitmap.

```
WriteableBitmap colorImageBitmap = null;
```

The preceding statement creates a variable called *colorImageBitmap* that will refer to the *WriteableBitmap* it is using. The very first time that the program tries to draw an image, it must make *colorImageBitmap* refer to the bitmap that is going to be used to display the images.

```
if (colorImageBitmap == null)
{
    this.colorImageBitmap = new WriteableBitmap(
        colorFrame.Width,
        colorFrame.Height,
        96,  // DpiX
        96,  // DpiY
        PixelFormats.Bgr32,
        null);
}
```

If the *colorImageBitmap* reference is *null*, the program creates a new *WriteableBitmap*. The construction of the bitmap looks very much like the statement that we used to make the original *BitmapSource*. To update the display the program just has to write new image data to the bitmap.

```
this.colorImageBitmap.WritePixels(
    new Int32Rect(0, 0, colorFrame.Width, colorFrame.Height),
    colorData, // video data
    colorFrame.Width * colorFrame.BytesPerPixel, // stride,
    0   // offset into the array - start at 0
    );
```

If your program uses just a single writeable bitmap that is updated in this way, the program will not generate the "old" bitmaps and will use memory much more efficiently.

> **Sample Code: Writeable Bitmap Demo** The sample project in the "01 Writeable Bitmap Demo" directory in the resources for this chapter (see the "Code Samples" section in the Introduction) holds a Kinect Camera program that allows you to change between using the writeable bitmap and the older version of the program. You will notice that if you turn off the Writeable Bitmap checkbox, you will see in Task Manager how the memory usage of the program changes.

Controlling the Color of the Pixels

The image data that the program receives from the Kinect sensor is held in an array of bytes. The programs described in the preceding pages copy the bytes from the *ColorFrame* value received from the Kinect sensor into an array called *colorData*.

Each element of the *colorData* array is a byte of memory that can hold a single 8-bit value. The bitmap that is delivered by the camera uses a format of data called BGR32. This means that each pixel is described as a 32-bit value in the order blue byte, green byte, and red byte. The final byte (which makes the pixel 32 bits in size) is the transparency value. This is used in computer displays to allow an image to show through the image underneath it. For the purposes of this example, you can ignore the transparency value.

Figure 4-2 shows how the bytes are arranged in memory. The first group of four values gives the colors for the first pixel on the screen. The next four values give the colors for the next pixel and so on across the screen. The pixels are stored in a long line, but they are mapped onto the screen a row at a time as they are drawn. This means that every fourth byte in the memory is a particular color. You can use this to do some image processing on the picture:

```
for (int i = 0; i < colorData.Length; i = i + 4)
{
    colorData [i] += 50;
}
```

Blue	Green	Red	Alpha	Blue	Green	Red	Alpha
0	1	2	3	4	5	6	7

FIGURE 4-2 Pixel color storage.

This code works down the array, adding 50 to every fourth byte, starting at 0. The effect of this is to make all the blue values in the image larger, giving the image displayed a blue tint.

> **Sample Code: Kinect Camera with Extra Blue** The sample project in the "02 KinectCam with Extra Blue" directory in the resources for this chapter (see the "Code Samples" section in the Introduction) holds a Kinect Camera program that makes the image bluer.

If you run the extra blue program, you will notice something interesting about the pictures. Very bright patches of blue will appear strange, perhaps turning yellow. This is because the 8-bit byte variables that hold the color values will wrap around if the program tries to put a value in them that is greater than 255. Thus, if an area of the screen has a blue value of *210* (quite a bright blue), when the program adds 50, the result is 260. Unfortunately, this is outside the range of the byte type holding the value that wraps around to give the value *4*. This causes very bright values to have less blue than they should have, making them appear yellow.

This effect looks a bit like a photographic technique called *solarization,* which partially reverses the brightness of an image. If you don't want this in your picture, you have to add some code to stop the blue value from exceeding 255:

```
int newColor;

for (int i = 0; i < colorData.Length; i = i + 4)
{
    int oldColor = colorData [i];
    newColor = (int) colorData [i] + 50;
    if (newColor > 255) newColor = 255;

    colorData [i] = (byte)newColor;
}
```

This code is a little more complicated. It uses an integer to calculate the new color value, and if this exceeds 255 it pulls the value back down to *255*. This is called *clipping*. Note that when the program puts the *newColor* value back into the array, it has to cast the value into a byte.

You can increase the amount of other colors in the program by updating different bytes in the image. If the program works through memory starting from a different byte in the image array, it will change that color instead. You can do this by changing the initial value of the loop counter.

```
for (int i = 1; i < colorData.Length; i = i + 4)
{
    // if we start at byte 1 we will work on the green byte
}
```

The preceding loop would work through the array starting at the byte with the offset 1, which is the green byte. By starting at position 2, the program would increase the brightness of the red in the image. If you change the starting value in the sample program, you can see how this works.

Creating a Color Adjustment Program

You now know how to change the appearance of a color on the screen by modifying the value that represents that color. You can use this ability to create a program that lets the user change the brightness of each color by using a slider to control the change in each color:

```
<Slider Name="redSlider" Orientation="Vertical"
ValueChanged="redSlider_ValueChanged"
Background="Red" Minimum="-255" Maximum="255" Height="480"></Slider>
```

The preceding XAML creates a vertical slider on the display that can be used to control the brightness of the red element in the image. The minimum of the slider is –255, and the maximum is 255. The slider also has a method bound to the *ValueChanged* event that is produced by the slider. When the slider is adjusted, the method will run and read the new offset value from the slider:

```
private void redSlider_ValueChanged(object sender,
    RoutedPropertyChangedEventArgs<double> e)
{
    redOffset = (int)redSlider.Value;
}
```

Note that because the value of a slider is provided as a double precision value, the program must cast this into an integer. The *redOffset* value is used to change the value of the red component of the image as shown here:

```
newValue = colorData [i+2] + redOffset;
if (newValue < 0) newValue = 0;
if (newValue > 255) newValue = 255;
colorData [i+2] = (byte)newValue;
```

This code contains a test to ensure that if the value becomes less than 0 it is clipped at 0. There are versions of the same statements for the blue and green components and a slider for each of these colors, too.

Figure 4-3 shows the image adjustment program. If you move all the sliders up together, this has the effect of boosting all the colors and making the image brighter overall.

> **Sample Code: Color Tweaker Program** The sample project in the "03 Color Tweaker" directory in the resources for this chapter (see the "Code Samples" section in the Introduction) holds a Kinect Camera program that has three sliders that let you change the brightness of the red, green, and blue components of the image.

FIGURE 4-3 An image adjustment program.

Improving the Speed by Writing Unsafe Code

The program you have made works well, but if you run it on a low-powered computer you might notice that the computer struggles to keep up. On my fairly powerful desktop machine, the image processing program takes around 25% of the processor when it runs. The problem is that for each pixel in the image received from the Kinect sensor, the program does quite a bit of computation. The image contains 307,200 pixels, and they are being produced at more than 20 times per second. This means that the program is processing over six million pixels per second. When you have a piece of code that is being called this frequently, it is worth taking a look at the statements to see if their performance can be improved.

```
newValue = colorData [i+2] + redOffset;
if (newValue < 0) newValue = 0;
if (newValue > 255) newValue = 255;
colorData [i+2] = (byte)newValue;
```

The preceding code performs the update of the red pixel on the screen. The code itself is fine, but it is not very efficient. The main problem with the code is that it reads from and writes to the *colorData* array. To make matters worse, the subscript for the array access is actually calculated twice as the result of the sum of *i + 2*. If you think about the amount of work the program has to do when it gets a hold of an element in an array, you can start to see the problem. Consider one statement in the sequence:

```
colorData [i+2] = (byte)newValue;
```

To perform this one statement, the program must do the following when it runs:

1. Calculate the value of *i + 2*. This will be the subscript for the array access—that is, the number of the element in the array to which is to be written.

2. Find the start of the *colorData* array in memory.

3. Work out the location of the element of the array that is to be changed.

4. Ensure that this element is inside the bounds of the array.

5. Store the value of *newValue* in this element.

This sequence of actions happens every time the array is used, which is many millions of times per second. The good news is that the C# compiler will do lots of clever things to make this sequence run as quickly as possible. However, using arrays to work on large blocks of memory is not very efficient. Fortunately C# provides a means by which a program can work through a block of memory in a much more efficient way. The bad news is that to use this you have to venture into writing *unsafe* code.

Managed Code and Unsafe Code

C# programs normally run as managed code. This means that before a program is started it is very carefully checked to ensure that it does not contain any untoward code and when the program runs it is monitored to ensure it doesn't do anything damaging to the system in which it is running. An untoward program would attempt to do things like change parts of the computer memory used by the operating system or take direct control of the low-level hardware in the computer. This bad behavior could be the result of the programmer not getting the program right, or it could be something more sinister such as the actions of a virus program trying to attack the computer system. Either way, in a managed code environment a program is not allowed to directly access any hardware or know where objects are located in memory. If a program breaks these rules, an exception will be thrown that will stop the program in its tracks.

However, to make the image processing program run more quickly it would be very useful to be able to directly access the memory where the *colorData* array is held. If a program could do this, it would not have to use the C# array mechanism to get hold of pixel values. To allow this, you can mark a C# project as "unsafe."

Figure 4-4 shows the Build properties for the KinectCam project. In the middle you can see the Allow Unsafe Code checkbox. This has been checked to tell the C# compiler and the managed code runtime that the program contains unsafe code.

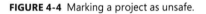

FIGURE 4-4 Marking a project as unsafe.

Some languages, for example C++, are inherently unsafe in the way they work, allowing the programmer more direct access to the memory of the computer. A program running as unsafe does not mean that it will necessarily crash your computer if it goes wrong. Modern operating systems such as Windows 7 are very good at isolating programs from each other and protecting important operating system components. However, when an unsafe program goes wrong the errors that it produces can be highly confusing. Some operating environments—for example, XNA on Windows Xbox 360 and programs running on Windows Phone 7—are not allowed to run code that has been marked as unsafe.

The programs that you are going to write next will do quite a lot of manipulation of the video image, and for this reason (and to make this run as quickly as possible), it makes sense to use pointers and work in unsafe mode.

References and Pointers

The use of unsafe code requires an understanding of pointers. A pointer is essentially a stripped-down reference. Just as you can make a car go faster by removing the bodywork, you can make a reference go faster by converting it into a pointer.

A reference is a lump of data that describes the location of an object in memory. When a reference is created, it is given the type of the object to which it refers:

```
KinectSensor myKinect;
```

The variable *myKinect* is declared in the *KinectCam* project and refers to the Kinect object being used by the program. Whenever the program uses the myKinect variable, the system will ensure that a variable of the correct type is being used and will then find that object.

```
byte* imagePosition;
```

In contrast, the variable *imagePosition* is a pointer that can refer to a byte in the memory of the computer. You can think of a pointer as the numeric address of a location in memory. If your computer has 4 gigabytes of memory, the memory hardware contains around 4,000 million addressable locations. Each of the locations has a different address. A pointer can hold a number that refers to one of those locations. When a pointer is used, no checking is performed to ensure that it is being used correctly; the program just gets a hold of the memory location that the pointer identifies. The lack of checking makes the program run more quickly, but it also increases the possibility that incorrect code can affect the way a program runs. This is why such code is branded as unsafe.

Working with pointers is quite easy. If a pointer is incremented, it now points to the next location in memory:

```
imagePosition++;
```

This preceding statement would move on to the next byte in the image. To use the location in memory that a pointer refers to, the * character is added to "dereference" the pointer:

```
*imagePosition = *imagePosition + 50;
```

This statement would have the effect of increasing by 50 the color value that *imagePosition* is pointing at.

> **Note** When you understand the effect of adding the * to your program, you truly understand pointers. The code *imagePosition++* will move the pointer down memory one location. The code **imagePosition++* will increase by 1 the byte value at which *imagePosition* is pointing.

Appropriate use of pointers will remove the need for a program to do any array calculations and will greatly speed things up.

Pointers and Fixed Memory Locations

One reason why C# programs are not able to know where an object is located is that when a managed code program is running, the tendency is for things to move around memory. During program execution the Garbage Collector process is constantly looking for unused objects and moving data around to make the best use of any free space. You saw it in action previously in this chapter. This means that references to objects are liable to change at any moment.

A program that uses pointers must work on the basis that what is being pointed at is not going to move about in memory. C# provides a keyword, *fixed*, that allows a program to fix a particular data item in memory while that item is worked on. This is also how the program can set a pointer with the location of a particular item in memory.

```
fixed (byte* imageBase = colorData)
{
    // For the duration of this block the pointer
    // imageBase points to the video image bytes
}
```

The preceding code shows how this is used. The variable *imageBase* is a pointer that is set to the location in memory of the first element of the *colorData* array. This array contains the video image received from the Kinect camera. The statements in the block that follow the *fixed* keyword will be performed with the *colorData* array at that position. In other words the *colorData* array is guaranteed not to move while the statements in the block are performed.

> **Note** When a program fixes a block of code in memory, it adds a constraint to the way that memory management can operate. A program should only fix items in memory for the shortest possible time.

The use of pointers makes it much easier to create a method that processes image bitmaps.

```
unsafe void updateImage(byte [] colorData)
{
    int noOfPixelBytes = colorData.Length;

    fixed (byte* imageBase = colorData)
    {
        // For the duration of this block the pointer
        // imageBase points to the video image by
        byte* imagePosition = imageBase;
        byte* imageEnd = imageBase + noOfPixelBytes;

        int newValue;

        while (imagePosition != imageEnd)
        {
            // Process Blue
            newValue = *imagePosition + blueOffset;
            if (newValue < 0) newValue = 0;
            if (newValue > 255) newValue = 255;
            *imagePosition = (byte)newValue;
```

```
            // Move on to green
            imagePosition++;
            // Do the green process here

            // Move on to red
            imagePosition++;
            // Do the red process here

            // skip past the alpha
            imagePosition++;
            imagePosition++;
        }
    }
}
```

In the preceding code, you can see the image processing method that performs color adjustment using pointers to access the image bytes. Within the *fixed* block a program can create other pointer variables. In this case the block uses the variable *imagePosition* to point at the byte being updated and the variable *imageEnd* is set to point at the end of the buffer. This makes testing for the end of the image processing very easy; the program just has to stop when the position reaches the end.

You can also see that after processing each byte the program moves on to the next one. The pointer is increased four times during each pass through the loop, as each color is represented by four values. Note that the method has been marked as *unsafe*. C# requires any method that uses unsafe code to be flagged in this way.

> **Sample Code: Performance Color Tweaker** The sample project in the "04 Performance Color Tweaker" directory in the resources for this chapter (see the "Code Samples" section in the Introduction) holds a Kinect Camera program that uses pointers instead of arrays to process the image data.

This code is much more efficient than the version that used arrays to access the bitmap data. I find that on my machine it reduces processor loading from 25% to around 15%.

Using 32-Bit Integer Pointers

The preceding program works with the byte color values of each pixel. This means that to move an entire pixel it has to perform four operations: one each for the blue, green, and red values followed by a final operation for the alpha value. To move a single pixel from one place to another would be a lot of work. For example, it might be nice to have a mirror effect on your Kinect camera, like the one in Figure 4-5.

FIGURE 4-5 Making a mirror camera.

Creating the mirror effect is quite easy. You can create a method, perhaps called *reflect*, that will copy pixels from one side of the image to the other, reversing the order as it copies. The problem is that if the method tried to copy the bytes, it would need to ensure that the blue, green, red order of the bytes is maintained. It would be much easier if the program could move the pixels in 32-bit chunks, so that all the information could be moved in one action. Fortunately, this is easy to do.

If we use pointers to types that occupy more memory, the program will move more memory when it works with them. The *int* type in C# is represented as a 32-bit value, so when working with integer pointers each access will move 4 bytes of data. If the reflect method uses an *int* pointer rather than a *byte* pointer, it will move the image data in 32-bit pixels rather than individual color values.

The image is supplied as an array of bytes, but in C# a program can cast a value from one type to another, so a *byte* pointer can be converted into an *int* pointer.

```
fixed (byte* imageBase = colorData)
{
    int* imagePosition = (int*)imageBase;
    // imagePosition now refers to complete 32 bit pixels
}
```

The preceding code fixes a byte pointer at the base of the image data bytes and then creates an integer pointer from that value. This means that to copy all the data bytes for a single pixel from one place to another, the program can use a single statement:

```
*toPos = *fromPos;
```

The variables *toPos* and *fromPos* are both integer pointers, and so 4 bytes are transferred in one action. Furthermore, when the pointers are updated, they are moved to the next integer location in the image.

```
fromPos++; // move towards the middle
toPos--;   // move back from the right edge
```

This means that the loops to copy the pixels only need to go around one-fourth as many times.

```
unsafe void reflectImage(byte[] colorData, int width, int height)
{
    fixed (byte* imageBase = colorData)
    {
        // Get the base position as an integer pointer
        int* imagePosition = (int*)imageBase;

        // repeat for each row
        for (int row = 0; row < height; row++)
        {
            // read from the left edge
            int* fromPos = imagePosition + (row * width);
            // write to the right edge
            int* toPos = fromPos + width - 1;
            while (fromPos < toPos)
            {
                *toPos = *fromPos; // copy the pixel
                fromPos++; // move towards the middle
                toPos--;   // move back from the right edge
            }
        }
    }
}
```

The method *reflectImage* reflects an image from left to right. It is given the length and width properties of the image bytes so that it would work with image areas of any size.

> **Note** The program uses integer variables, but at no time does it manipulate the values in the variables. Instead, the variables are used as containers that are 32 bits in size.

Saving the Image to a File

You now have a program that can be used to get some interesting, if not artistic, images. It would be nice if these could be saved into a file.

```
private void saveButton_Click(object sender, RoutedEventArgs e)
{
    // Set the flag to trigger a snapshot
    takePicture = true;

    // Configure save file dialog box
    Microsoft.Win32.SaveFileDialog dlg = new Microsoft.Win32.SaveFileDialog();
    dlg.FileName = "SnapShot"; // Default file name
    dlg.DefaultExt = ".jpg"; // Default file extension
    dlg.Filter = "Pictures (.jpg)|*.jpg"; // Filter files by extension

    // Process save file dialog box results
    if (dlg.ShowDialog() == true)
    {
        // Save document
        string filename = dlg.FileName;
        using (FileStream stream = new FileStream(filename, FileMode.Create) )
        {
            JpegBitmapEncoder encoder = new JpegBitmapEncoder();
            encoder.Frames.Add(BitmapFrame.Create(pictureBitmap));
            encoder.Save(stream);
        }
    }
}
```

The preceding method is connected to a Save button. When the button is pressed, the event first sets a flag to tell the camera capture method to take a copy of the currently displayed bitmap. The program uses a flag in this way because the images are being captured in a separate thread to the one dealing with the button-pressed event.

If the user happens to press the button while the color data from the camera was being updated, the program may save a frame that contains a corrupted image. So, instead, the handler that runs when the Save button is pressed just sets a flag to request that the next bitmap captured should be copied so that it can be stored:

```
if (takePicture)
{
    pictureBitmap = BitmapSource.Create(
        colorFrame.Width, colorFrame.Height, 96, 96, PixelFormats.Bgr32, null,
        colorData, colorFrame.Width * colorFrame.BytesPerPixel);
    takePicture = false;
}
```

The preceding statements are in the event handler that runs when the Kinect sensor has a new image available. The variable *pictureBitmap* holds the bitmap picture that is to be saved to disk. If the *takePicture* flag is set to true, the event handler method makes a new bitmap and saves it there. It then clears the *takePicture* flag so that next time the method runs the image is not overwritten with another one.

The *saveButton_Click* method displays a file save dialog that allows the user to select a file to put the picture in. The method then creates a *JpegBitmapEncoder* that is used to save a jpeg image containing the picture.

Sample Code: Kinect Photo Booth The sample project in the 05 Kinect Photo Booth directory in the resources for this chapter (see the "Code Samples" section in the Introduction) holds a Kinect Camera program that allows you to use reflection and to turn off the clipping of color values so that you can make some interesting images. It also allows you to save the images into jpeg files.

Improving Video Quality

If you look closely at the video image on your screen, you will notice quite a bit of noise on the picture. This is produced in the camera sensor. When the electrical signals are read from the chip inside the Kinect sensor bar, noise will always be present along with the signal. You see this as flickering speckles on top of the picture. It is particularly obvious on darker areas of the scene. One way to improve the video quality is to take the average of a number of camera readings. This works because the noise is randomly distributed across a single image. If a program averages the values from a number of frames, the effect of the noise will be cancelled out, leading to significantly better quality pictures. This might not work too well for moving subjects, but we can have quite a lot of fun with this anyway.

A problem with averaging the video signal is that this is a slow process. To compute the average of a series of numbers, a program has to add them all together and then divide by the size of the series. This means that the computer must perform a number of additions and a divide calculation for every pixel, which is a lot of extra work.

One way to speed things up is to buffer all the values that you are averaging and keep a rolling total of those numbers. Each time we add a new number to the sequence we subtract the oldest one from the total and add the new one. This means that the program never has to add up all the numbers to work out the total; it simply has to perform a subtraction and an addition. The amount of work the program does is independent of the number of values it is averaging—although the more values that are averaged, the more memory is required.

The most efficient way to do this is to use blocks of memory to hold all the images and the buffer, and then use pointers to manage the movement through them.

The sample program will average the pixels from up to 50 images. Since the Kinect camera operates at around 30 frames a second, this has a magical effect on the picture. People walking past the camera appear as ghosts. If they stand still, they mysteriously appear, and when they move away, they slowly vanish.

The program provides an extra slider on the right of the red, green, and blue intensity images. This slider lets you set the number of averages that the program uses to work out the color of each pixel. The higher the slider, the more values are averaged, up to a maximum number of 50. If you move this slider up to the top, you get a ghost camera, where changes to the picture in front of the camera take a few seconds to register.

The program also has two new checkboxes, for Funky and Super Funky. If you set the Funky checkbox, the program doesn't clear the average values for a pixel when the slider is used to adjust the number of averages to use. If you set the Super Funky checkbox, the program doesn't clear the total values for a pixel. By clicking these boxes and then moving the averages slider up and down, you can get some amazing video effects, particularly if the subjects are moving, as illustrated in Figure 4-6.

FIGURE 4-6 One type of video effect obtained from a Funky camera.

Improving Performance by Waiting for Each Kinect Frame

One problem with the preceding program is that even though it uses the fastest possible memory access, it still needs quite a powerful computer to run smoothly. If you run the sample program on a low-performance laptop, you will find that the display updates very slowly. It may not work at all. The Kinect SDK will deliver a new frame at regular intervals, and serious problems can result if a program is not able to process each frame before the next one arrives.

You can fix this problem by changing the way that the program obtains frames from the Kinect SDK. Rather than waiting for an event that indicates a new frame has arrived, a program can request a new frame from the Kinect SDK.

```
ColorImageFrame colorFrame = myKinect.ColorStream.OpenNextFrame(10);
```

The method *OpenNextFrame* will request a frame from the video stream. The method is provided with a parameter that is the number of milliseconds to wait before a frame becomes available. If the camera cannot produce a frame in that time, the *OpenNextFrame* method will return a *null* result. This allows you to prevent a program from getting completely stuck if a new frame isn't available. The great thing about this way of working is that the program will only request a second frame when it has finished processing the first one, and so on. The best way to do this is to make a loop that repeatedly fetches frames and displays them, before moving on to the next one.

You can see how this works in the following code. The *videoDisplay* method contains a loop that runs as long as the *displayActive* flag is *true*. Each time around the loop, the program fetches a new frame and then displays it. Then it fetches another frame. If a program ever needs to stop the loop, it can do this by setting the *displayActive* flag to *false*. When the flag becomes false, the display loop will end.

```
bool displayActive = true;

void videoDisplay ()
{
    while (displayActive)
    {
        using (ColorImageFrame colorFrame = myKinect.ColorStream.OpenNextFrame(10))
        {
            if (colorFrame == null) continue;

            // process and display the frame
        }
    }
}
```

The advantage of this technique is that the computer is never in danger of being overwhelmed by messages from the Kinect SDK. The program only fetches a new frame when it has finished processing the previous one.

Creating a Video Display Thread

Up until now you have used the *Window_Loaded* method to allow your program to run code when your program starts up. This is where your programs have obtained a Kinect sensor and started it running. You might think that this method is a good place to put in a call to the *videoDisplay* method. This would mean that once the Kinect sensor had been set up, the program could then start displaying video. However, this would not work. The *Window_Loaded* method is called as part of the setup for the window on the screen of the computer. If the *Window_Loaded* method never returned (which is what would happen if it called the *videoDisplay* method), the program would not display properly.

The way to solve this problem is for the *Window_Loaded* method to create a new *thread* of execution that will update the display. If you think of a program as a rail network, you can think of a thread as a train running on that network. The train runs through the statements in the program one at a time. A program can call a method to start another thread running. This would be like the driver of a train making a request to the rail network controller to start a new train running at a particular station. The two trains would then run simultaneously on the rail network.

The .NET Framework provides a set of classes that implement threads. These classes are used a lot by the operating system. Whenever you print a document from your word processor, you are using threads. One thread is providing the editor user interface that lets you keep working while another thread is sending the text out the printer. If your computer only has one processor, the operating system will switch between active threads many times per second to give you an illusion that the threads are active at the same time. If your computer has multiple processors it will actually run multiple threads in parallel.

The threading classes are described in the *System.Threading* namespace, which you can add to your C# program.

```
using System.Threading;
```

A *Thread* is an object that describes a particular thread of execution on the computer. It holds the place that the thread has reached in the program (the position of the train on the track).

```
Thread updateVideoThread;
```

The preceding statement declares a variable that can refer to a thread object. At the moment the variable *updateVideoThread* does not refer to anything, the next thing the program must do is create the thread.

```
updateVideoThread = new Thread(new ThreadStart(videoDisplay));
```

The preceding statement creates a new *Thread* value. When a program creates a thread, it must identify the method to run when the thread is started. The method that is to be started is specified using a *ThreadStart* value. The *ThreadStart* type is a *delegate* type. A delegate is a kind of reference that can refer to methods. In the preceding statement a new *ThreadStart* value is created that refers to the *videoDisplay* method, which will read frames from the Kinect and use them to update the display. This is the same as telling a train driver the station from which to start running the train.

```
updateVideoThread.Start();
```

This is the final statement the program needs to get the thread running. The *Start* method causes the thread to begin running. When the thread starts, it will call the *videoDisplay* method.

Updating the Image from a Different Thread

This thread business looks quite simple. In fact, you might be wondering why I haven't mentioned it until now. The reason is that the program must deal with another layer of complexity, and this has to do with the way that the Windows Presentation Foundation display works.

The code that actually displays the components on the screen has a very difficult job to do. It must ensure that at any instant the window on the screen exactly reflects the state of the objects that represent the components. If your program changes the text in a *TextBox*, it is the display manager that must change the appropriate pixels on the screen to match. The last thing the display manager wants is something else diving in and changing display elements behind its back. This means that the *videoDisplay* method is unable to update the content of an image on the screen if it is running on a different thread than the Display Manager.

Fortunately this is quite easy to sort out. The first step is to create a method that actually does the display update:

```
void updateDisplay()
{
    if (colorImageBitmap == null)
    {
        this.colorImageBitmap = new WriteableBitmap(
            640,
            480,
            96,  // DpiX
            96,  // DpiY
            PixelFormats.Bgr32,
            null);
        kinectVideo.Source = colorImageBitmap;
    }

    colorImageBitmap.WritePixels(
        new Int32Rect(0, 0, 640, 480),
        averagedImage, // video data
        640 * 4, // stride,
        0   // offset into the array - start at 0
        );
}
```

This method takes a new set of data from the *averagedImage* array and puts it on the screen. The next thing to do is add a statement that asks the Display Manager to call this method at some point in the future when it is updating the display:

```
Dispatcher.Invoke(new Action(() => updateDisplay()));
```

The preceding statement creates a new *Action* that refers to the *updateDisplay* method and then asks the *Dispatcher* object to *Invoke* this. The result of this statement is that the *updateDisplay* method is called at some point in the future within the context of the Display Manager. You will find out more about the Display Manager and the Action type in Chapter 5.

```
void videoDisplay ()
{
    while (displayActive)
    {
        using (ColorImageFrame colorFrame = myKinect.ColorStream.OpenNextFrame(10))
        {
            if (colorFrame == null) continue;

            if (colorData == null)
                colorData = new byte[colorFrame.PixelDataLength];

            colorFrame.CopyPixelDataTo(colorData);

            if (clipping)
                updateImageClip(colorData);
            else
                updateImage(colorData);

            if (mirror)
                reflectImage(colorData, colorFrame.Width, colorFrame.Height);

            averagedImage = imageAverage(colorData, colorFrame.Width,
                                         colorFrame.Height);

            if (takePicture)
            {
                pictureBitmap = BitmapSource.Create(
                    colorFrame.Width, colorFrame.Height, 96, 96,
                    PixelFormats.Bgr32, null,
                    averagedImage, colorFrame.Width * colorFrame.BytesPerPixel);
                takePicture = false;
            }

            Dispatcher.Invoke(new Action(() => updateDisplay()));
        }
```

```
        }
}
```

In the preceding code, you can see the complete *videoDisplay* method. This performs the image processing and then calls the *updateDisplay* method to put the new image on the screen.

Stopping the Background Thread

If you built the program using the preceding threaded technique, you would find that it is much more responsive, particularly on low-powered machines. However, you would also notice another problem, which is that the program does not seem very keen to stop. The usual way to stop a program like this is to click on the red X in the top-right corner of the window to close it. Unfortunately, if you do this the window will close but the program doesn't seem to stop properly. If you use Windows Task Manager to see what is running inside your machine, you will probably find that the program is still active, even though it is not displaying anything.

The reason for this problem is that the thread you created to update the screen is still running, even though the window that it is part of has been closed. To stop the thread from running, the program just has to set the *displayActive* flag to *false*. This will end the *while* loop in the *videoDisplay* method, which will cause the method to return. When the method finishes, the thread running it is stopped, because it has nothing left to do at that point.

The best way to get control when a program is stopping is to connect a method to the *Closing* event that is generated by a form when it is closed. This works in exactly the same way as the *Loading* method:

```
private void Window_Closing(object sender, System.ComponentModel.CancelEventArgs e)
{
    displayActive = false;
}
```

When the user closes the window, the *displayActive* flag is set to *false*, which will end the *videoDisplay* loop. The method can then also close down the Kinect sensor by calling the *Stop* method on it.

```
void videoDisplay ()
{
    while (displayActive)
    {
        // fetch the frame and process it
    }
    // when we get here the program is ending - stop the sensor
    myKinect.Stop();
}
```

> **Sample Code: High-Performance Image Tweaker** The sample project in the "07 High Performance Image Tweaker" directory in the resources for this chapter (see the "Code Samples" section in the Introduction) holds a Kinect Camera program that uses the preceding threading techniques to create a camera that works by requesting images from the Kinect rather than responding to image frame events. I have found that it works well even on lower-powered computers.

Summary

In this chapter you have discovered the form of the data that the camera produces and the fastest way to process this data. You have also discovered how to save an image in a file and investigated some video noise reduction techniques that can also be used to make an image very funky. Finally, you learned how to improve the performance of a program by changing the way that it obtains image frames from the Kinect SDK.

In Chapter 5 we will improve our image-processing skills to use the camera as a sensor to detect movement.

Moving Pictures

After completing this chapter, you will:

- Understand how programs can detect movement in video images

- Appreciate the effects of noise on video signals and how this can be dealt with

- Play alarm sounds from programs on your Windows PC

- Create a program that can take and store photographs when movement is detected

Detecting Movement in Video Images

ONE POSSIBLE USE FOR THE Microsoft Kinect camera would be as a movement-sensitive camera; in other words, any movement in the area viewed by the camera would trigger a photograph. This could be extended to create a motion-sensitive burglar alarm. To get this to work, a program will have to analyze video images and detect changes to the picture being received from the Kinect camera. The basic sequence that the program will perform is shown in Figure 5-1.

The idea illustrated in Figure 5-1 is that the program will compare each new image with the previous one. The sequence starts at the entry point at the top (the filled black dot). The first thing it does is fetch an image from the camera. The very first time it runs, the program will not have a previous image to compare the latest image with, and so it must set the previous image to the latest one. The next time around the loop, the latest image is compared with the previous one. If a change is detected (i.e., something in the new image is different from the previous one), the program will sound an alarm. After the comparison has been performed, the latest image becomes the previous one. The sequence repeats until the alarm program is stopped.

You are going to create a method called *differenceCount* that will be called to count the number of differences between the latest image and the previous one. In other words it will perform the actions in the middle of the preceding sequence. The method will also make a copy of the image for use next time it is called.

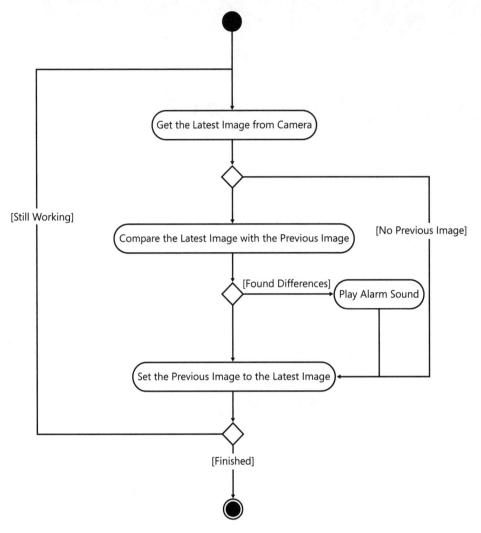

FIGURE 5-1 Detecting differences in images.

Storing a Video Image in Program Memory

A video image is actually just an array of byte values organized in a particular sequence. An image can be represented in a number of different ways. The Kinect camera produces bytes in the sequence blue, green, red, and the alpha (transparency) value. If you want to refresh your knowledge of this, take a look at Figure 4-2 in Chapter 4.

If a program needs to store a video image, it can do this by creating a byte array of the appropriate size. You have already used one program that does this. The sample project "Image Tweaker and Ghost Camera" in the section "Improving Video Quality" makes a number of byte arrays that it uses to store images that it is working on. Now you are going to see how this works.

```
byte[] previousFrameBytes = null;
```

The variable *previousFrameBytes* is a reference to an array of bytes. This array will hold a copy of the previous frame that the Kinect camera captures. The program must set *previousFrameBytes* to refer to a byte buffer of the appropriate size when it starts running. The program that you are going to create will contain a method called *differenceCount* that will count the number of pixels that are different between the latest image and the previous one.

```
unsafe int differenceCount(byte [] videoImageBytes)
{
    int differences = 0;

    // Make the previous frame buffer if we need to

    if (previousFrameBytes == null)
    {
        previousFrameBytes = new byte[videoImage.Length];
        Buffer.BlockCopy(videoImage, 0, previousFrameBytes, 0, videoImage.Length);
        // return  0 as we don't have any differences yet
        return 0;
    }

    // the rest of differenceCount goes here

}
```

The very first time that *differenceCount* is called, the reference to *previousFrameBytes* will be *null*. The method creates a new buffer array and then copies the current frame into it, ready for the next time the method is called. You can see how this works in the preceding code. The *BlockCopy* method is a useful way of copying bytes from one place to another. You just have to give it the source and destination arrays, whereabouts in the array to start copying, and the number of bytes to copy. The *BlockCopy* method is given the number of bytes to copy, which in this case is the length of the *videoImageBytes* array. Because the very first time the method is called there is no previous frame to compare with, the method can just return 0 at this point. The next time the method is called, it can compare the new image with the one that has just been stored and count the number of pixels that have changed.

Detecting Changes in Video Images

You might think that creating a program that detects changes in a video image would be easy. All the program would have to do is compare the color of a pixel with the color that it saw in the previous frame. If the program "sees" any change at that point, this means that something has changed in the image. The code to do this would be very simple to write:

```
if (previousRed != red)
    differences++;
```

This tiny piece of C# compares the red component of a pixel with the previous value. If the values are different, the code increments a counter variable called *differences*, which is keeping track of the number of differences in this image. However, this code would not work very well, and the reason for this is noise.

Dealing with Noise

Noise is a problem whenever computers get signals from the real world. Noise appears as speckles on images and as background hiss and crackle on audio signals. When a program tries to make sense of the signals coming in from the real world, it must deal with the fact that some of that information will be corrupted by noise. In Chapter 4 you saw a program that worked out the average value of the colors of each pixel in a scene over a large number of frames. This greatly improved the quality of the image, but it did mean that the sensor took longer to create the picture and the camera did not cope well with the effects of movement (although this did make for some interesting video effects when the video values held in memory got out of step with the image).

There is an important difference between analog and digital signals. Digital signals inside a computer are either *true* or *false*. A program that loads the contents of a digitally stored variable can have complete confidence in the value that it is receiving. There is no likelihood of noise if only two values are possible.

Unlike a digital signal, the value of an analog signal can be one among an infinite range of possible values. When a computer wants to use analog signals from the outside world, the first thing it must do is convert the analog value into a pattern of digital bits that represent the signal level as closely as possible.

The image data from the Kinect camera provides 8 bits of data for each of the three primary colors. This means that the intensity of each color is represented as a number in the range 0 to 255. You might think that if the picture remains the same, the intensity value received from the Kinect camera would remain the same, but unfortunately this is not the case.

The video capture process, along with the signal itself, results in noise appearing in the data that a program receives. This means that it is very unlikely that a particular pixel will have exactly the same color in successive frames. If your movement detection program triggered an alarm every time it detected a single pixel change in the image, the alarm would be continuously switched on.

Using Change Thresholds to Filter Out Noise

One way to reduce the problem of noise is to filter out small changes in the intensity of each pixel. Any changes below a particular threshold value would be ignored, as they would be attributed to noise and not movement. For example, if the red intensity of a pixel changes by 4, this change is probably going to be caused by noise and not something changing in the image.

```
byte greenChangeThreshold = 20;
byte blueChangeThreshold = 20;
byte redChangeThreshold = 20;
```

In the preceding code, you can see three threshold values: one each for green, blue, and red. Any changes below 20 in the color intensity of a pixel will be ignored by the program. These intensity values might seem very generous, in that a change of 20 is around one-tenth of the total range of brightness values that are available. However, as you will discover, the program does need to have this range of tolerances to be effective.

```
if (red > previousRed)
    redDiff = red - previousRed;
else
    redDiff = previousRed - red;
```

The preceding statement sets the value of *redDiff* to the difference between the current and the previous values of the red pixel. It decides which way to perform the calculation so that the result is always positive. The program can then compare this value with a threshold to see if the difference is large enough to mark a change in the image at that point.

```
if (greenDiff > greenChangeThreshold || blueDiff > blueChangeThreshold ||
    redDiff > redChangeThreshold)
{
    differences++;
    *greenPos = 255;
    *bluePos = 255;
    *redPos = 255;
}
```

The preceding code tests the difference values against their thresholds for all the colors at a pixel. If any difference value has changed too much, the program increments the *differences* counter and then sets the color of that pixel on the display to white. It does this by using three pointers: *greenPos*, *bluePos*, and *redPos*. These have been set to point at the pixel values in the display buffer. The color created by adding together bright red, green, and blue is white.

It should be possible to find some threshold values that will filter out noise in the signal but still allow for movement detection. The program can use another threshold value to determine the number of changes that must be detected before a movement is recognized. You could use this to make the alarm react to large objects such as people but not to small objects such as your cat.

> **Note** This means that the movement detection can be defeated if the image is only changed gradually by the item moving through it. For example, burglars could do things to reduce the changes that they cause in a picture. One behavior would be to move very slowly. The second would be to wear very plain-colored clothing, as any pattern in an item of clothing would cause many more changes in the image when it moved. This might be why prisoners are sometimes made to wear striped outfits, but I'm not sure.

Sounding the Alarm

When a significant difference between two frames is detected, the program should sound an alarm. The alarm sound that you want to play must be held in a WAV file, which is the sound file format used on Windows computers. You can use the Sound Recorder program supplied with Windows 7 to record your own sounds if you wish. A very good tool for working with sound files is Audacity, a freely available open-source program that you can download from the following site:

http://audacity.sourceforge.net

I'm presently using an alarm sound I call "ding," which I made by hitting a saucepan with a wooden spoon, but you can create whatever sound you like. To add sound to any program you can follow the sequence explained next.

Adding Sound Playback to a Project

Once you have your sound sample, you need to add it to the Visual Studio project that contains your solution and then write the code that will play the sound.

1. The best way to do this is to drag the file from its folder and drop it into the Visual Studio Solution Explorer.

2. The next thing you need to do is make sure that when the program is deployed, the sound sample file is stored as well. You can do this by modifying the Properties of the sound file that you have added to the project. Right-click the sound file and select Properties from the menu that appears. Now view the properties for the file.

3. Change the "Copy to Output Directory" setting to the one shown in the following graphic.

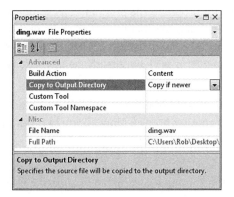

4. The sound playback itself is performed by the *SoundPlayer* class that is defined in the *System. Media* namespace. To get access to this namespace, add a using statement to your program.

```
using System.Media;
```

5. The program can now declare a variable of type *SoundPlayer* that will hold the sound to be played. This will be declared in the *MainWindows.xaml.cs* class alongside all the other data members of the class.

```
SoundPlayer alarmPlayer;
```

6. When the program starts, it can create a new *SoundPlayer* instance that contains this alarm sound:

```
alarmPlayer = new SoundPlayer("ding.wav");
```

 Note If the filename is not correct, the program will compile correctly but will fail when it runs.

7. Playing the sound is very simple; an instance of the *SoundPlayer* class provides a method called Play. This will start the sound playing.

```
alarmPlayer.Play();
```

A program can contain many sound effects; you just have to create a new SoundPlayer variable for each one. A Windows PC can play many sounds at the same time. The *SoundPlayer* class provides methods that allow you to make a sound play continuously, which can be useful for background sounds in games. The complete alarm program in the next section uses the *SoundPlayer* class to play the sound alarms when movement is detected.

A Complete Alarm Program

You now know enough to create a motion detector program. The program can capture an image from the Kinect camera and then count the number of pixels that have changed in each successive frame. If the number of changed pixels exceeds a particular threshold, then the program could sound an alarm. Fortunately for you, there is no need to do this as I have already made one for you.

> **Sample Code: Color Motion Detector** The sample project in the "01 Color Motion Detector" directory in the resources for this chapter holds a Kinect Camera program that will sound an alarm if movement is detected by the camera.

Figure 5-2 shows how the program is used. The first three vertical sliders allow the user to control the thresholds for the red, green, and blue elements of the picture. The rightmost slider allows you to change the total number of differences that must be detected before the alarm triggers. The colored panel will display red when the alarm is triggered and green when not. The display shows the pixels that have changed by coloring them white. It is interesting to reduce the threshold values and watch the image disappear into a sea of white noise.

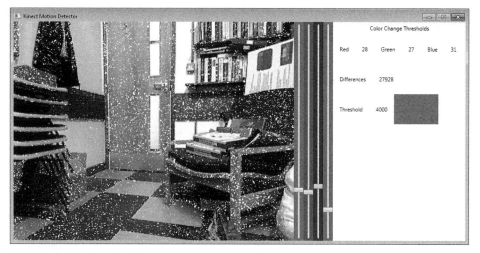

FIGURE 5-2 Kinect motion detector.

The method *updateDisplay* is called after each frame to update the screen of the application.

```
SolidColorBrush OKBrush = new SolidColorBrush(Colors.Green);
SolidColorBrush AlarmBrush = new SolidColorBrush(Colors.Red);

void updateDisplay()
{

    differenceValue.Content = differences.ToString();
    thresholdValue.Content = alarmThreshold.ToString();
```

```
greenValue.Content = greenChangeThreshold.ToString();
blueValue.Content = blueChangeThreshold.ToString();
redValue.Content = redChangeThreshold.ToString();

if (differences > alarmThreshold)
{
    if (alarmLabel.Background != AlarmBrush)
    {
        alarmPlayer.Play();
        alarmLabel.Background = AlarmBrush;
    }
}
else
{
    alarmLabel.Background = OKBrush;
}

if (colorImageBitmap == null)
{
    this.colorImageBitmap = new WriteableBitmap(
        640,
        480,
        96,  // DpiX
        96,  // DpiY
        PixelFormats.Bgr32,
        null);
    kinectVideo.Source = colorImageBitmap;
}

colorImageBitmap.WritePixels(
    new Int32Rect(0, 0, 640, 480),
    currentImageBytes, // video data
    640 * 4, // stride,
    0    // offset into the array - start at 0
    );
}
```

This method displays the threshold values and the total number of differences on the screen, and it also sets the background color of the alarm label to a red brush or a green brush. If it detects that the color of the brush has changed from green to red because the alarm has been triggered, it plays the alarm sound. It also displays the image from the camera.

```
int differences;

bool displayActive = true;

Thread updateVideoThread;
```

```
void videoDisplay()
{
    while (displayActive)
    {
        using (ColorImageFrame colorFrame = myKinect.ColorStream.OpenNextFrame(10))
        {
            if (colorFrame == null) continue;

            if (currentImageBytes == null)
                currentImageBytes = new byte[colorFrame.PixelDataLength];

            colorFrame.CopyPixelDataTo(currentImageBytes);

            differences = differenceCount(currentImageBytes);

            Dispatcher.Invoke(new Action(() => updateDisplay()));
        }
    }
}
```

The program uses the same thread-based technique as the one at the end of Chapter 4. The *videoDisplay* method repeatedly loads an image from the Kinect video camera, calls the *differenceCount* method to compare the new frame with the previous one, and then invokes the *updateDisplay* method to update the window. As you saw at the end of Chapter 4, in the section "Updating the Image from a Different Thread," it is not possible for the *videoDisplay* method to call *updateDisplay* directly because the method is running on a different thread from the Windows Presentation Foundation window manager. The *updateDisplay* method would like to change the settings on some display elements on the screen, and only threads running in the window manager are allowed to do this.

Windows manages hundreds of different threads when a computer is running, giving each thread control for a fraction of a second. Some are managing the memory; others are looking after the hard disk and network connections, and so on. When the Kinect program is running, one thread is fetching image data from the Kinect camera and another will be acting as the window manager for the application. The problem is that if every program was allowed direct access to the screen, this would not end well. It is important that changes to the display be carefully coordinated to fit in with the needs of the hardware that is actually performing the drawing.

You can think of the window manager as a bit like a DJ at a party. If everyone at the party could stop and start tracks playing, nobody would hear any music. Instead the DJ is the one person in charge of the music and those present put in requests to be played later, in sequence. In the case of the Kinect program, the way it puts in a request to the window manager is by using the *Dispatcher. Invoke* method. The *Dispatcher* is the part of the window manager that delivers messages to all the windows components that make up the display. This includes delivering mouse movement information and informing display components that their content has changed. A program can ask the Dispatcher to deliver a message for it. In the following case, the message is a request to run the method that will update the display:

```
Dispatcher.Invoke(new Action(() => updateDisplay()));
```

This message asks the window manager to run a method at some point in the future. The parameter to the *Invoke* method is a delegate that refers to the method to be called. A delegate is a special kind of reference that refers to methods. The *Action* type is a delegate type that can refer to methods that have no parameters and do not return a result. The preceding statement creates a new *Action* delegate that refers to the *updateDisplay* method.

The *Invoke* method puts this delegate value onto a list of things to do, just like a DJ accepts a particular request. Later, when the window manager thread is active, it can call the method that is able to update the display. This all happens very quickly, and as far as the user is concerned the display just updates as they would expect.

Switching to Black and White

The preceding color motion detector works quite well, and you will be able to find settings for the thresholds that allow movement to be detected. However, there is a way to improve performance with very little effort, and that is to convert the image to black and white before testing for changes.

In a black-and-white image, each pixel is represented by a single value, which is the brightness of the scene at that point. A very simple way to convert a pixel into its black-and-white equivalent would be to add up the amounts of the red, green, and blue pixels:

```
int whiteLevel = red + blue + green;
```

One problem with this approach is that it produces a value that is now much larger than a single byte can hold. In other words, if red, green, and blue were both at the value *200*, the sum of the three would be *600*, which would not fit into a single byte. To make the result fit into a byte, we can divide the value by 3:

```
byte whiteByte = (byte)(whiteLevel / 3);
```

The value *whiteByte* now contains a byte value that represents the brightness of a particular pixel. If the red, green, and blue pixels are all loaded with this value, the result is a pixel that has an appropriate brightness.

```
*greenPos = whiteByte;
*bluePos = whiteByte;
*redPos = whiteByte;
```

The conversion from black and white that I have used is not completely accurate. The preceding code treats each color equally, so that the final intensity is made up of one-third each of the red, green, and blue components. In real life the human eye is more sensitive to some colors than others. Our eyes are much more sensitive to green than any other color, and so a proper conversion would be made up of 0.59 green, 0.3 red, and 0.11 blue. However, this would slow down the conversion, so I have left it out. However, if you want to create programs that produce photographic-quality black-and-white images from your Kinect sensor, then you should bear this in mind.

Using black and white in this way does seem to reduce the amount of noise detected for each pixel. This is probably because the value of each pixel is now averaged over three values (red, green, and blue).

> **Sample Code: Black-and-White Motion Detector** The sample project in the "02 Black and White Motion Detector" directory in the resources for this chapter holds a Kinect Camera program that will sound an alarm if movement is detected by the camera. This converts the image information into black and white before performing the tests.

Triggering Pictures with Motion Capture

Rather than sound an alarm when the program detects motion, it might be more useful to take a picture of the scene. In Chapter 4 the Photo Booth program contained code that enabled a program to save an image into a file; this can be used to save images here as well. The only problem is that if the program detects motion several times, it will have to store the pictures in different files. It would not be useful if the program kept overwriting one file with each new picture. One way to solve this is to use a frame counter that is increased after each shot has been taken:

```
int frameNo = 1;
```

The program can use the following code to create a different filename for each photograph:

```
string destDir = System.IO.Path.GetDirectoryName(fileNameTextBox.Text);
string destFile = System.IO.Path.GetFileNameWithoutExtension(fileNameTextBox.Text);
string fileName = destDir + @"\" + destFile + frameNo.ToString() + ".jpg";
frameNo++;
```

The preceding program code uses the contents of *fileNameTextBox* as the starting filename. It then gets the destination directory and the filename and constructs a new filename that contains the frame number. The user selects the filename, and then the program produces a sequence of numbered image files. This code uses a very useful *Path* class, which is held inside the *System.IO* namespace. It provides a set of methods that you can use to manipulate filenames. The preceding program code uses the Fully Qualified Name for the *Path* class so that it can be distinguished from the *Path* class in the Windows *Shapes* namespace.

> **Sample Code: Motion Detector Camera (Figure 5-3)** The sample project in the "03 Motion-Activated Camera" directory in the resources for this chapter holds a Kinect Camera program that will sound an alarm and take a picture if movement is detected by the camera. Users must select a destination for the file and then the program will produce a numbered set of shots, one for each time movement is detected.

FIGURE 5-3 Kinect motion-detecting camera.

Capturing Multiple Frames

The motion detecting camera works very well. You could use it to find out who keeps taking all the milk from the fridge. However, it does have one problem: the program just takes a single picture as soon as movement is detected in a frame. This means that rather than capturing the face of the milk-stealing miscreant, it will probably just capture the person's foot while walking into the picture. This might not produce enough to secure a conviction. You could program the software to capture frames every time it sees movement, but this could produce many thousands of pictures and fill up a hard disk with photographs that might not mean much.

One way to fix this would be to have the camera capture a sequence of frames each time it detects a new movement. This would not fill up the computer's disk with pictures and would generate enough pictures to provide conclusive evidence.

```
int picturesToTake = 0;
```

Rather than using a flag to tell the program when to take a picture, this version of the program uses a variable called *picturesToTake*. When the program detects movement, it sets the value of *picturesToTake* to *5*. The program can then save frames as long as the value of this variable is greater than 0, and it can reduce the counter by 1 each time a frame has been saved.

```
if (picturesToTake > 0 )
{
    saveFrame(videoImage);
    picturesToTake--;
}
```

> **Sample Code: Motion Detector Camera** The sample project in the "04 Motion Activated Camera Multiple Frames" directory in the resources for this chapter holds a Kinect Camera program that will sound an alarm and take five consecutive pictures if movement is detected by the camera. Users must select a destination for the file, and then the program will produce a numbered set of shots, five for each time movement is detected.

As an exercise, you might want to investigate how you could add a *TextBox* to the program that would allow the user to select how many pictures are taken when movement is detected. To improve the chances of catching the criminal in the act, you could also add code that took a sequence of pictures at longer intervals after the sensor was triggered.

Summary

In this chapter you have learned more about how images are held and manipulated in the computer, and how a program can detect changes in them.

You have also learned about noise and how this is present on all signals that are used by a computer when working with data from the real world.

Finally, you created a program that generates sound alarms and captures images when movement is detected in video signal.

In Chapter 6, you are going to investigate the Kinect depth sensor and how we can use this to create some amazing applications.

Fun with the Depth Sensor

After completing this chapter, you will:

- Understand how the depth sensor delivers depth information

- Combine depth and image information to trigger a camera when an object moves close to it

- Use the depth camera to make a program that lets you draw with your fingertip

- Make use of the depth sensor to detect objects

- Create an XNA game where you are the controller

Visualizing Kinect Depth Information

YOU HAVE SEEN HOW THE Kinect video camera works. At regular intervals the video camera sensor produces a lump of data containing a set of values for the red, green, and blue intensity for each pixel in the scene it is capturing. This data describes a single frame of video. A program can use the pixel values in the frame to display an image for the viewer. The video information can also be used as data values to do other things, such as detect movement. In this chapter you will see how the Kinect depth sensor works and how you can use information from this sensor to do interesting things with your programs.

The Kinect Depth Sensor

The Kinect depth sensor generates data in a way very similar to the video camera. At regular intervals it produces a frame of information. Each frame contains a number of pixel values, only rather than giving the red, green, and blue intensity values for each point in a scene, a pixel value gives the distance of that point in the scene from the camera. It is as if the Kinect sensor took a tiny tape measure and measured the distance to every point in the scene in front of it and then assembled the results in an array of pixels. However, this is not actually how it works. The Kinect sensor projects out a grid of infrared dots and then works out how the dots have been displaced by objects in front of the camera, as demonstrated in Chapter 1, in the section "The Depth Sensor."

The distance readings are given in millimeters (mm), and the sensor uses 13 bits to represent each value. This means that, in theory, the Kinect depth sensor can register objects up to 25 feet (8 meters) from the sensor. However, in reality the usable range of the present sensors is half of this, up to about 12 feet (4 meters). It is not possible to resolve objects closer to the sensor than 24 inches (800 mm) because of the way that the sensor works. This is because at short distances, the infrared camera that is used cannot focus on individual dots in the grid, just like your eye can't focus on things held very close to it. In tests, I've found that I can get good distance results between 3 feet (1 meter) and 12 feet (4 meters) from the sensor.

All the distance measurement takes place inside the Kinect sensor bar; in other words, a program in the computer that uses the distance information just has to process the incoming frames of depth data that the Kinect produces.

Obtaining Depth Information from the Sensor

To obtain the depth information from the Kinect sensor, a program uses exactly the same technique as was used to read the video data in the earlier chapters.

```
KinectSensor myKinect = KinectSensor.KinectSensors[0];
myKinect.DepthStream.Enable();
```

The preceding statements select a Kinect sensor and then enable the depth camera. A program can enable both the video and the depth stream at the same time; later you will create an application that does this. The program can then connect a method to an event that is raised each time a new depth reading is available.

```
myKinect.DepthFrameReady +=
    new EventHandler<DepthImageFrameReadyEventArgs>(myKinect_DepthFrameReady);
```

Each time that a new depth frame is available, the method *myKinect_DepthFrameReady* will be called. This method call delivers a depth frame that contains a set of distance values: one for each depth reading produced by the depth sensor. These readings can then be copied into an array for the program to use.

```
short[] depthData = null;

void myKinect_DepthFrameReady(object sender, DepthImageFrameReadyEventArgs e)
{
    using (DepthImageFrame depthFrame = e.OpenDepthImageFrame())
    {
```

```
        if (depthFrame == null) return;

        if (depthData == null)
            depthData = new short[depthFrame.PixelDataLength];

        depthFrame.CopyPixelDataTo(depthData);

        // the depth values are now in the array depthData
    }
}
```

The preceding *myKinect_DepthFrameReady* method obtains the depth data values from the sensor and stores them in an array called *depthData*. This is an array of *short* integer values, each of which is 16 bits in size. The C# *short* data type is used to hold values that have a smaller range than the *int* type, which is more commonly used to store integer values in programs. The *int* data type allows a C# program to work with integer values in the range plus or minus 4,000,000,000 or so. An *int* variable uses 32 bits to store each value. The *short* data type uses 16 bits to represent each value. This is a closer fit to the 13 bits of data that make up each depth reading. If the program used the *int* type to hold the values, it would waste 19 bits in each value.

The designers of the Kinect SDK have found a use for the 3 spare bits in each 16-bit depth value. These bits identify the image data values corresponding to a particular player standing in front of the sensor. The system can track up to six players and provide skeleton information about two of these players. (You will discover how to do this in Chapter 8.) The value in these 3 bits identifies the player of which this depth value is part. If the value is zero, it means that this depth value is not part of any of the players.

Figure 6-1 shows how the depth value and the player number are combined in a single 16-bit value. The bits labeled "P" are the player data bits and are the bottom 3 bits. The bits labeled "D" are the depth data values and are in the remaining 13 bits. The numbers at the bottom of the diagram give the value that each bit represents.

Bit 15	Bit 14	Bit 13	Bit 12	Bit 11	Bit 10	Bit 9	Bit 8	Bit 7	Bit 6	Bit 5	Bit 4	Bit 3	Bit 2	Bit 1	Bit 0
D	D	D	D	D	D	D	D	D	D	D	D	D	P	P	P
4096	2048	1024	512	256	128	64	32	16	8	4	2	0	4	2	0

16-bit depth value

FIGURE 6-1 16-bit depth and player data.

Later on you will use the player data bits to make a program that can isolate the picture of a player from the background. For now the program does not need to use these values, and so they must be discarded. A program can do this by shifting the combined 16-bit value to the right by 3 bits. This causes the player information to drop off the end, while leaving the bits that represent the depth value.

```
int depthValue = depthData[depthPos] >> 3;
```

The preceding statement creates a depth value from the element with the subscript value *depthPos* in the *depthData* array.

Figure 6-2 shows the result of the shift. The "P" (player) values have disappeared, and the depth values are now in the correct position to provide a value with which the program can work. The top 3 bits of the value (bits 15, 14, and 13) are set to 0 by the shifting operation.

Bit 15	Bit 14	Bit 13	Bit 12	Bit 11	Bit 10	Bit 9	Bit 8	Bit 7	Bit 6	Bit 5	Bit 4	Bit 3	Bit 2	Bit 1	Bit 0
			D	D	D	D	D	D	D	D	D	D	D	D
			4096	2048	1024	512	256	128	64	32	16	8	4	2	0

13-bit depth value

FIGURE 6-2 13-bit depth data.

Depth Data Values

Because of the way it works, the Kinect sensor cannot always get a good depth reading. Sometimes part of the image from the infrared projector is in shadow or an object in front of the sensor is too distant or too close. The Kinect SDK uses a set of special values that are given in the depth data to reflect these situations. A program must check for these values. You are going to make the program display colors to indicate these error conditions. The indicator values are provided as properties of the *DepthStream* member in the Kinect sensor:

```
if (depthValue == myKinect.DepthStream.UnknownDepth)
{
    // the depth values for this pixel could not be obtained
}
```

The preceding statements check if a depth value is unknown. This means that the depth sensor did not get a reflection of the projected infrared dot at this position. Other possible values are *TooFarDepth* and *TooNearDepth*. Any other value in the depth stream will be the depth of the pixel at that position in the image.

Visualizing Depth Information

Now that you know the meaning of the data values received from the sensor, you can create a program that creates a view of them. You are going to create a program that will show graphically the results from the distance camera. In formal computer terms this is called *visualization*. You are creating a view of some data. Humans use visualization a lot. Whenever you look at a graph of values, you are actually seeing an artificial construction created to help you understand what the numbers mean.

You are going to make a program that displays an image representing the numbers that the distance sensor is producing. You can start with a simple mapping of distance to brightness. The farther away the object is, the darker it will be drawn on the screen. This will result in a picture that looks like an image of the scene, but it actually shows how far objects are away from the Kinect sensor bar. You are going to do this by creating an array of pixel color values that will be converted into an image to be displayed.

Figure 6-3 shows the arrangement of memory that the depth visualization program is going to create. Each of the items is an 8-bit intensity value for the color of that pixel. Figure 6-3 shows the data for two pixels that take up a total of 8 bytes of memory. This is the same figure that you saw in Chapter 4 when you investigated camera output. What the depth-viewing program is going to do is set color intensity values into the array. It will use depth values from the camera to make the colored pixels. This is exactly how the display in your computer works. The picture that you see on the screen is actually made up of numbers held in a block of memory that tells the graphics card what color to paint the screen at each point in the display.

Blue	Green	Red	Alpha	Blue	Green	Red	Alpha
0	1	2	3	4	5	6	7

FIGURE 6-3 Creating pictures.

The program is going to draw the image so that the closer parts of the scene look brighter. To do this it will set the red, green, and blue values of the scene to a value that is larger the closer an object is to the camera. Unfortunately these brightness values are only 8 bits in size. In other words, the 8-bit brightness value is in the range 0–255, but the 13-bit depth information is in the range 0–8191. The program must remove the "least significant" 5 data bits from the 13-bit depth information to leave 8 bits that give an intensity value that represents the entire range of distance values. The good news is that this is very easy to do using shift. If you shift a 13-bit value to the right five times, the rightmost 5 bits will drop off the end, leaving an 8-bit value that can be used to represent the intensity of the color.

```
byte depthByte = (byte)(depthValue >> 5);
```

The preceding statement creates a *depthByte* value that holds an 8-bit value representing the depth value.

Figure 6-4 shows the final 8-bit version of the depth data, once it has been shifted to the right to remove five of the bits. Of course this means that the program will lose a lot of precision in the depth data. A difference of one between two depth values now reflects a change in distance of 32 mm rather than the 1 mm distance in the original data. You can increase the resolution of the depth display by only shifting the value 4 bits instead. This works because although the sensor values can deliver results in the range of 12 feet (4 meters) to 24 feet (8 meters), this is very rarely useful in practice, whereas an improvement in resolution to 16 mm will provide a better-quality image. Of course if you wanted to write a program that actually uses the depth value to recognize the position of objects, you would use the full-size versions of the depth values.

Bit 15 Bit 14 Bit 13 Bit 12 Bit 11 Bit 10 Bit 9 Bit 8 Bit 7 Bit 6 Bit 5 Bit 4 Bit 3 Bit 2 Bit 1 Bit 0

| | | | | | | | | D | D | D | D | D | D | D | D |

128   64   32   16   8   4   2   0

8-bit depth value

FIGURE 6-4 An 8-bit version of the depth information.

The program has to do just one last thing to the value to make it work properly. At this stage, the color intensity will be larger the farther away an object is from the sensor. The idea is that the program will show closest objects as brighter, and so the program must make the intensity increase for objects that are closer to the depth sensor. This is easily achieved by adding a tiny bit of extra math to the statement that calculates the depth byte.

```
byte depthByte = (byte)(255-(depthValue >> 4));
```

This statement subtracts the depth value from 255. This means that as the depth value gets larger, the brightness value will get smaller. You now know how to work out a brightness value that represents a particular depth value; however, the program must do this for each pixel in the display. The simplest way to do this is to use a loop that works through the array received from the depth sensor. This will create pixel values that are stored in an array that can be displayed.

```
void myKinect_DepthFrameReady(object sender, DepthImageFrameReadyEventArgs e)
{
    using (DepthImageFrame depthFrame = e.OpenDepthImageFrame())
    {
        if (depthFrame == null) return;

        if (depthData == null) depthData = new short[depthFrame.PixelDataLength];

        if (depthColorImage == null)
            depthColorImage = new byte[depthFrame.PixelDataLength * 4];

        depthFrame.CopyPixelDataTo(depthData);

        int depthColorImagePos = 0;

        for (int depthPos = 0; depthPos < depthFrame.PixelDataLength; depthPos ++)
        {
            int depthValue = depthData[depthPos] >> 3;
            // Check for the invalid values
            if (depthValue == myKinect.DepthStream.UnknownDepth)
            {
                depthColorImage[depthColorImagePos++] = 0; // Blue
                depthColorImage[depthColorImagePos++] = 0; // Green
                depthColorImage[depthColorImagePos++] = 255; // Red
            }
```

```
        else if (depthValue == myKinect.DepthStream.TooFarDepth)
        {
            depthColorImage[depthColorImagePos++] = 255; // Blue
            depthColorImage[depthColorImagePos++] = 0; // Green
            depthColorImage[depthColorImagePos++] = 0; // Red
        }
        else if (depthValue == myKinect.DepthStream.TooNearDepth)
        {
            depthColorImage[depthColorImagePos++] = 0; // Blue
            depthColorImage[depthColorImagePos++] = 255; // Green
            depthColorImage[depthColorImagePos++] = 0; // Red
        }
        else
        {
            byte depthByte = (byte)(255 - (depthValue >> 4));
            depthColorImage[depthColorImagePos++] = depthByte; // Blue
            depthColorImage[depthColorImagePos++] = depthByte; // Green
            depthColorImage[depthColorImagePos++] = depthByte; // Red
        }
        // transparency
        depthColorImagePos++;
    }

    // we now have a new array of color data

    if (depthImageBitmap == null)
    {
        this.depthImageBitmap = new WriteableBitmap(
            depthFrame.Width,
            depthFrame.Height,
            96,  // DpiX
            96,  // DpiY
            PixelFormats.Bgr32,
            null);
        kinectDepthImage.Source = depthImageBitmap;
    }

    this.depthImageBitmap.WritePixels(
        new Int32Rect(0, 0, depthFrame.Width, depthFrame.Height),
        depthColorImage, // video data
        depthFrame.Width * 4, // stride,
        0   // offset into the array - start at 0
        );
    }
}
```

The preceding method, *myKinect_DepthFrameReady*, displays a color image that contains the depth information. The variable *depthPos* is used to count through the depth sensor values, and the variable *depthColorImagePos* is used to count through the pixels in the image that is created.

Note The version of the preceding code does not use unsafe code and pointers to manipulate the data. This means that it is less efficient than it might be, but it is also much easier to understand. If you are concerned about performance you might like to consider how you could convert it to use pointers as in Chapter 4, in the section "Improving Performance by Waiting for Each Kinect Frame."

Figure 6-5 shows the results of pointing the depth sensor at a chair in my office.

FIGURE 6-5 Depth sensor view showing a chair.

Using the Depth Information to Detect Intruders

A program can use the depth information directly to do some fun things. Writing an alarm that is triggered by someone moving too close to the sensor is very easy. The program just has to work through the depth information looking for the smallest value. If this is less than a particular threshold, the program will sound the alarm. Unlike the video movement alarm that you created earlier, this one is much harder for a burglar to defeat. The video movement alarm had to put thresholds around the input values so that it was not triggered by noise. A slow-moving burglar would be able to beat the video movement detector because it would be hard to distinguish the intruder from noise. However, a depth alarm will detect when a depth value reaches a particular number, and there is not much that a burglar can do about that.

The logic to detect the closest object to the camera is very simple. Each time a new depth value is calculated, it is compared with the current minimum distance. If it is smaller than the smallest distance seen so far, it is the new smallest distance.

```
if (depthValue < minDistance)
    minDistance = depthValue;
```

The preceding test will do this. Note that this code does the test for one pixel; to get the closest pixel a program will have to work through all the pixels in the scene.

Using the Depth and Video Sensors at the Same Time

The best way to use the depth information would be to trigger Kinect to take a picture when something moves close to the camera. To do this, the program must activate both input sensors and connect event handlers to each.

```
if (KinectSensor.KinectSensors.Count == 0)
{
    MessageBox.Show("No Kinects detected", "Camera Viewer");
    Application.Current.Shutdown();
}

try
{
    myKinect = KinectSensor.KinectSensors[0];

    myKinect.DepthStream.Enable();
    myKinect.ColorStream.Enable();

    myKinect.Start();

    myKinect.DepthFrameReady +=
        new EventHandler<DepthImageFrameReadyEventArgs>(myKinect_DepthFrameReady);
```

```
    myKinect.ColorFrameReady +=
        new EventHandler<ColorImageFrameReadyEventArgs>(myKinect_ColorFrameReady);
}
catch
{
    MessageBox.Show("Kinect initialise failed", "Depth Viewer");
    Application.Current.Shutdown();
}
```

This code runs when the program starts running. The Kinect sensor instance is told that both distance and depth sensors will be used:

```
myKinect.DepthStream.Enable();
myKinect.ColorStream.Enable();
```

It is now possible to connect handlers to the events that fire when new frames of information are available from either sensor.

> **Sample Code: Depth-Activated Camera** The sample project in the "02 Depth-Activated Camera" directory in the resources for this chapter (see the "Code Samples" section in the Introduction) holds a Kinect Camera program that displays a depth and a video view. When the camera detects an object closer than the set threshold, it will take a sequence of pictures of it. Note that for this to work well you have to make sure that that closest thing the Kinect will see is the item to be detected. In other words, this works best in wide open spaces.

Drawing in the Air

You can modify the previous program slightly to create one that lets you draw on the screen just by moving your finger in the air. If you stand and point your finger toward the depth sensor, your fingertip is the closest item to the sensor. A program can work out whereabouts this point is in the image and then draw pixels at this point. You have already seen that a program can create an array of bytes that is then displayed as an image. This is how you created the depth camera view earlier. Now you are going to use the depth information to control a drawing action in an array of bytes.

```
// Image Size
const int fingerPaintImageWidth = 640;
const int fingerPaintImageHeight = 480;
const int fingerPaintImageByteSize =
    fingerPaintImageHeight * fingerPaintImageWidth * 4;
```

```
// Image buffer
byte[] fingerPaintImageBytes = new byte[fingerPaintImageByteSize];
```

This is the declaration of the byte array that holds the image that will be drawn. The size of the image has been set as the same size as the resolution of the Kinect sensor depth camera, as 6,400 pixels wide and 480 pixels high.

To draw in the image, all the program has to do is change the color values of the pixel that it wants to draw.

```
void drawFingerPaintPixel(int drawPos, byte blue, byte green, byte red, byte alpha)
{
    fingerPaintImageBytes[drawPos] = blue;
    drawPos++;
    fingerPaintImageBytes[drawPos] = green;
    drawPos++;
    fingerPaintImageBytes[drawPos] = red;
    drawPos++;
    fingerPaintImageBytes[drawPos] = alpha;
}
```

The *drawFingerPaintPixel* method is given the draw position and the color and transparency (alpha) values to be put at that pixel. The Kinect depth information and the draw buffer that was created for the finger-painted pictures are arranged in a similar way. The very first items in the arrays refer to the top-left corner of the screen. A program can directly map pixels in the depth image into the drawn image. If you think about it, this must work because otherwise the images from the depth camera that you created earlier would look wrong. This means that all the program has to do is to draw something when it finds a point that is closer than the draw threshold.

```
if (depthValue < fingerDrawDistance)
{
    drawFingerPaintPixel(depthPos * 4, bluePen, greenPen, redPen, alphaPen);
}
```

The preceding code tests the depth value, and if it is less than the draw distance it will call *drawFingerPaintPixel* to draw a pixel using the current settings of the pen color. The value of *depthPos* identifies the position of the pixel in the depth buffer. This is multiplied by four to give the position of the pixel in the output bitmap. This multiplication is there because the depth buffer uses one value per pixel (a 16-bit depth value in a short value) but the output image uses 4 bytes per pixel (3 color bytes and 1 transparency byte).

It turns out that this is not really a finger-painting program as such; you can paint with your whole body if you move into the drawing range.

> **Sample Code: Simple Finger Painting** The sample project in the "03 Simple KinectFingerPaint" directory in the resources for this chapter (see the "Code Samples" section in the Introduction) holds a Kinect Camera program that you can use to perform finger painting in the air. The draw distance has been set at 1 meter from the sensor. This version of the program is very primitive (but fun to play with). You will be developing this program later as you learn more about the Kinect features.

You might like to experiment with changing the drawing color as the program is used.

Detecting Objects

You know that the Kinect sensor can detect people and other objects in the frame of view. Now it is time to find out how to do this in your programs. This sounds like a very hard problem to solve, but it turns out to be easy to get something that works quite well. You start by making some assumptions about the scene in front of the Kinect sensor:

- The object to be detected will be the largest thing in front of the sensor.

- The object to be detected will be fairly flat.

- The object to be detected will be facing the sensor.

If you put all these assumptions together, you can get one working principle for the object detector you are going to build:

- The object to be detected is described by a large set of depth readings that are all around the same distance from the sensor.

If you think about it, this makes very good sense. If you want the Kinect sensor to detect your movement, you need to stand in front of the sensor and move everything else out of the way. Because you are going to face the sensor—and humans are fairly flat—the sensor will receive a large number of readings that are all about the same distance from it. The floor, ceiling, and walls of a room all recede into the distance, away from the sensor, and do not have a large set of specific depth readings associated with them. Of course, this technique will fail if you stand close to a wall. In that case your depth readings will be difficult or impossible to distinguish from the wall itself.

Figure 6-6 shows the output from a program that reads the depth sensor and then plots the frequency of readings at 31 different distances from the sensor. You can see that in slot 13, something would seem to be much larger than the other objects in the scene. In fact, bearing in mind that there are high readings around this point, it would seem reasonable to assume that these are part of the object as well.

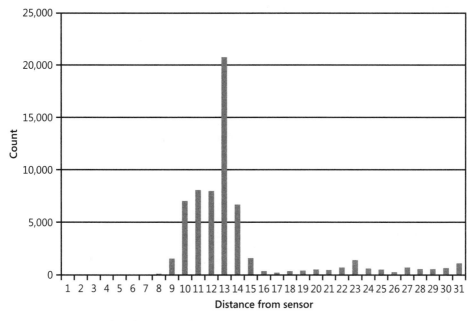

FIGURE 6-6 A graph of the frequency of depth values.

Counting Depth Values

The Kinect sensor can produce depth values over 4,000. The preceding program splits this range into 32 different "slots" and then keeps a counter for each slot. It makes rather clever use of the shift operation to create and manage the slots.

```
const int slotSizeFactor = 7;
const int noOfSlots = 4096 >> slotSizeFactor;
```

The variable *slotSizeFactor* sets the number of shifts that will be used to reduce depth values. If it held the value *1*, there would be 2,048 slots. Each time *slotSizeFactor* gets one bigger, it halves the number of slots. A *slotSizeFactor* of seven gives us slots that are about 5 inches (128 mm) deep, which seems to work quite well. You get a figure of 128 mm because the sensor gives readings in millimeters (mm). There are 4,096 possible depth values, and 4,096 divided by 32 is 128. Using the shift operator in this way is very efficient, as shifting is much faster than performing a division.

To count the elements at each depth, the program must work through all the depth values and increase the counter in the slot that corresponds to that depth value.

```
// Clear the depth counters in each slot
for (int slotNo = 0; slotNo < SlotCounts.Length; slotNo++)
{
    SlotCounts[slotNo] = 0;
}
```

```
// Make a pass through the image counting depth pixels

for (int depthPos = 0; depthPos < depthData.Length; depthPos++)
{
    int depthValue = depthData[depthPos] >> 3;
    // Check for the invalid values

    if (depthValue == myKinect.DepthStream.UnknownDepth ||
        depthValue == myKinect.DepthStream.TooFarDepth ||
        depthValue == myKinect.DepthStream.TooNearDepth)
    {
        continue;
    }

    // Got a valid depth value
    // Find the slot and increase the counter

    int slotNumber = depthValue >> slotSizeFactor;
    SlotCounts[slotNumber]++;
}
```

The first part of the program sets all the elements in the *SlotCounts* array to zero. The program then works through the depth values. The interesting part is where the *depthValue* is shifted right by the *slotSizeFactor*. This produces the number of the slot that must be incremented. At the end of this code, the program will have built an array that contains histogram heights like the ones seen in Figure 6-6. The next thing it must do is find the slot that contains the largest number of depth values. This will give the distance from the camera of the largest object in the scene.

```
// Now find the depth with the most pixels
int maxCount = 0;
int maxPos = 0;

for (int slotNo = 0; slotNo < SlotCounts.Length; slotNo++)
{
    if (SlotCounts[slotNo] > maxCount)
    {
        maxCount = SlotCounts[slotNo];
        maxPos = slotNo;
    }
}
```

This loop works through the slots while looking for the largest count values. Each time it finds a new largest value, it records the position in the array and then sets the new maximum.

When this loop has completed, the program knows the approximate distance from the Kinect sensor to the largest object in the scene. It can now make another pass through the data and generate a depth display that displays all the parts of the image which are that distance away.

```
// Now color those pixels red in the image

int depthColorImagePos = 0;

for (int depthPos = 0; depthPos < depthData.Length; depthPos++)
{
    int depthValue = depthData[depthPos] >> 3;
    // Check for the invalid values

    if (depthValue == myKinect.DepthStream.UnknownDepth ||
        depthValue == myKinect.DepthStream.TooFarDepth ||
        depthValue == myKinect.DepthStream.TooNearDepth)
    {
        // Color invalid pixels black
        // Blue
        depthColorImage[depthColorImagePos] = 0;
        depthColorImagePos++;
        // Green
        depthColorImage[depthColorImagePos] = 0;
        depthColorImagePos++;
        // Red
        depthColorImage[depthColorImagePos] = 0;
        depthColorImagePos++;
    }
    else
    {
        byte depthByte = (byte)(255 - (depthValue >> 4));

        if (depthValue >> slotSizeFactor == maxPos)
        {
            // Blue
            depthColorImage[depthColorImagePos] = 0;
            depthColorImagePos++;
            // Green
            depthColorImage[depthColorImagePos] = 0;
            depthColorImagePos++;
            // Red
            depthColorImage[depthColorImagePos] = depthByte;
            depthColorImagePos++;
        }
        else
        {
```

```
      // Blue
      depthColorImage[depthColorImagePos] = depthByte;
      depthColorImagePos++;
      // Green
      depthColorImage[depthColorImagePos] = depthByte;
      depthColorImagePos++;
      // Red
      depthColorImage[depthColorImagePos] = depthByte;
      depthColorImagePos++;
    }
  }
  // transparency
  depthColorImagePos++;
}
```

This loop works through the image data and builds the picture that will be displayed by the program. If the depth value is in the *maxPos* slot, the pixel is drawn using only the red color. If it is not in that slot, the pixel is drawn using all colors and shows as gray. You might want to experiment with slots of different sizes; a *slotSizeFactor* that is larger will handle objects in a greater range of depths.

> **Sample Code: Object Detection** The sample project in the "04 Object Detector" directory in the resources for this chapter (see the "Code Samples" section in the Introduction) holds a Kinect Camera program that uses the preceding code to perform object detection. It works quite well, particularly if the scene around the Kinect sensor is not cluttered. You can experiment with different slot sizes. The program also has a "Dump" button that will dump the contents of the slot counter for you to analyze. The Dump button produces a comma separated value (CSV) file that can be imported into a spreadsheet program, for example Microsoft Excel. The file contains a single row of values. Each value is the count for that particular "slot." The graph in Figure 6-6 was produced by plotting a histogram of one set of such values.

Making You into the Controller

One of the claims made about Kinect is that it "makes you into the controller." Now you are going to find out how to do this. The controller that you are going to make simply uses the position of the object in the frame to control the left–right movement of a paddle on the screen. Remember that there is nothing magical happening here; it is just very simple math based on an assumption about the situation. The assumption that you are making is this: the actual *x* position of the object is the average of all *x* position values in the object.

This assumption works on the basis that people are generally symmetrical. In other words if I stand facing the camera, as much of me will be on one side as on the other side. To get a value that represents my position, a program just has to take the *x* readings of all the positions, and that should lie on the line that bisects me. Of course if I hold one arm out and leave the other by my side, this will not work too well, but in practice it is surprisingly effective. To calculate an average, you need to add up all the *x* values.

```
int xTotal;
```

The variable *xTotal* will hold the total of all the *x* values for the points in the object that is being tracked.

```
xTotal = 0;

for (int depthPos = 0; depthPos < noOfPixelBytes; depthPos += 2)
{
    int depthValue = depthData[depthPos] >> 3;


    if (depthValue >> slotSizeFactor == maxPos)
    {
        // Add the x position of this pixel to the total
        xTotal = xTotal + (depthPos % image.Width);
    }
}

xPosition = xTotal / SlotCounts[maxPos];
```

The preceding code works out the average of all the *x* values in the object. The total is initially set to zero, and then the program works through the depth buffer looking for values that are in the same slot as the object being tracked. If it finds an object in the slot, it works out the *x* position of the object by using the modulus operator. The modulus operator gives the remainder when the left-hand value is divided by the right-hand one. This is the value that gives the position of this depth value across the depth frame. The method then adds this to the total of all the *x* positions it has found. At the end of the loop, the total is divided by the total number of points at this depth to give the *x* position of the object. This is set to the value of the variable *xPosition*. This value can be used as a control input to a game.

Using the Kinect Sensor with an XNA Game

Until now, all the programs that you have written in this chapter for the Kinect have been Windows Presentation Foundation (WPF) applications. However, you can use Kinect in XNA games as well. In fact, you can use the technology in any Windows application. XNA is a framework you can use to create games. Versions of XNA are available for Windows PC, Windows Phone, and Xbox 360. If you want to find out more about the XNA framework, you could take a look at *Microsoft XNA Game Studio 4.0: Learn Programming Now!*, published by Microsoft Press (ISBN 0735651574).

To make this easier, it makes sense to create a *KinectController* component that can be added to any game.

```
class KinectController
{
    Runtime myKinect;

    private GraphicsDevice graphicsDevice;

    public string ErrorMessage;

    public KinectController(GraphicsDevice graphicsDevice)
    {
        this.graphicsDevice = graphicsDevice;
        ErrorMessage = "";
    }
}
```

The *KinectController* class will control the Kinect device. In the preceding code, you can see the constructor for the class. When a game makes an instance of this class, it must supply a reference to the *graphicsDevice* in use in the game. This is because the class creates an XNA texture for display by the game, and the class needs to use the *graphicsDevice* from the game to do this. The *KinectController* class exposes an *ErrorMessage* string that can be used to inform the game of any problems encountered with the sensor.

```
public bool SetupKinect ()
{
    // Check to see if a Kinect is available
    if (Runtime.Kinects.Count == 0)
    {
        ErrorMessage = "No Kinects detected";
        return false;
    }

    myKinect = Runtime.Kinects[0];

    // all the other Kinect setup code goes here
    return true;
}
```

When a game wants to use the Kinect sensor, it calls the *SetupKinect* method. This returns *true* if the Kinect sensor was set up successfully. If the method returns *false*, something went wrong and the *ErrorMessage* field will describe the error. The code in the setup method is exactly the same code that you saw in previous programs that used the Kinect sensor bar.

An XNA game can set up the Kinect controller in the *LoadContent* method. If you have not used XNA before, the *LoadContent* method is called when a game starts running. It has the job of loading all the textures, sounds, and other assets that the game requires.

```
protected override void LoadContent()
{

    // all the other content loading code goes here

    if (!kinect.SetupKinect())
    {
        message = kinect.ErrorMessage;
        state = GameState.error;
    }
}
```

The *SetupKinect* method returns *false* when the Kinect could not be initialized. The method detects this and sets the state of the game to *GameState.error*. In this state the game does not run, and instead just displays the error message.

Getting the Control Value from the Kinect

When the *KinectController* is active, it is constantly processing depth data and updating the *x* position of an object that it detects. This is converted into an XNA gamepad value by the following property exposed by the *KinectController* class.

```
public float X
{
    get
    {
        return (xPosition - halfWidth) / halfWidth;
    }
}
```

An XNA gamepad returns *x* values in the range −1 (for fully left) through to +1 (for fully right). The preceding code takes the position of the object that has been detected and does some math to create a result in this range. The variable *halfWidth* is used in this calculation. It is set to half the width of the depth image.

In the Kinect-controlled game, the user manages the position of a paddle by moving from left to right. The *x* property of the *KinectController* is used to control the movement of the bat on the screen.

```
batRectangle.X += (int) (kinect.X * batSpeed);
```

In an XNA game, the position of an object can be described by a *Rectangle* class that has an *x* property. The preceding statement updates the *x* position of the bat rectangle using the *x* position provided by the Kinect controller.

Drawing the Kinect Depth Image in XNA

In the preceding programs, you have used an Image display element in the Windows Presentation Foundation (WPF) programs that you have written. You discovered that a program can create an image from the Kinect video camera or the Kinect depth camera by building an array of bytes that hold the blue, green, red, and transparency (alpha) values for each pixel.

An XNA game can do the same thing. In XNA an image is held in an object of type *Texture2D*. These can be created from arrays of bytes in exactly the same way as the images you have made before. The only difference is that an XNA texture is created from an array that holds the pixel colors in the order red, green, and blue.

```
if ( DepthTexture == null )
    DepthTexture = new Texture2D(graphicsDevice,
        myKinect.DepthStream.FrameWidth,
        myKinect.DepthStream.FrameHeight);
DepthTexture.SetData(depthColorImage);
```

The preceding statements create a depth texture from the *depthColorImage* byte array. Note that to create a texture, a program must have a reference to the *graphicsDevice* in use by the game. This is the class that provides the link between the program and the screen display hardware. Also note that this code creates a new XNA texture the first time it is called. After the first call, the same texture will be used for successive images.

> **Sample Code: Kinect-Controlled BlockBuster** The sample project in the "05 Simple KinetBlockBuster" directory in the resources for this chapter (see the "Code Samples" section in the Introduction) holds an XNA breakout game that can be controlled by the player moving to the left and right to move the paddle.

The sample game does allow the player to control the paddle by moving, but it is not very precise in operation. It turns out that the Kinect SDK provides much better ways of getting movement information, and you will explore these later. However, I hope that it makes it clear to you that there is no magic happening when a Kinect sensor follows you around the room. All that is happening is that the computer is doing math based on some assumptions that have been made about the scene and the items in it. You will find out how to use these more advanced features of the Kinect SDK later in this book.

> **Note** If you have not written an XNA game before, it is not a problem. You can learn quite a lot about XNA from the preceding sample code. If you want to find out more about this powerful game creation tool, a number of good books about the XNA framework are available, including one by yours truly, that you might like to investigate. You can use the *KinectController* class in any program where you want to use the *x* position of an object in front of the Kinect sensor to control a program.

Summary

In this chapter, you learned how the Kinect sensor provides depth information to your programs and how to use this to provide simple program behaviors.

You have also seen that by making some simple assumptions about a situation and then creating a program that works using these assumptions, you can create something that appears to recognize things.

You have also discovered how the Kinect behavior can be placed into a software component that can then be used in other programs—in this case an XNA game where the gamepad is replaced by the user moving around the scene.

In Chapter 7, you will investigate the sound sensor to discover how you can use it to provide another level of control to your programs.

Fun with the Sound Sensor

After completing this chapter, you will:

- Understand the nature of sound waves and how they are transferred through the air

- Use the Kinect to capture and play back some sound

- Create a program that shows the sound waves on the screen

- Add a sound recorder function to the intruder detector program that allows the user to create customized alarm messages

Capturing Sound Using Kinect

THE KINECT SENSOR BAR CONTAINS four high-quality microphones and some powerful sound-processing hardware. This makes it able to do clever things like cancel noise and work out from whereabouts in front of the sensor a particular sound signal is coming. You will find out a bit more about how this works later; for now you are going to write a simple program that captures some sound and does things with it.

Sound and Computers

Before you can start to write programs that manipulate sound, it is worth taking some time to consider what sound is.

Figure 7-1 shows what a sound might look like. Sound travels through the air in pressure waves. The graph shows how the air pressure at a point in the path of the sound wave changes over time as a single cycle of a sound wave moves through the air. Sound is made by something that vibrates (perhaps a guitar string or your vocal chords) and pushes against the air around it. This creates a pressure wave that moves through the air. The wave consists of areas of high pressure (where the line

103

on the graph in Figure 7-1 is above the middle line) and low pressure (where the line on the graph is below the middle line). When a sound wave hits something, the changes in pressure it produces cause the object to vibrate. When a sound wave arrives at your ear, it vibrates the eardrum, which is connected to nerve endings that send signals into the brain to let you hear the sound. A microphone takes a sound wave and converts it into an electrical signal that changes over time in a way that reflects the original sound.

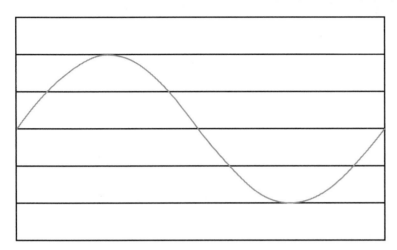

FIGURE 7-1 A simple sound wave.

You could get a sound signal that looks like the one in Figure 7-1 by getting someone, preferably a soprano, to sing "Oooooh" into a microphone. The wave is a sine wave—that is, a single clear tone. The pitch of the "Oooooh" that is sung gives the rate at which the signal goes up and down. The higher the pitch of the note, the more peaks and troughs you would see in a particular time period.

Figure 7-2 shows two sopranos singing at the same time. One soprano is singing louder than the other. The loudest singer is producing the note that has the greatest distance between the peak and trough of each wave. The two singers are also singing at different pitches. The louder note has a lower pitch as it only has five sets of peaks and troughs on the graph, whereas the quieter note has six.

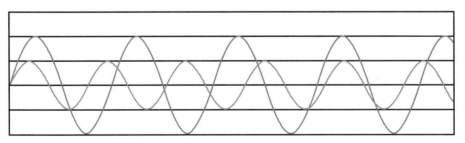

FIGURE 7-2 Two sopranos singing together.

If a soprano sings the note A, the wave will go up and down 440 times a second. This is called the frequency of the sound signal. The unit of frequency is the Hertz (Hz). Hertz gives the number of times the wave completes a cycle in 1 second. This means that the note A has a frequency of 440 Hz. The human ear can hear sounds in the frequency range of 20 Hz to around 20,000 Hz, although as we get older the upper range starts to decline.

You have seen that a video camera records an image by breaking it into a number of individual pixels. Each pixel represents the color and brightness of a point in the image. The pixel is represented by three numbers that give the red, green, and blue brightness of that point in the scene. When a computer converts a sound into a digital representation, it uses a number to represent the level of the sound at a particular instant. A device that converts an audio signal into a set of digital values is sometimes called a *sound sampler*. The name is a good one, in that the sampler produces a sequence of numbers by sampling the level of the sound at regular intervals.

Figure 7-3 shows what a sampler could produce if it was given the audio signal in Figure 7-1 to process. The height of each column gives the level of the sound at that particular point in time. Each of the height values is represented by a number. The idea is that this set of numbers will allow a computer to re-create the wave that was recorded.

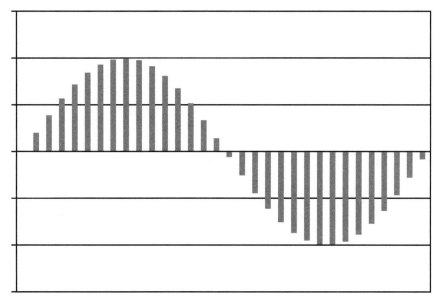

FIGURE 7-3 Sound sampler.

Of course, the numbers stored by a sampler can only ever be an approximation of the original sound signal. If you joined together each of the columns in Figure 7-3, you would get a wave that looked rather like the one in Figure 7-1, but the shape of the wave would not be exactly the same. You could improve the quality of the sample by taking more readings and making each measurement more precise.

In digital sound terms, the sampling rate is given as the number of samples per second. If you want CD quality sound, you need to sample at a rate of 44,000 Hz and produce samples of 16-bit resolution. You have seen resolution before. In Chapter 6 you saw that the depth sensor produced depth data with 13 bits of resolution, which meant the sensor could deliver distance values between 1 millimeter (mm) and 4 meters. The more bits that a computer uses to represent a value, the more accurately that value can be held. The Kinect audio sensor produces 16-bit samples at a rate of 16,000 samples per second. This is not quite recording-studio quality, but it does allow very high-quality voice signals, which is just what the Kinect sensor bar was designed to work with.

> **Note** You might think that the Kinect sensor contains multiple microphones so that it can record multichannel sounds. You know that to record stereo signals you need two microphones: one for left and one for right. However, the multiple microphones in the Kinect are not used to record multichannel sounds. Instead they are used to allow audio processing components in the sensor bar to detect and reject echoes. The signals from the microphones can also be combined by software running in the sensor bar to produce a microphone array that can be "aimed" at a particular sound source.

Receiving Sound Signals from Kinect

The *KinectSensor* class contains an *AudioSource* property that is of type *KinectAudioSource*. The type *KinectAudioSource* provides methods and properties that can be used to allow a program to respond to and work with sound signals. The first method you are going to use is the *Start* method. This starts the audio sampling process and supplies a program with a *Stream* from which the program can read sound data.

```
KinectSensor myKinect = KinectSensor.KinectSensors[0];
```

This statement creates a variable called *myKinect* that refers to the first Kinect sensor attached to the computer. You have seen this statement in every program that you have written that uses the Kinect sensor.

```
Stream kinectAudioStream = myKinect.AudioSource.Start();
```

This statement calls the *Start* method on the *AudioSource* property provided by the sensor. The *Start* method starts the audio hardware producing sound data. It also returns a reference to a *Stream* that will deliver the audio data to the program.

The Kinect SDK provides audio data in the form of a *Stream* because audio data is not the same as video or depth data. The Kinect SDK produces video and depth data as frames that appear at regular intervals. Every $\frac{1}{30}$ second, the Kinect sensor generates a new frame for a program to handle. However, audio data is not like this. Audio data is produced continuously, at a rate of 16,000 sample values per second. A program that wants to work with the audio data is not able to wait for a frame of such data; instead, it must read the data continuously.

One way that a program can obtain data is by reading values from a file stored on the hard disk of the computer. The program can open the file and then read the values and work on it. This happens whenever your computer plays a music file for you. The program, perhaps Windows Media Player, will open the file on the disk, read values from it, and then convert those values into sound. You can think of the Kinect audio stream as a never-ending file which contains sample values that are being produced by the microphones in the Kinect sensor. Every time a program reads the audio stream, it will get the latest set of values.

The *Stream* class is part of the .NET Input/Output library and is used whenever a program wants to have access to a stream of bytes from a source. The *Stream* class itself is abstract, which means a program will never actually create a *Stream* instance. Instead lots of classes have behavior based on the *Stream*. These classes provide *Stream*-based access to files, network connections, and, in the case of Kinect audio, the stream of values produced by the sound sensor. Because all these classes are child classes of the *Stream* parent, they all provide a common set of *Stream* methods, including one to read bytes from the stream.

This means that an audio program never has to worry exactly what kind of *Stream* is being provided to the data. An audio-processing program that uses Kinect sound input could consume sound data from any *Stream*-based source, including a recorded file of sound data. When a program wants some audio data from the Kinect, it can request this from the stream by calling the *Read* method on the stream variable.

```
byte [] soundSampleBuffer = new byte[5000];

int count = kinectAudioStream.Read(soundSampleBuffer, 0, soundSampleBuffer.Length);
```

The preceding statements read a buffer full of sound information into the *soundSampleBuffer* array. The *Read* method returns how many bytes were successfully read from the stream. The *Read* method is provided with a buffer array to hold the sound bytes, the start position in the buffer to store the data, and the number of bytes to be read from the stream. The preceding statements would store 5,000 bytes of sound data in a byte array called *soundSampleBuffer*. Although the stream could return individual bytes of sound data, it would be very inefficient if the program called the *Read* method for each byte in turn. A buffer size of 5,000 is a good one for a start. Later, in the section "Sound Signals and Latency," you will find out how the size of this buffer affects the performance of the program.

If you wanted to create a sound recorder, you could just save this buffer into a file. But to start, you are going to play the sound back through the Windows PC sound system.

Playing Sound Using XNA

The easiest way to play sound from a PC is to use the *DynamicSoundEffectInstance* class that is part of the XNA Game Framework. This class can be used by game programs to play back sounds that have been dynamically generated. For example, a game might want to generate a slightly different sound effect for different laser blasters in a space shooter game. The *DynamicSoundEffectInstance* class allows the game to play sound waveforms that have been created by software. This is exactly what you need to make a program that will generate sound output from sound data that has been obtained from the Kinect sensor.

You saw the XNA framework for the first time in Chapter 6, where it was used to create a game that used the player as the controller. The framework provides a set of classes for sound effect generation, including the *DynamicSoundEffectInstance* class that makes it very easy to take a stream of sound values and play them directly.

```
DynamicSoundEffectInstance soundEffectOutput;

soundEffectOutput = new DynamicSoundEffectInstance(16000, AudioChannels.Mono);
```

When a *DynamicSoundEffectInstance* is created, the program must set the sample rate (you are using 16,000 samples a second) and the format of the data (you are using mono). A program can now give the dynamic sound effect arrays of sound sample vales for it to play back through the PC speaker.

```
soundEffectOutput.SubmitBuffer(soundSampleBuffer, 0, count);
```

This statement would use the *DynamicSoundEffectInstance* value to play the buffer that was read from the Kinect stream. A complete sound playback method would repeatedly read sound from the Kinect and then immediately play it back. It would look like this:

```
void pumpAudio()
{
    // Create a buffer to hold the sound data
    byte[] soundSampleBuffer = new byte[1000];

    // Create a Kinect audio source and a sound input stream
    Stream kinectAudioStream;

    // Start the source and connect the stream to it
    kinectAudioStream = myKinect.AudioSource.Start();

    // Create an output soundeffect to play the audio
    DynamicSoundEffectInstance soundEffectOutput;
    soundEffectOutput = new DynamicSoundEffectInstance(16000, AudioChannels.Mono);

    // Start the soundeffect playing
    soundEffectOutput.Play();
```

```
    // Repeatedly read the sound in and then play it
    while (true)
    {
        int count = kinectAudioStream.Read(soundSampleBuffer, 0,
                                        soundSampleBuffer.Length);
        soundEffectOutput.SubmitBuffer(soundSampleBuffer, 0, count);
    }
}
```

The *pumpAudio* method would run forever. It creates the input stream and the output sound effect and then repeatedly reads a buffer from the sound stream and sends it to the sound effect output. It is not the kind of code I would recommend that you write. It has no error handling. If the Kinect cannot be located or the sound effect created, it will not display anything useful to the user; it will just produce an exception and stop. However, it should give you a good understanding of just how simple it is to get a program that takes in audio and then plays it back.

Now that you have the *pumpAudio* method, you next need a way to get it to run. To avoid any clicks and buzzes on the sound stream, it is important that the method run as quickly and smoothly as possible. The best way to do this in a program is to create a separate thread that runs this method independently of the rest of a program.

You have already seen threads in action. In Chapter 5, in the section "A Complete Alarm Program," you saw that the video processing activities in the program ran on a thread separate from the user interface. This meant that your program had to contain extra code to perform communication between the video processing methods and the user interface. In this case, you need to know how to create a new thread and start it running.

The thread management classes are in the *System.Threading* namespace. They provide resources that will let a program start and manage new threads of execution. If a program wants to use these resources, it can add the namespace.

```
using System.Threading;
```

A thread is a piece of "living" code. When a C# program starts, it is "brought to life" by the operating system making a call of the *Main* method in the program. Code in the *Main* method will then go on to call other methods and the program. It is important to remember that all programs start running this way. Even the Windows Presentation Foundation (WPF) applications that you created have a *Main* method at their heart. This is the method that creates the windows on the screen and sends them the messages that get them started.

A running program can bring another piece of code to life by creating a new thread to run that code. When the new thread is active, it will run alongside the existing program. The Windows operating system will manage the execution of the new thread. If a computer has more than one processer, the threads may run in parallel. Alternatively, the operating system will switch rapidly between the active threads in a program. The thread itself is represented by an object of type *Thread*.

```
Thread audioThread = new Thread(new ThreadStart(pumpAudio));

audioThread.Priority = ThreadPriority.Highest;

audioThread.IsBackground = true;

audioThread.Start();
```

The preceding code creates a new thread and starts it running the *pumpAudio* method. The first statement creates the audio thread. When a thread is created, it must be told the method that it will run when it starts. The *ThreadStart* class is a delegate type that can hold a reference to a method in an object. In this case it is created to hold a reference to the *pumpAudio* method, which is the method that the thread will run.

The second statement sets the priority of the thread to indicate that this thread must run with high priority. This asks the Windows operating system to run this thread as quickly as it can. If the thread is interrupted, this may cause parts of the audio stream to be missed, which would result in the program producing clicks and silences on the audio output.

Note This priority is relative to other threads running in your program only. The *Priority* property of a thread does not provide a way that you can make a thread that can run in preference to other programs on the computer.

The third statement makes the thread into a background thread. This means that the thread will terminate automatically when the program ends. The final statement starts the thread running. When the *Start* method runs, the program asks the Windows operating system to start a new thread and the *pumpAudio* method will be called and begin running. At this point the Kinect sensor stream will be read and sound output generated.

Threads are very useful in situations when a program wants to do something in parallel with an existing task. They are frequently used when a program wants to provide a responsive user interface but the selected task will take a while to complete. The foreground task may display a status indicator while the background task gets on and does the job. When a program is stopped by the user, all the background threads that it has created are stopped as well.

Stopping the Program

Every XNA game contains an *Update* method that is repeatedly called to update the game world. In a driving game the *Update* method would move the car along the track, check throttle input, and so on. In a space-shooter game, the *Update* method would move all the game objects, check for collisions, destroy any aliens that the player had destroyed, and adjust the score. In the sound playback game that you are creating, the *Update* method must check to see if the user is stopping the program.

You create a new XNA game by using one of the XNA templates in Visual Studio 2010. This generates a Game class which contains an *Update* method that you can use as the basis of your game update behavior. The *Update* method contains a test that will stop the game if the Back button is pressed on an Xbox gamepad that is connected to the PC. You can connect a wired Xbox gamepad to a Windows PC via a USB connection. When the player presses the Back button on the gamepad, the *Update* method calls the *Exit* method to end the game. You can add an extra test that will cause the program to stop when the Escape key is pressed on the keyboard.

```
protected override void Update(GameTime gameTime)
{
    // Allows the game to exit
    if (GamePad.GetState(PlayerIndex.One).Buttons.Back == ButtonState.Pressed ||
        Keyboard.GetState().IsKeyDown(Keys.Escape))
    {
        this.Exit();
    }

    base.Update(gameTime);
}
```

You can see the *Update* method in the preceding sound playback program. This will cause the game to end if the Back button is pressed on the Xbox 360 gamepad or the Escape key is pressed on the keyboard. The code that has been added reads the state of the keyboard and checks to see if the Escape key is pressed.

Sample Code: Simple Sound Processor The sample project in the "01 Simple Sound Processor" directory in the resources for this chapter (see the "Code Samples" section in the Introduction) holds an XNA program that uses the preceding method to play sound received by the Kinect sensor from the speaker on your computer.

Sound Signals and Latency

If you run the sample program, you will notice that your speech does not come out of the speaker at exactly the same instant that you say it to the Kinect sensor. This happens because it takes a small, but noticeable, time for the signal to be read by the sensor, transferred into the program, and then replayed. Delays of this kind are referred to as *latency,* and they are inevitable whenever we create systems that process real-world signals. You will most often notice problems with latency when you see a video where the sound and the picture aren't in sync. Humans are very good at spotting when the lip movements and the sound of a person talking do not match, and a lot of effort is spent making sure that video and audio components are synchronized.

The reason for the delay in the preceding program is that the program always reads a complete buffer full of sound data before it passes it on for playback.

```
int count = kinectAudioStream.Read(soundSampleBuffer, 0, soundSampleBuffer.Length);
soundEffectOutput.SubmitBuffer(soundSampleBuffer, 0, count);
```

The two preceding statements are at the heart of our sound playback. The first statement reads the sound data from the Kinect, and the second statement sends this sound data to be played back. The larger the *soundSampleBuffer,* the longer the latency, as the program will take longer to assemble the buffer before passing it on.

```
// Create a buffer to hold the sound data
byte[]soundSampleBuffer = new byte[1000];
```

The version of the preceding code creates a 1,000-byte buffer. This will have room for 500 sample values (remember that each sample takes up 2 bytes of storage) that will take around $\frac{1}{32}$ second to play (remember that 16,000 samples are played back every second). You could reduce the latency by reducing the size of the buffer, but this would increase the loading on the computer as the program would now spend more time calling the methods that read the stream and play the output. From my experiments, a buffer size of around 1,000 bytes is a good compromise between latency and computer loading. Not all the latency is caused by the program; the signal processing in the Kinect sensor bar and the Kinect SDK running on the Windows PC also introduce delays. The amount of latency that you will notice depends on the speed of your computer. The value of 1,000 works well on my machine with a 3-GHz processor.

Visualizing a Sound Signal in XNA

Because you now know that sound can be held in a computer as an array of numbers, you can think about creating a program that allows these numbers to be visualized in some way. In electronics a device that is used to visualize electrical signals that change over time is an oscilloscope. This displays a representation of an incoming signal by scanning a spot of light across a video screen and moving it up and down according to the level of the incoming signal. If the spot is moved quickly, it appears to draw a line that shows the representative shape of the signal. Using an oscilloscope, an audio engineer can view this shape and detect any distortion or noise that is present.

You can make your own audio oscilloscope by creating a program that works in exactly the same way. The Kinect audio stream can generate sound values that a program then uses to determine the Y positions of a sequence of dots drawn across the screen. This would allow the program to draw a picture of the sound wave similar to the one in Figure 7-1. You have already seen that a program can create its own textures from data produced by the Kinect depth camera. Now you are going to create a texture from an array of sound values.

```
Texture2D soundTexture = null;
byte[] soundTextureBytes;
byte soundRed = 255;
byte soundBlue = 255;
```

```
byte soundGreen = 255;
byte[] soundSampleBuffer ;
```

The preceding variables are the ones that your audio oscilloscope will use. The *soundTexture* value will hold the texture that shows the shape of the signal. To create this texture, the program will first make an array of bytes that contains the image of the trace. The program also has red, green, and blue values that set the color of the line drawn on the screen. The final value is the *soundSampleBuffer,* which is now shared between the *pumpAudio* thread and the XNA display update thread. When the program starts running, it must set up the texture bytes and the buffer that will hold the sound samples. It could use a method called *setupSoundDisplay* to do this.

```
void setupSoundDisplay()
{
    int width = GraphicsDevice.Viewport.Width;
    int height = GraphicsDevice.Viewport.Height;
    soundTextureBytes = new byte [width*height*4];
    soundSampleBuffer = new byte[width * 2];
}
```

This method creates the two arrays that are going to be used to create the oscilloscope display. The first of these is the texture bytes. This needs to have 4 byte values for each pixel. These bytes give the red, green, blue, and alpha (transparency) values for each pixel. The second array is the sample buffer that will hold the sound intensity values. This uses 2 bytes for each sound value because the sound is supplied as a 16-bit value.

Both of these arrays are dimensioned according to the width and height of the screen viewport. This means that the Kinect audio stream will produce a row of samples that can be displayed across the screen each time the program reads from it. To update the display, the program must create an array of bytes that contain the required pixel values.

```
void updateSoundDisplay()
{
    int width = GraphicsDevice.Viewport.Width;
    int height = GraphicsDevice.Viewport.Height;
    int halfHeight = height / 2;
    int rowPixelBytes = width * 4;

    // clear the screen from last time
    for (int i = 0; i < soundTextureBytes.Length; i++)
        soundTextureBytes[i] = 0;

    int samplePos = 0;
    // draw the scope trace on the screen
    for (int x = 0; x < width; x++)
    {
        // Compute the sound level
```

```
short soundLevel = (short)(soundSampleBuffer[samplePos] |
                           (soundSampleBuffer[samplePos + 1] << 8));

// move on to the next sound sample
samplePos += 2;

// Compute the position of this pixel
int soundY = ((soundLevel * height) / 65535) + halfHeight;
soundY = soundY * rowPixelBytes;
int pixelPos = (x * 4) + soundY;

// Set the color of the pixel
soundTextureBytes[pixelPos] = soundRed;
pixelPos++;
soundTextureBytes[pixelPos] = soundBlue;
pixelPos++;
soundTextureBytes[pixelPos] = soundGreen;
pixelPos++;
    }
    // Create a new texture for the latest display
    soundTexture = new Texture2D(GraphicsDevice, width, height);
    // Set the texture to the calculated oscilloscope display
    soundTexture.SetData(soundTextureBytes);
}
```

This method works through the sound sample values and calculates the pixel position of the "dot" that needs to be drawn. The variable *soundLevel* is used to hold the level of the audio signal at each point on the screen. This is calculated from the *soundSampleBuffer* values and then scaled to produce the Y position of the dot. This is then used to calculate where in the pixel bytes the dot should be drawn. Once the position has been calculated, the red, green, and blue values for the dot are set. Finally the byte values are used to create a new texture for display on the screen. The code is very similar to the loop that was used to display the depth information in the Simple Kinect BlockBuster program that you created at the end of Chapter 6.

> **Sample Code: Simple Audio Oscilloscope** The sample project in the "02 Simple Audio Oscilloscope" directory in the resources for this chapter (see the "Code Samples" section in the Introduction) holds an XNA program that uses the preceding method to play sound and display the shape of the waveform received by the Kinect sensor.

Figure 7-4 shows the oscilloscope display from the program when I sing "Oooooh" to it. This isn't quite a sine wave because I'm not actually a trained soprano. However it does show just what an audio signal looks like. You can use the program to view your singing voice and find out how close you can get to a sine wave.

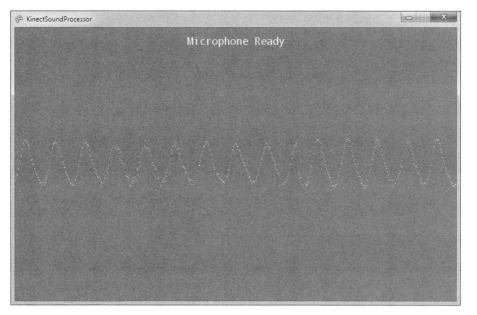

FIGURE 7-4 Oscilloscope output.

Figure 7-4 is also interesting because of what happened to the display around two-thirds of the way across the screen. The signal waveform seems to break just after the first wave. This is because the thread displaying the image and the thread capturing the audio are sharing the same buffer array. The display thread will have been working through the array and drawing the wave when the audio pump completed a read of the Kinect audio stream and dropped off a new set of sound values. These new values are then used for the remainder of the drawing operation.

In this program, the screen display is slightly corrupted but the program runs perfectly well. However, if you write a program in which multiple threads of data share a single data item, you need to be very careful to make sure that the threads don't affect each other in unexpected ways. If you wanted to create a program in which the display was not corrupted, you would have to add code to lock the shared memory for one thread to use at a time. However, this also creates the potential for problems if threads end up "fighting" over the same item. To keep it simple, I'm happy to live with the display corruption you can see in Figure 7-4.

Storing Sound Data in a File and Replaying It

The final thing you are going to do with the sound data is store it into a file. You are going to do this to allow users to customize the alarm sounds made by the motion-detecting alarm that you created in Chapter 4. The updated version of the alarm program will contain a button that can be pressed to record a new alarm sound.

```
bool audioCaptureActive = false;
```

```
private void recordSoundButton_Click(object sender, RoutedEventArgs e)
{
    if (audioCaptureActive) return;

    audioCaptureActive = true;

    Thread audioThread = new Thread(new ThreadStart(captureAudio));
    audioThread.Priority = ThreadPriority.Highest;
    audioThread.IsBackground = true;
    audioThread.Start();
}
```

The preceding code is the event handler for the record button in the alarm program. When the button is pressed, this code causes a new alarm sound to be recorded using the Kinect microphone. The first thing the method does is check the *audioCaptureActive* flag to make sure that the program is not already capturing audio. If the flag is set to true, the button press is ignored and the method returns immediately. It then sets the flag to indicate that audio capture is active and starts a thread that will perform the audio capture. When the thread finishes running, the *audioCaptureActive* flag is set to false again.

This code is just like the code that you used earlier to start the playback of audio in the XNA program. It runs the method *captureAudio* on a separate thread. This method captures audio from the Kinect and then saves it in a WAV file for use by the alarm program.

Creating a WAV File

When a program stores data in a file, it needs to make sure that the data can be used by other programs. It would be easy to just write a large number of sound byte values out to a file, but this would not be very useful if no other program could use the stored data. There are a number of different sound file formats; you are going to use the WAV file type to store the audio from the alarm. All the sound effects used by the Windows operating system are held in WAV files.

The format of the sound data that is stored in a WAV file is actually in the same format as the raw byte values that the Kinect sensor creates. However, storing the data is not just a question of saving the data bytes and giving the output file the type WAV. The program must also create a WAV file header that is stored at the beginning of the file and describes the sound content. The header is used by any program that wants to play the file. When a program opens the sound file, it uses the header to determine the number of sound channels, the sample rate, and the length of the sample. Fortunately, some standard methods can be used to create this header file, and you can add these to your program very easily.

```
void captureAudio()
{
    if (alarmSoundActive)
    {
        showAlarmSoundStatus("Cannot record - alarm sound active");
        return;
```

```
    }

    showAlarmSoundStatus("Recording");

    try
    {
        // Create a Kinect audio source and a sound input stream
        Stream kinectAudioStream = myKinect.AudioSource.Start();
        // Get the sound sample
        kinectAudioStream.Read(soundSampleBuffer, 0, soundSampleBuffer.Length);

        // Get the output stream
        using (var fileStream = new FileStream(alarmFileName, FileMode.Create))
        {
            WriteWavHeader(fileStream, recordBufferSize);
            fileStream.Write(soundSampleBuffer, 0, soundSampleBuffer.Length);
        }

        showAlarmSoundStatus("Recorded OK");
    }
    catch
    {
        showAlarmSoundStatus("Record Failed");
        return;
    }
    finally
    {
        audioCaptureActive = false;
    }
}
```

The preceding code is the *captureAudio* method that captures a block of sound and stores it in a file. The name of the file to be used is held in the variable *alarmFileName*. The code uses the method *WriteWavHeader* to create the WAV file header and the method *showAlarmSoundStatus* to display messages to the user. When the method finishes, it sets the *audioCaptureActive* flag to *false* so that further captures can take place.

The method uses the *try-catch-finally* construction to deal with any errors that might occur. It is important to perform error handling when writing into files as these actions can fail. For example, the storage device might fill up before the file is written. The catch part of the construction displays the error message. The finally part of the construction is always performed, whether or not an exception is thrown. The preceding code ensures that audio capture is turned off irrespective of how the file save turned out.

Playing a Recorded Sound

The original alarm program created an instance of the *SoundPlayer* class to play the alarm sound. Unfortunately the *SoundPlayer* class is not able to play WAV files in the format that the program creates. This is because the sound file only has a single sound channel, and *SoundPlayer* can only play back stereo sounds. Fortunately the *MediaElement* class can be used to play back mono sounds, and it has a number of other advantages that will help the program manage the sound play back. The *MediaElement* in the program is described in the XAML for the main windows form on the screen.

```
<MediaElement Name="alarmPlayer" MediaEnded="alarmPlayer_MediaEnded"/>
```

This creates a *MediaElement* called *alarmPlayer*. It also attaches an event handler to the *MediaEnded* event. This means that the method *alarmPlayer_MediaEnded* will run when the media finishes playing. This is very useful, as it provides a way for the program to stop the user from recording new alarm sounds when the alarm is sounding. You will see how this works in the section "Sound Playback Management" that follows.

Triggering the Sound Playback

The motion-sensitive alarm plays the alarm sound and takes pictures when the number of differences between the current camera image and the previous one exceeds a given threshold.

```
if (differences > alarmThreshold)
{
    if (!alarmSoundActive && !audioCaptureActive)
    {
        alarmPlayer.Source = new Uri(alarmFileName, UriKind.RelativeOrAbsolute);
        alarmPlayer.LoadedBehavior = MediaState.Play;
        alarmPlayer.UnloadedBehavior = MediaState.Close;
        alarmSoundActive = true;
        alarmLabel.Background = AlarmBrush;
        picturesToTake = 5;
    }
}
else
    alarmLabel.Background = OKBrush;
```

This is the code that triggers the alarm. The alarm is only triggered if the sound is not being played and no audio capture is active. If the alarm is triggered, it sets a flag to indicate that the alarm sound is now playing. Note that the alarm now triggers the playback of the sound as well. It does this by setting properties on the *alarmPlayer* object that define the source of the sound and then set the behaviors to begin the sound playback.

Sound Playback Management

When the alarm sound playback completes, the *alarmPlayer_MediaEnded* method is called automatically.

```
private void alarmPlayer_MediaEnded(object sender, RoutedEventArgs e)
{
    alarmSoundActive = false;
    alarmPlayer.Source = null;
}
```

This code turns off the alarm sound and sets the media source of the *alarmPlayer* to *null*. This has the effect of disconnecting the media player from the alarm sound file and makes it possible for the program to update this.

Figure 7-5 shows the user interface of the modified motion-detector program. The user will press the Record Sound button to record a new sound effect. The user will then record a 4-second alarm message that is stored by the program and used when motion is detected. The alarm sound is stored alongside the program in a file called alarm.wav.

> **Sample Code: Adjustable Sound Alarm** The sample project in the "03 Alarm with adjustable sound" directory in the resources for this chapter (see the "Code Samples" section in the Introduction) holds a motion-sensitive alarm that lets you configure the alarm sound.

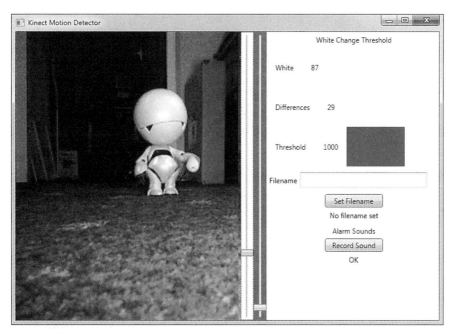

FIGURE 7-5 Recording sounds.

Summary

In this chapter you have learned a bit about sound waves and how they can be captured and stored inside a computer.

You have created a program that allows you to visualize the sound and another that lets you store and retrieve sound data for use by other programs.

You have also learned a bit more about the issues that need to be addressed when creating programs that contain threads that execute alongside each other and make use of shared resources.

In Chapter 8, you are going to investigate the way that the Kinect can provide detailed information about the position and movement of a human figure.

PART III

Creating Advanced User Interfaces

You now know the fundamentals of the sensors in the Kinect sensor bar, and how to use them in a program. In this section, you are going to find out how the sensor can be used to create genuinely new user interfaces, starting with skeleton tracking, moving on to voice control, and finally making use of multiple sensors at the same time to create augmented reality, where real world graphics are aligned with computer-generated content, using the Kinect to align the two.

Chapter 8

Body Tracking with Kinect

After completing this chapter, you will:

- Understand how the Kinect can register the position of a body and how the information is presented to a program

- Create a program that will track the head of a subject

- Make use of the Kinect body position information that is provided by the Kinect SDK

- Create programs that make use of body-tracking information to perform gesture recognition

- Create a program that will detect when two people kiss

Kinect Body Tracking

YOU HAVE SEEN HOW THE Kinect depth sensor generates distance data. Your program is given a picture of the view from the sensor. Each pixel in the picture contains a value that represents the distance from the sensor to an object in that direction. The Kinect depth sensor works by projecting a grid of infrared dots over the scene in front of it and viewing the reflection of each dot. Because the sensor knows the position of each dot in the grid, it can work out the distance to the reflection. If you are not familiar with this, take a look at the section "The Depth Sensor" in Chapter 1.

You have used the depth information to detect objects moving into and out of the space in front of the Kinect sensor. You have also discovered that a program can locate a person standing in front of the sensor by using the fact that in this situation, the person will be the largest object in front of the sensor.

The Kinect SDK can use the depth data stream from the Kinect sensor to perform body tracking. The software starts by locating the largest object in the scene, just like your programs did in Chapter 6 in "Detecting Objects." However, the Kinect SDK goes a lot further: it then looks at the pattern of depth values in the object and looks for cues that allow it to work out the position and orientation of a person standing in front of it. The people who created the Kinect sensor had to do a lot of research to find all possible human shapes and how they could be viewed. They then had to train the Kinect SDK with this information so that it can recognize you when you walk in front of it, no matter what your stature.

The Kinect SDK can produce skeleton-tracking information for two people standing in front of the sensor. The tracking information contains the position in 3D space of key positions in each person—for example, the position of the person's head, arms, and hands. The Kinect SDK can also provide some limited tracking for up to four other body shapes that it might see in front of it. The limited tracking information gives just the position of those people. This is because it would require a lot of computing power to track six figures in detail.

Note The software does not work for very small children. This is not because they are too small to be seen by the Kinect sensor, but because their size and shape are outside the range of body shapes that the software has been programmed to recognize. The sensor can also become confused if the clothing being worn can obscure the person's shape. Items such as skirts, jackets, and baggy tops make it harder for the software to work out the skeleton of the person wearing them. To get the best results, it is best to dress in a way that helps the Kinect system recognize the shape.

The position information for a person is provided by the Kinect SDK in a number of different ways. Your program can tell which elements of a frame of depth information are from a particular person in the scene. A program can also get information about the position of all the body parts of someone standing in front of the Kinect sensor by using the Kinect skeleton information.

Kinect Skeleton Information

An average human contains 206 bones fitted together to form the skeleton that supports the body. Bones have joints between them so they can move—for example, at the knee and the elbow. The Kinect SDK simplifies the human figure down to 19 "bones" that are connected to 20 "joints."

Figure 8-1 shows how the Kinect SDK connects the bones. A program is given the position of each of the 20 joints that the Kinect SDK tracks. The program can draw a stick figure like the one in Figure 8-1 by joining the joints together. You will do this later in the chapter.

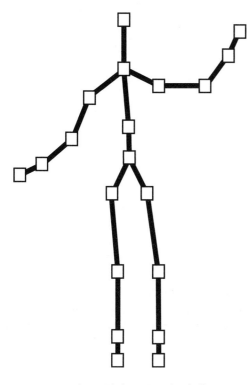

FIGURE 8-1 A Kinect "skeleton" waving hello.

Kinect Joint Positions

The program is given the tracking state of each joint, along with its position in 3D space. The 3D value gives the X, Y, and Z coordinates that specify the location of that joint in the space in front of the sensor. The coordinates are expressed according to the skeleton space coordinate system.

Figure 8-2 shows how the space coordinate system works. The Kinect sensor is placed where the X, Y, and Z lines intersect. The sensor is looking out in the direction of Z. If a person standing in front of the sensor moves to the right, the X part of the joint position will increase. If the person stands on tiptoes, the Y position of the head will increase, and if the person backs away from the sensor, the Z position of the head will increase. You can actually see this in action by having a go with a program that displays the coordinate information for the head of a skeleton that is being tracked by Kinect. That is the program you are going to build next.

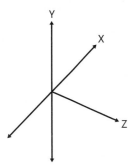

FIGURE 8-2 The skeleton space coordinates.

A Head Tracking Program

The program you are going to create will configure the Kinect sensor to perform skeleton tracking. It will then display the position of the head of a skeleton that is being tracked in a Windows Presentation Foundation (WPF) window on the screen. You can use it to get familiar with the position information that is produced by the Kinect SDK. To start, the program must get the Kinect running.

```
KinectSensor myKinect;

private void Window_Loaded(object sender, RoutedEventArgs e)
{
    // Check to see if a Kinect is available
    if (KinectSensor.KinectSensors.Count == 0)
    {
        MessageBox.Show("No Kinects detected", "Head Position Viewer");
        Application.Current.Shutdown();
        return;
    }

    // Get the first Kinect on the computer
    myKinect = KinectSensor.KinectSensors[0];

    // Start the Kinect running and select the skeleton stream
    try
    {
        myKinect.SkeletonStream.Enable();
        myKinect.Start();
    }
    catch
    {
        MessageBox.Show("Kinect initialise failed", "Head Position Viewer");
        Application.Current.Shutdown();
```

```
    }

    // connect a handler to the event that fires when new frames are available

    myKinect.SkeletonFrameReady +=
            new EventHandler<SkeletonFrameReadyEventArgs>(
                    myKinect_SkeletonFrameReady);
}
```

The preceding method is connected to the *Window_Loaded* event in the head-tracking program. This method will run when the program is first opened. It creates a *KinectSensor* instance and then configures it to track the skeleton.

```
myKinect.SkeletonStream.Enable();
```

This is exactly the same pattern as you saw in programs that use the video and depth cameras. When the skeleton stream is enabled, it can generate an event each time it has new skeleton data for your program. The program can connect an event handler to this method.

```
myKinect.SkeletonFrameReady +=
            new EventHandler<SkeletonFrameReadyEventArgs>(myKinect_SkeletonFrameReady);
```

The method *myKinect_SkeletonFrameReady* is connected to the *SkeletonFrameReady* event and will run each time that the skeleton tracking code in the Kinect SDK has completed the analysis of the scene in front of the sensor. Just because the skeleton tracking code has finished analyzing the scene does not necessarily mean that a person was successfully identified and tracked. The code in the *myKinect_SkeletonFrameReady* method must check the skeleton data to find out what, if anything, was identified in the scene. Your first skeleton tracking program will display just the X, Y, and Z position values of the head joint of the skeleton.

```
void myKinect_SkeletonFrameReady(object sender, SkeletonFrameReadyEventArgs e)
{
    string message = "No Skeleton Data";

    Skeleton[] skeletons = null;

    using (SkeletonFrame frame = e.OpenSkeletonFrame())
    {
        if (frame != null)
        {
            skeletons = new Skeleton[frame.SkeletonArrayLength];
            frame.CopySkeletonDataTo(skeletons);
        }
    }
```

```
    if (skeletons == null) return;

    foreach (Skeleton skeleton in skeletons)
    {
        if (skeleton.TrackingState == SkeletonTrackingState.Tracked)
        {
            Joint headJoint = skeleton.Joints[JointType.Head];
            SkeletonPoint headPosition = headJoint.Position;

            message = string.Format("Head: X:{0:0.0} Y:{1:0.0} Z:{2:0.0}",
                headPosition.X,
                headPosition.Y,
                headPosition.Z);
        }
    }

    StatusTextBlock.Text = message;
}
```

When the method is called, it is given an argument of type *SkeletonFrameReadyEventArgs*. This contains a method called *OpenSkeletonFrame* that provides access to the frame of skeleton data. This works in exactly the same way as the video and depth cameras. The event handler can request a *SkeletonFrame* that contains the skeleton-tracking information available to your program.

The Kinect SDK can keep track of up to six skeletons at any time. Two of them are fully tracked with information about the position of skeleton joints. The other four are tracked in terms of their position only. The preceding method uses a *foreach* construction to work through each of the skeletons and looks for ones that have the state *Tracked*. The other two states are *Untracked*, which means there is no data for this skeleton, and *PositionOnly*, which means that no joint information is available for this skeleton. The program checks to see if the skeleton it is working on is being tracked:

```
if (skeleton.TrackingState == SkeletonTrackingState.Tracked)
```

If this is true, the program then obtains the *Joint* instance that describes the position of the head from the *Joints* collection provided by the *Skeleton* class.

The Joints Collection and C# Dictionaries

The 20 *Joint* values that describe the position of each part of the skeleton are accessed in a similar manner to items held by the *C# Dictionary* collection class. A *C# Dictionary* is worth knowing about because of its usefulness. In real life a dictionary is a place, perhaps a book, where you can look up words. One great trick involving a traditional dictionary like this is to tell someone "The word *gullible* is not in any dictionary." Of course the person will rush off to find the word and prove you wrong, which can be very amusing. Or at least I find it so.

In programming terms, a dictionary collection works in exactly the same way as a traditional one. You can create a dictionary instance that will hold a collection of items indexed on a particular key value. You could implement a traditional dictionary by creating a dictionary instance that contained strings (the definition of the word) indexed on another string (the word itself).

```
Dictionary<string, string> RobsWords = new Dictionary<string,string>();
```

The *Dictionary* class provides an *Add* method that is used to add key and value pairs to it.

```
RobsWords.Add("gullible",
    "Will look up a word in a dictionary just because I say it isn't there");
```

A program can then get the definition of a word by using the word to index the dictionary.

```
string wordDefinition = RobsWords["gullible"];
```

If a program tries to find a key that does not exist in the dictionary, the program will throw an exception. The *Dictionary* class provides a method called *ContainsKey* that a program can use to check to see if the key is present.

```
if (RobsWords.ContainsKey("jabberwocky") == false)
{
    // If we get here the dictionary does not contain the word
}
```

The really powerful thing about dictionaries is that you can create any type of item and key. So if you wanted to keep track of the employees of a company, you could create a dictionary that contained a collection of employees indexed by employee name:

```
Dictionary<string, Employee> CompanyEmployees = new Dictionary<string, Employee>();
```

In the case of the Kinect skeleton information, the SDK contains a collection class called *JointCollection* that works in a way similar to *Dictionary*. A program can use a value of type *JointType* to index the collection and obtain information about a particular joint in the collection. One of the values of the *JointType* type is *JointType.Head*.

```
Joint headJoint = skeleton.Joints[JointType.Head];
```

The variable *headJoint* now contains the joint information describing the head. This includes the position of the head, as a value of type *SkeletonPoint*.

```
SkeletonPoint headPosition = headJoint.Position;
```

The preceding code gets the *Position* element of the joint information for the head. It can now go ahead and build a string to display the X, Y, and Z values giving the head position.

Using Format Strings to Build a Message

```
message = string.Format("Head: X:{0:0.0} Y:{1:0.0} Z:{2:0.0}",
    headPosition.X,
    headPosition.Y,
    headPosition.Z);
```

It is worth spending some time on this statement, as you might find it a bit confusing when you first see it. The first thing you need to understand is how the message string is created. The *Format* method is part of the *string* class and allows a program to lay out values for display. The first parameter given to the *Format* method is the format string. This contains text to be displayed along with placeholders for the values of variables that are to be inserted. There are three placeholders: one each for the X, Y, and Z values to be displayed. The placeholder *{0:0.0}* means "Use the first value and display one digit before the decimal point and one digit after the decimal point."

> **Note** Remember that in the C# language everything is numbered starting at zero. So although the X value is the first one that the program should display, it will have an index of 0.

The preceding *Format* method has four parameters: the formatting string and the X, Y, and Z values to be displayed. If you need to display a different number of values, you can use a different number of parameters. If the program tries to use an element that is not there—for example, the format string contains a placeholder for a fifth item, but there are only four data values—the program will throw an exception when it runs.

You can have a lot of fun with formatting strings. You can display text in fields of a particular width, add leading zeros or spaces, and even insert commas into numbers to print out thousands correctly. The main reason I am using the preceding formatting is so that only a small number of digits are displayed.

The next thing you need to understand is how the information for each joint is held. This is provided in a *Joints* dictionary that holds 20 items, one for each joint that is tracked.

> **Sample Code: Head Tracker** The sample project in the "01 KinectHeadTracker" directory in the resources for this chapter (see the "Code Samples" section in the Introduction) holds an XNA program that tracks the head of one skeleton.

The preceding Head Tracker application displays only one decimal place, which means that positions are given to a precision of one-tenth of a meter, or 100 mm.

Figure 8-3 shows the output from the program. You can test it by moving around the space in front of the sensor and seeing how the values for X, Y, and Z change. You will find that they work according to the directions described in Figure 8-2. Remember that the program will only display the head tracking information when it is able to track an entire skeleton, so you will need to give the sensor a clear view of your entire body for this program to work.

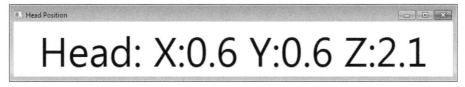

FIGURE 8-3 Displaying the head position.

Skeleton Information Quality

You have already seen that a skeleton value provides a *Tracked* property that can be used to check whether or not the skeleton is being tracked.

```
if (skeleton.TrackingState == SkeletonTrackingState.Tracked)
{
    // Joint information is available for this skeleton
}
```

It is also possible to detect if any of the skeleton information is not visible to the sensor. The *ClippedEdges* property of a skeleton gives information that a program can use to ask the user to move in order to be seen properly. The property is of type *FrameEdges,* which is an enumerated type with a range of values that describe the quality of the skeleton information.

If the *ClippedEdges* value is *FrameEdges.None,* this means that all of the skeleton joints are being tracked by the sensor. The Kinect SDK will set values into this property that a program can use to give the user instructions so that they can change position:

```
if (skeleton.ClippedEdges == FrameEdges.None)
{
    qualityMessage = "Good Quality";
}
else
{
    if ((skeleton.ClippedEdges & FrameEdges.Bottom) != 0)
        qualityMessage += "Move up ";
    if ((skeleton.ClippedEdges & FrameEdges.Top) != 0)
        qualityMessage += "Move down ";
    if ((skeleton.ClippedEdges & FrameEdges.Right) != 0)
        qualityMessage += "Move left ";
```

```
    if ((skeleton.ClippedEdges & FrameEdges.Left) != 0)
        qualityMessage += "Move right ";
}
```

The program tests the *ClippedEdges* value. If it is *FrameEdges.None,* the message "Good Quality" is displayed. If there is some clipping, the code uses the arithmetic & (and) operator to check particular bits in the quality message. The actual enum values are defined in the Kinect for Windows SDK as follows:

```
public enum FrameEdges
{
    None = 0,
    Right = 1,
    Left = 2,
    Top = 4,
    Bottom = 8,
}
```

Each quality state is represented by a particular power of two. The & operator uses the state as a mask to test particular bits. For example, if the quality value was set to nine, this means that the skeleton data was clipped on the right side (because if you use the & operator to combine nine and one, you get one) and clipped on the bottom (because if you use the & operator to combine nine and eight, you get eight). In this case, the preceding code would display Move Left and Move Up. If you are standing too close to the sensor so that the depth camera can't see your feet or your head, the program might display both Move Up and Move Down at the same time. You might want to investigate how you would change the program to display Move Back in this situation.

Joint Tracking State

The skeleton data also includes information about the quality of the information about each individual joint. The information is exposed in the form of a *TrackingState* property that will have one of three possible values:

- **Tracked**   The Kinect SDK can see the joint in the depth data and is able to work out where it is from this data.

- **Inferred**   The Kinect SDK is not able to see this joint, but it can work out where it should be, based on the position of other joints and what it knows about the skeleton. The position of joints will be inferred if the subject is wearing clothing that stops the sensor from seeing the joints directly.

- **NotTracked**   The Kinect SDK is unable to determine where this joint is.

You can use this information to improve the head tracking program:

```
SkeletonPoint headPosition = headJoint.Position;

message = string.Format("Head: X:{0:0.0} Y:{1:0.0} Z:{2:0.0}",
    headPosition.X,
    headPosition.Y,
    headPosition.Z);

if (headJoint.TrackingState == JointTrackingState.Inferred)
{
    message = message + " I";
}
```

This version of the head tracking program only displays the head position if it is being tracked successfully. If the position is inferred, the program puts the letter *I* after the position value.

> **Sample Code: Head Tracker with Status Display** The sample project in the "02 KinectHeadTrackerStatus" directory in the resources for this chapter (see the "Code Samples" section in the Introduction) holds an XNA program that tracks the head of one skeleton and displays clipping prompts to the user. It also appends an I to the head position information if the head position is out of range.

Drawing a Skeleton

The head tracking program works quite well, but at the moment you have to take on faith that it is actually tracking properly. One way to prove that your skeleton is being sensed correctly is to draw it on the screen. To do this, your program will have to draw some lines.

Drawing Lines in WPF

A WPF program can draw lines very easily. They are drawn on a Canvas that is added to the WPF page like any other display element.

```
<Canvas Name="skeletonCanvas" Width="640" Height="480" HorizontalAlignment="Center" />
```

This line of XAML (eXtensible Application Markup Language) describes the canvas you are going to use to draw the skeleton. The canvas has a width of 640 pixels and a height of 480 pixels, and it is being placed in the center of the window.

A canvas is a container element that can hold things that it will draw. At the moment the canvas doesn't hold anything, so when it is drawn it appears empty. A program can create display elements and add them to the canvas so that they are drawn when the canvas is updated.

```
Line testLine = new Line();
testLine.Stroke = new SolidColorBrush(Colors.Red);
testLine.StrokeThickness = 5;
testLine.X1 = 0;
testLine.Y1 = 0;
testLine.X2 = 200;
testLine.Y2 = 100;
```

The preceding statements create and configure a new *Line* value that is called *testLine*. It will be drawn using a solid red brush and will be 5 pixels thick. The line will extend from the origin (0,0) to the point that is 200 pixels across the screen and 100 pixels down.

At this moment, the line is not being drawn, as it is not connected to any display elements on the screen. You want to draw it on the skeleton canvas, so you need to add the line to the *Children* of that canvas.

```
skeletonCanvas.Children.Add(testLine);
```

A container can hold many objects; each one is added using the preceding method. The WPF manager will update the screen automatically, as required. When the display is updated, the canvas will draw the line on the display with the properties set in the program.

Figure 8-4 shows the top-left corner of the Skeleton Viewer program when it runs. Remember that in computer graphics, the origin (the coordinate 0,0) is the top-left corner of the display.

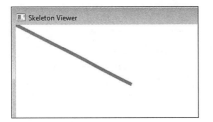

FIGURE 8-4 Drawing a line on a canvas.

Converting Joint Positions to Image Coordinates

The preceding program draws a line between the points (0,0) and (200,100). You can see in Figure 8-4 that this makes a line that goes 200 pixels across the screen and 100 pixels down it. The position of the start and end points of the line are given using two coordinates: X and Y. This is because a picture is a two-dimensional image.

However, the position of the joints in a skeleton are expressed using three coordinates. When you stand in front of the Kinect sensor, your head will be some distance to the left or right of the sensor (X), some distance above or below the sensor (Y), and some distance away from the sensor (Z). Later you will use these three-dimensional (3D) values to allow your programs to detect movement and gesture, but for now you need a way to convert the 3D position of an object into a 2D position that you can draw on a screen.

Artists do this when they paint a picture. They look at the scene in front of them and then transform their view into a series of lines and points on the painting that represent what they see. In graphical terms, this is projection. You can think of it as a form of transformation. The 3D X, Y, and Z values that describe the position of your head must be transformed into a 2D value that gives the starting point of a line on the image.

The good news is that the Kinect SDK provides a method that will perform this transformation for you. It is given a value that contains the X, Y, and Z values that describe a 3D position and converts this into X and Y values that give the position in an image frame. The method is called *MapSkeletonPointToColor,* and it maps the position of a skeleton joint onto coordinates that match positions provided by the video camera. Another method—*MapSkeletonPointToDepth*—can map 3D joint positions into the depth image frame. Both of these methods return point types (*ColorImagePoint* and *DepthImagePoint,* respectively) that give the X and Y positions of the joint in the respective image.

The *MapSkeletonPointToColor* method can be used to allow a program to create applications where the position of a person in front of the Kinect sensor is aligned with the image from the video camera. You will do this in Chapter 10, "Augmented Reality with Kinect." For now you are just going to use the X and Y coordinate values to draw the skeleton on the screen.

```
ColorImagePoint headPoint = myKinect.MapSkeletonPointToColor(headJoint.Position,
                        ColorImageFormat.RgbResolution640x480Fps30);
```

The method has two parameters. The first is a *SkeletonPoint* giving the position information of the joint, and the next is the format of the image into which the position is to be mapped. This sets the range of the width and height values that will be produced. Using the preceding format, a skeleton joint on the far right would have an X value of 640, because this is the maximum X value. The method returns a value of type *ColorImagePoint* that has X and Y properties giving the position of the point. The complete line can be created as follows:

```
Line backBone = new Line();
backBone.Stroke = new SolidColorBrush(Colors.Red);
backBone.StrokeThickness = 5;

ColorImagePoint headPoint = myKinect.MapSkeletonPointToColor(headJoint.Position,
ColorImageFormat.RgbResolution640x480Fps30);
backBone.X1 = headPoint.X;
backBone.Y1 = headPoint.Y;

ColorImagePoint hipPoint = myKinect.MapSkeletonPointToColor(hipCenter.Position,
ColorImageFormat.RgbResolution640x480Fps30);
backBone.X2 = hipPoint.X;
backBone.Y2 = hipPoint.Y;

skeletonCanvas.Children.Add(backBone);
```

The preceding statements create a *Line* called *backBone* that joins the head with the center of the hips. This line is added to the skeleton canvas.

Sample Code: Head Tracker with Backbone Drawing The sample project in the "03 Kinect Backbone Viewer" directory in the resources for this chapter (see the "Code Samples" section in the Introduction) holds an XNA program that tracks the head of one skeleton and displays clipping prompts to the user. It also draws the backbone of the player on the screen.

When you run the program, you should see your backbone being drawn on the screen. If you lean left and right you should see the line move to match.

Clearing the Canvas

If you take a look inside the preceding demo program, you will notice that each time the skeleton is drawn, the canvas is cleared so that the previous line is replaced with a new one.

```
skeletonCanvas.Children.Clear();
```

Turning Yourself into a Paintbrush

You might find it interesting to remove this statement from the backbone viewer program. This means that successive lines will pile up on the screen, turning your body into a huge paintbrush. As you move around the area in front of the sensor, you can fill in the screen with red lines. You could change the program so that, rather than using your backbone to draw, it uses your left or your right arm. This would allow you to produce more detailed pictures.

Drawing a Complete Skeleton

To draw a complete skeleton, a program just has to join up the correct joints with lines. You could just block copy the preceding code and change it to create each line individually, but this would be a lot of work, and if you make any mistakes in your copying the drawing will not look right. A much better approach is to create a helper method called *addLine* that is used to draw one line between two joints:

```
Brush skeletonBrush = new SolidColorBrush(Colors.Red);

void addLine(Joint j1, Joint j2)
{
    Line boneLine = new Line();
    boneLine.Stroke = skeletonBrush;
    boneLine.StrokeThickness = 5;

    ColorImagePoint j1P = myKinect.MapSkeletonPointToColor(j1.Position,
                    ColorImageFormat.RgbResolution640x480Fps30);
```

```
    boneLine.X1 = j1P.X;
    boneLine.Y1 = j1P.Y;

    ColorImagePoint j2P = myKinect.MapSkeletonPointToColor(j2.Position,
                            ColorImageFormat.RgbResolution640x480Fps30);
    boneLine.X2 = j2P.X;
    boneLine.Y2 = j2P.Y;

    skeletonCanvas.Children.Add(boneLine);
}
```

This method contains the code that you have already seen, but it is given the joints to work on as parameters. It uses a brush that is created once and stored as part of the program. Now that you have the method, you just have to make a number of calls of it to draw the entire skeleton:

```
// Spine
addLine(skeleton.Joints[JointType.Head], skeleton.Joints[JointType.ShoulderCenter]);
addLine(skeleton.Joints[JointType.ShoulderCenter], skeleton.Joints[JointType.Spine]);

// Left leg
addLine(skeleton.Joints[JointType.Spine], skeleton.Joints[JointType.HipCenter]);
addLine(skeleton.Joints[JointType.HipCenter], skeleton.Joints[JointType.HipLeft]);
addLine(skeleton.Joints[JointType.HipLeft], skeleton.Joints[JointType.KneeLeft]);
addLine(skeleton.Joints[JointType.KneeLeft], skeleton.Joints[JointType.AnkleLeft]);
addLine(skeleton.Joints[JointType.AnkleLeft], skeleton.Joints[JointType.FootLeft]);

// Right leg
addLine(skeleton.Joints[JointType.HipCenter], skeleton.Joints[JointType.HipRight]);
addLine(skeleton.Joints[JointType.HipRight], skeleton.Joints[JointType.KneeRight]);
addLine(skeleton.Joints[JointType.KneeRight], skeleton.Joints[JointType.AnkleRight]);
addLine(skeleton.Joints[JointType.AnkleRight], skeleton.Joints[JointType.FootRight]);

// Left arm
addLine(skeleton.Joints[JointType.ShoulderCenter],
    skeleton.Joints[JointType.ShoulderLeft]);
addLine(skeleton.Joints[JointType.ShoulderLeft], skeleton.Joints[JointType.ElbowLeft]);
addLine(skeleton.Joints[JointType.ElbowLeft], skeleton.Joints[JointType.WristLeft]);
addLine(skeleton.Joints[JointType.WristLeft], skeleton.Joints[JointType.HandLeft]);

// Right arm
addLine(skeleton.Joints[JointType.ShoulderCenter],
    skeleton.Joints[JointType.ShoulderRight]);
addLine(skeleton.Joints[JointType.ShoulderRight],
    skeleton.Joints[JointType.ElbowRight]);
addLine(skeleton.Joints[JointType.ElbowRight], skeleton.Joints[JointType.WristRight]);
addLine(skeleton.Joints[JointType.WristRight], skeleton.Joints[JointType.HandRight]);
```

If you were drawing a stick figure, you would draw lines that connect all the various parts of the body. The preceding sequence of calls to *addLine* draws each part of the body in turn.

> **Sample Code: Head Tracker with Skeleton Drawing** The sample project in the "04 Kinect Skeleton Viewer" directory in the resources for this chapter (see the "Code Samples" section in the Introduction) holds an XNA program that tracks the head of one skeleton and displays clipping prompts to the user. It also draws the skeleton of the player on the screen.

Figure 8-5 shows the output from the program, displaying a skeleton along with head position information and the quality information that you saw in the previous program.

> **Note** The preceding program will draw the skeleton and works well, even on low-powered machines. However, it is not using the WPF drawing mechanism in the most efficient way. Each successive frame that is drawn is made up of a brand-new set of lines. A more efficient version of the drawing program would place the lines on the canvas the first time the skeleton is drawn and then update their position to reflect changes in the position of the skeleton. This would make the program slightly more complicated (it would have to keep track of the lines), but it would make it much more efficient.

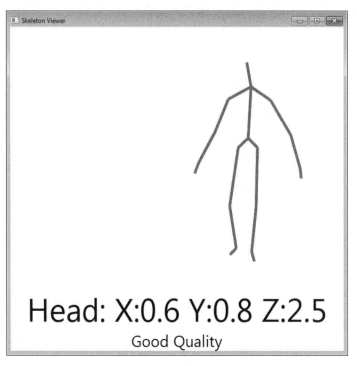

FIGURE 8-5 Drawing a skeleton.

Detecting Gestures

You now know how a program can obtain and use skeleton information. Next, you are going to write a program that interprets user gestures. One kind of gesture is a movement such as waving your hand in the air. You could write a Kinect program that detects this; in fact, the Xbox 360 Kinect user interface works this way. However, this is difficult to do. The program has to track the movement of the hand over time and compare the path that it sees with the path for that particular gesture.

A better kind of gesture is one where the user moves two body parts close together. You are going to create a program named *TinHead,* which will play a sound when the user taps his or her head. The program will detect when the user brings the right hand close to the head and will play a sound effect when this happens. To make this work, you will need a way of measuring the distance between two joints in the skeleton. This turns out to be very easy to do, once you have reminded yourself of some trigonometry that you learned ages ago.

Calculating the Distance Between Two Points in Space

Our program will have the position of two points (the right hand and the head) and must calculate the distance between those two points. The actual position values will be given as 3D coordinates (X, Y, and Z), but for simplicity we are going to start by considering how we would decide the distance between two positions in two dimensions using just the coordinates X and Y. A program could work out the differences between two joint locations by subtracting the X and Y components as follows:

```
float dX = first.Position.X - second.Position.X;
float dY = first.Position.Y - second.Position.Y;
```

This gives the distance across and the distance up that you need to move when traveling from one point to the other.

Figure 8-6 shows how this works. To get from the top point to the bottom, you could take the long way around by moving down by *dY* and across by *dX*. However, the program needs the value of distance to use as a trigger for the TinHead sound playback.

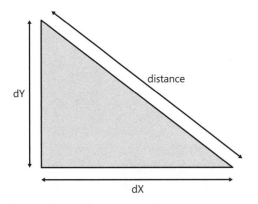

FIGURE 8-6 Triangles and distances.

The Pythagorean theorem for right-angled triangles states that "The square of the hypotenuse is equal to the sum of the squares of the other two sides." In Figure 8-6, the distance value is the hypotenuse (the side opposite the right angle) and X and Y are the other two sides. If you express this as an equation, you see the following:

```
(dX*dX) + (dY*dY) = (distance * distance)
```

We have the values of *dX* and *dY* and want to calculate the value of distance. This turns out to be very easy to do:

```
distance = Math.Sqrt((dX * dX) + (dY * dY));
```

The *Math* library in .NET provides a square root method called *Sqrt* that provides the distance value. It turns out that the Pythagorean theorem works in three dimensions as well; you just have to add the distance in the third dimension. You can use all this to create a method that will return the distance between two joints.

```
private float jointDistance(Joint first, Joint second)
{
    float dX = first.Position.X - second.Position.X;
    float dY = first.Position.Y - second.Position.Y;
    float dZ = first.Position.Z - second.Position.Z;

    return (float)Math.Sqrt((dX * dX) + (dY * dY) + (dZ * dZ));
}
```

Using a Gesture to Trigger an Action

Now that a program can measure the distance between two joints, it becomes very easy to trigger an action:

```
float distance = jointDistance(skeleton.Joints[JointID.Head], skeleton.
Joints[JointID.HandRight]);

if (distance < 0.4f && oldDistance > 0.4f)
{
    dingPlayer.Play();
}

oldDistance = distance;
```

This program will play a sound when the user moves one hand within 0.4 meters of his or her head. This value seems to work reliably without many false triggers. The program uses a variable called *oldDistance* that keeps track of the distance value that was measured from the previous skeleton.

This allows the program to only play the sound when the hand reaches the head and not all the time that the hand is close to the head. The sound effect is loaded into the program and played in just the same way as the sound effects that you used to make the burglar alarm in previous chapters.

> **Sample Code: "Tin Head"** The sample project in the "05 Kinect TinHead" directory in the resources for this chapter (see the "Code Samples" section in the Introduction) holds an XNA program that plays a sound effect when the user moves the right hand close to the head.

Biometric Recognition with Kinect

Biometrics is a branch of technology that uses physical characteristics of people—for example, height, fingerprints, hair color, facial features, or voice—to recognize them. Now that you can measure the distance between joints, you might be able to use the Kinect as a rough-and-ready biometric system. By using a set of characteristic distances—for example, the length of the leg bones and the spine—you can make a program that will obey your commands but refuse to work for your little sister or your bigger brother. To do this, you just need to use the *jointDistance* method with those joints rather than the hand and the head.

Creating a "Kiss-Detecting" Program

The programs that you have written so far have only tracked one skeleton. Now it is time to find out how a program can track two people and make decisions based on how close they are together. You will do this by creating a "chaperone" program that will detect when two skeletons move their heads close together, as they would do if they were kissing. This program will make use of the ability of the Kinect SDK to track two skeletons. Because a program is given the position of each joint in a skeleton in the 3D space in front of the sensor, it can calculate the distance between the positions. The actual content of the program will be very similar to the TinHead program.

Finding Two Skeletons That Are Being Tracked

The kiss-detecting program will use the joint positions of the two heads that are being tracked. To do this it will need to obtain the two skeletons standing in front of the sensor.

```
// find two trackedSkeletons
List<SkeletonData> trackedSkeletons = new List<SkeletonData>();

foreach (SkeletonData skeleton in e.SkeletonFrame.Skeletons)
{
    if (skeleton.TrackingState == SkeletonTrackingState.Tracked)
        trackedSkeletons.Add(skeleton);
}
```

The preceding code creates an empty list of skeletons and then works through all the skeleton results looking for any that are being tracked. If it finds a tracked skeleton, it adds it to the list.

Next the program must detect if the heads of the skeletons are too close together. It must also draw the skeletons.

```
if (trackedSkeletons.Count < 2)
    status = string.Format("{0} person(s) present", trackedSkeletons.Count);
else
{
    drawSkeleton(trackedSkeletons[0], new SolidColorBrush(Colors.Red));
    drawSkeleton(trackedSkeletons[1], new SolidColorBrush(Colors.Blue));

    float distance = jointDistance(trackedSkeletons[0].Joints[JointType.Head],
        trackedSkeletons[1].Joints[JointType.Head]);

    if (distance < 0.4f)
    {
        status = "Steady on now";

        if (oldDistance > 0.4f)
        {
            alarmPlayer.Play();
        }
    }
    else
    {
        status = "OK";
    }

    oldDistance = distance;
}
```

If fewer than two skeletons are in the list that has been created, not enough people are present to detect kissing, so the program just sets the status message accordingly.

If two skeletons are detected, the program calculates the distance between their heads. If this value is less than the trigger threshold, the program will display a status message and play a warning sound effect.

The skeleton drawing behavior has been moved into a method called *drawSkeleton*. You can use this in any program where you need to draw a skeleton on a canvas. The method is provided with a skeleton to draw and the brush with which to draw it.

> **Sample Code: "Kinect Kiss Detector"** The sample project in the "06 Kinect Kiss Detector" directory in the resources for this chapter (see the "Code Samples" section in the Introduction) holds an XNA program that plays a sound effect when two tracked skeletons try to kiss. I'm not guaranteeing that it will always work, but it is certainly fun to test.

You could improve the kiss-detection program to display different warnings as the skeletons got closer and to detect when people are "just holding hands."

Summary

In this chapter, you have learned how the Kinect performs skeleton tracking and how this information is made available to your programs.

You have discovered how a *C# Dictionary* collection works and how the skeleton *Joints* collection provides you with easy access to joint positions.

You have also learned how to draw lines in WPF programs and then have used this to project the 3D joint location onto a 2D image that can show skeletons on the screen.

Finally, you have learned how to work out the distance between joints and use this to make interesting program behaviors.

In Chapter 9, you are going to learn how you can use real voice commands to control your programs via the Kinect sensor.

Chapter 9

Voice Control with Kinect

After completing this chapter, you will:

- Understand how to configure speech recognition in a C# program

- Create a gesture-controlled painting program that uses voice input to select commands

- Improve the painting program so that it also outputs messages using speech synthesis

Using the Microsoft Speech Platform

THE MICROSOFT SPEECH PLATFORM IS very powerful. It comprises a set of components that make it easy to create programs to recognize speech input and produce spoken output. Components in the Speech Platform are interchangeable and configurable so that the platform can work with different languages and locales. You can find out more about the Microsoft Speech Platform here:

http://msdn.microsoft.com/en-us/library/hh361572.aspx

The Kinect for Windows SDK uses Version 11 of the Microsoft Speech Platform. The platform contains three components:

1. Microsoft Speech Platform Runtime. This allows programs running on a Windows PC to make use of the speech recognition features provided by the Microsoft Speech Platform. This is provided as part of the Kinect for Windows SDK.

2. Language Packs. A language pack provides the dictionaries that map sounds from a particular language onto words that the program can understand and act on. The Kinect for Windows SDK provides an updated English language pack that has been customized to work with the sensor. If you want to use other languages, you can download language packs from here:

http://www.microsoft.com/download/en/details.aspx?id=27224

3. Microsoft Speech Platform SDK. You will be developing programs that use the Microsoft Speech Platform. To do this you will need to install the SDK. You can download the Microsoft Speech Platform SDK from here:

   http://www.microsoft.com/download/en/details.aspx?id=27226

Testing Voice Recognition

You can test voice recognition by using the Kinect Audio Demo that is provided as part of the Kinect for Windows SDK. To run this demonstration program, you can use the Kinect SDK Sample Browser. You used this in Chapter 2 in the section "Testing the Kinect Sensor Bar." Start the sample browser and find the "Kinect Audio Demo" item. Click the Run Sample button to start the sample running.

Figure 9-1 shows the demo program in action. The display at the top shows the direction from the Kinect sensor to the voice source that is detected. The program can recognize the words *red*, *green*, or *blue*. When you say these words, the direction indicator moves to point toward you.

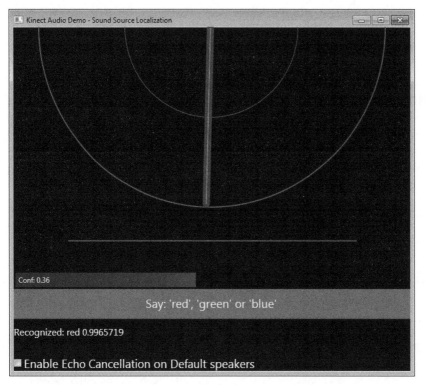

FIGURE 9-1 The Kinect audio demo.

Creating a Program That Recognizes Color Names

The Speech Platform can be used to create programs that understand grammar as well as single words. This means that you could design a structure that would allow a program to respond to a complex command such as "Open the door." You would do this by creating a construction that gives the structure of the command. It would describe the options available at the start of the command (perhaps Open or Close) and the things that could be opened and closed (door, window, etc.).

However, you are going to keep things simple by making a program that just responds to individual words. It seems that the traditional demonstration application for Kinect voice control is a program that recognizes the names of colors as they are spoken by the user. That is what you are going to create first. However, you are then going to put this to good use, to make a body-controlled painting program where the user can select colors using speech input.

It is very important that you install both the 64-bit (x64) *and* the 32-bit (x32) versions of the Microsoft Speech SDK. If you only install one of them, the Kinect for Windows SDK documentation warns that your programs may not run correctly after you have built them. The installers can be found on the Microsoft Speech Platform pages at the Microsoft Download Center:

http://www.microsoft.com/download/en/details.aspx?id=27226

Adding the Speech Platform SDK Assemblies to a Project

Before you can use the classes from the Speech Platform SDK, you must add the speech assemblies to your Visual Studio project. You can do this by following the same process as described in Chapter 3, "Creating a New Visual Studio Project for Kinect." The classes for speech recognition are held in the following library, and it is the one you should add to your project:

C:\Program Files\Microsoft SDKs\Speech\v11.0\Assembly\Microsoft.Speech.dll

Once you have added the library, you can add some include statements to your project to make the library classes easier to use:

```
using Microsoft.Speech.AudioFormat;
using Microsoft.Speech.Recognition;
```

> **Note** The Kinect SDK installation automatically adds part of the Speech SDK to your system. This is so that the speech sample programs will work correctly. However, if you wish to develop and debug speech applications, you should install the Speech SDK.

Creating a Speech Recognition Engine

The *SpeechRecognitionEngine* class is the part of the Microsoft Speech Platform that performs voice recognition. If a program needs to convert spoken words to text, it can create an instance of the *SpeechRecognitionEngine* class to do the work.

```
SpeechRecognitionEngine recognizer;
recognizer = new SpeechRecognitionEngine(kinectRecognizerInfo);
```

When a new *SpeechRecognitionEngine* is created, the constructor is given a lump of data that describes the particular recognizer that is to be used. In the preceding statements, this data is supplied in the variable called *kinectRecognizerInfo*. This variable is of type *RecognizerInfo*.

```
RecognizerInfo kinectRecognizerInfo;
```

The *RecognizerInfo* class holds lots of information about a particular speech recognizer, including the language it recognizes and the audio formats with which it can work. You can think of this as the résumé of a particular recognizer if you like. A program that wants to recognize a particular language can check through all the recognizers that are installed on a system to find one that will do the job.

This way of working makes very good sense. The designers of the Speech Platform are addressing the challenge that a system will have to respond to spoken commands in a variety of different languages. It would be impossible to create one program that could understand all possible languages. Instead of doing this, the platform breaks down the problem so that each language is handled by a custom recognizer for that language.

A program can get a list containing all the recognizer descriptions on a particular machine by using the *InstalledRecognizers* method exposed by the *SpeechRecognitionEngine* class:

```
var recognizers = SpeechRecognitionEngine.InstalledRecognizers();
```

The preceding statement sets the variable *recognizers* to a collection of *RecognizerInfo* values that describes all the recognizers available on that particular computer.

Rather than declare the *recognizers* variable as a collection type, I have declared it as of type *var*. A variable of type *var* automatically adopts the correct type depending on how it is used in a program. The compiler will infer the type to be used based on what is put into the variable.

```
var thisIsInt = 1;
var thisIsString = "Hello World";
```

In the preceding statements, the *thisIsInt* variable will be used as an integer and the variable *thisIsString* will be used as a string, despite them both being declared with the "same" type of *var*. However, the compiler is well aware of what is going on in this situation and will still detect any programming mistakes involving these variables. If your program tries to combine the variables in a way that their adopted types do not permit, the program will fail to compile.

```
thisIsInt = thisIsString;
```

This statement tries to put the *"Hello World"* string from *thisIsString* into the integer variable *thisIsInt*. This is an action that you know is not possible. The compiler would refuse to compile this statement and would instead produce the error message *"Cannot implicitly convert type 'string' to 'int'"*. In other words, as the compiler checks your program, it works out what a variable of type *var* is being used for and then enforces this throughout the program.

The *var* type is useful in situations where the type of the variable is not particularly important and you want to keep the code simple. You can think of the keyword *var* as being short for *variable* and letting you create "Variable variables."

Since the *recognizers* value is a collection, a program can use the *foreach* construction to work through it.

```
var recognizers = SpeechRecognitionEngine.InstalledRecognizers();

foreach (RecognizerInfo recInfo in recognizers)
{
    // look at each recInfo value to find the one that works for Kinect
}
```

Each time round the loop, the value of *recInfo* is set to the next recognizer in the list. The program must look for a *RecognizerInfo* value that describes a recognizer that would work with the Kinect sensor. This is the same behavior as you looking through a pile of résumés to find a translator who can speak Spanish and can use Microsoft Word to type a translation.

```
var recognizers = SpeechRecognitionEngine.InstalledRecognizers();
```

A suitable Kinect recognizer has the string "True" associated with the dictionary key "Kinect" in its *AdditionalInfo* property. The *AdditionalInfo* property of a *RecognizerInfo* value tells you more information about a recognizer, including things like the company who created it and the speaking style with which it works best. You have seen dictionaries before, such as the *Joints* collection in a Kinect skeleton, which is a dictionary that lets a program look up the position of a particular joint.

In this case, the *AdditionalInfo* property lets a program look up information about a particular recognizer. The first thing the program must do is check to see if there is an entry about Kinect in the *AdditionalInfo* property. Then, if the information is present the program must make sure that the value of the property is set to *true*. There is a second requirement for a workable recognizer, which is that the *Culture* setting for the recognizer must be set to *"en-US,"* which means "English-United States."

```
if (recInfo.AdditionalInfo.ContainsKey("Kinect"))
{
    string details = recInfo.AdditionalInfo["Kinect"];
    if (details == "True" && recInfo.Culture.Name == "en-US")
```

```
    {
        // If we get here we have found the info we want to use
    }
}
```

This code performs the required tests. It first looks to see if the Kinect is supported and then tests for the required culture. You can use all this to create a method that will find and return the information about the recognizer that is required.

```
private RecognizerInfo findKinectRecognizerInfo()
{
    var recognizers = SpeechRecognitionEngine.InstalledRecognizers();

    foreach (RecognizerInfo recInfo in recognizers)
    {
        // look at each recognizer info value to find the one that works for Kinect
        if (recInfo.AdditionalInfo.ContainsKey("Kinect"))
        {
            string details = recInfo.AdditionalInfo["Kinect"];
            if (details == "True" && recInfo.Culture.Name == "en-US")
                // If we get here we have found the info we want to use
                return recInfo;
        }
    }
    return null;
}
```

The method will either return the information describing the required recognizer or the value *null*. This means that to create a speech recognizer for your program, you can use the following two statements:

```
kinectRecognizerInfo = findKinectRecognizerInfo();
recognizer = new SpeechRecognitionEngine(kinectRecognizerInfo);
```

> **Note** These two statements greatly simplify the operation. In a proper program you would need to make sure that if the *RecognizerInfo* was not found, the program did not try to create a recognizer. You would also have to make sure that any problems setting up the *SpeechRecognitionEngine* were handled correctly. This has been done for you in the sample programs.

Building the Commands

You are going to create a very simple speech recognition system that recognizes a set of words. The next thing your program must do is set up the words that are to be recognized. The *Choices* class is provided by the Microsoft Speech Platform as a way of creating a collection of words that are to be recognized. You can get the system to recognize any word by adding it to the choices to be used in a system.

```
Choices commands = new Choices();
```

The *Choices* class is a container that will hold all the words that are to be recognized at a point in a conversation. You are not going to have anything more than just the one set of commands in this program.

```
commands.Add("Red");
commands.Add("Green");
commands.Add("Blue");
commands.Add("Yellow");
commands.Add("Cyan");
commands.Add("Orange");
commands.Add("Purple");
```

The preceding statements add the command options that you want to use in your program. If you want to use additional commands, such as "Clear" or "Exit," you just have to add them. When a word is recognized by the speech recognition engine, your program is given the command word back so that it can act on it.

Creating a Grammar

The Speech Platform can recognize complex commands. It does this by allowing the programmer to create a "grammar" that describes the command structure and the words that it contains. Grammar is the part of a language that describes how the various elements fit together.

In the English language we talk about verbs and nouns, where verbs are "doing" words that describe actions and nouns are words that identify things. The statement "open the door" makes sense to us because we know that "open" is a verb and "door" is a noun that identifies something that could be opened. Grammar gives us the rules that allow us to see that "door the window" is not sensible because neither "door" nor "window" are verbs and a sentence like this needs a verb. In similar fashion, "open the close" would also be nonsensical, as that contains verbs but no nouns.

To allow the Speech Platform to understand command phrases that work in this way you could create a grammar that says that *open* and *close* are verbs and can work on *doors* and *windows*. However, for your first program you are going to create a very simple grammar that just contains the commands to select a particular color.

In the Speech Platform a grammar is actually created by a *GrammarBuilder* class. This allows more flexibility. The *GrammarBuilder* is given the higher-level description of the required statement and then produces a grammar that suits a particular culture. This makes it easier to deal with a wide range of languages.

```
GrammarBuilder grammarBuilder = new GrammarBuilder();

grammarBuilder.Culture = kinectRecognizerInfo.Culture;
grammarBuilder.Append(commands);

Grammar grammar = new Grammar(grammarBuilder);

recognizer.LoadGrammar(grammar);
```

The preceding statements create a *GrammarBuilder* called *grammarBuilder*. This is then set to the same culture as the recognizer we are using (in this case, U.S. English) and then used to create a *Grammar* value that is loaded into the *recognizer*.

Getting Audio into the Speech Recognizer

In Chapter 7, in the section "Receiving Sound Signals from Kinect," you saw that the Kinect audio source produces a stream of audio values. The first program that you wrote in that section opened a stream of audio values and displayed them on the screen. Later you saved those values in a file so that the audio could be played back later. In the following program, the audio stream is connected to the recognizer:

```
private void setupAudio()
{
    try
    {
        myKinect = KinectSensor.KinectSensors[0];
        myKinect.Start();

        kinectSource = myKinect.AudioSource;
        kinectSource.BeamAngleMode = BeamAngleMode.Adaptive;
        audioStream = kinectSource.Start();
        recognizer.SetInputToAudioStream(audioStream, new SpeechAudioFormatInfo(
                                        EncodingFormat.Pcm, 16000, 16, 1,
                                        32000, 2, null));
        recognizer.RecognizeAsync(RecognizeMode.Multiple);
    }
    catch
    {
        MessageBox.Show("Audio stream could not be connected","Kinect Speech Demo");
        Application.Current.Shutdown();
    }
}
```

The method *setupAudio* creates and configures a Kinect sensor to produce audio data. The microphones are configured to work as an adaptive beam. This means that sound-processing hardware in the sensor will analyze the audio signals received from the microphones and work out from where the sound source is coming. The sensor bar will then process the sound signals to remove echoes and unwanted noises that come from other directions.

There are three possible *BeamAngleMode* values:

- **Automatic**   The system selects the beam direction that corresponds to the sound source. This angle is selected by the Windows media drivers.

- **Adaptive**   The system selects the beam angle using custom-written software that is part of the Kinect SDK. This gives the best results.

- **NotTracked**   The program sets the beam direction. Unless you want your program to control the beam direction based on other input—for example, skeleton tracking—you should set the mode to Adaptive.

Next, the audio stream is connected to the recognizer so that sound from the Kinect is analyzed by it. Working with streams in this way makes it possible for the recognizer to read text from a file, but in this case it will work with the live sound stream from the user.

Finally, the recognizer is configured to recognize words repeatedly and asynchronously.

Responding to Recognized Words

You have now reached the point where everything has been set up to allow voice recognition in your Kinect program. To recap what has been done so far:

1. The Speech Platform SDK has been installed on the system.

2. The program project contains a reference to the Speech Platform libraries.

3. When the program runs, it locates the recognizer information and creates a speech recognition engine using the appropriate recognizer.

4. The program sets up a list of the commands that are to be recognized.

5. The program creates a *GrammarGenerator* and then a *Grammar* that is assigned to the speech recognizer.

6. The program starts the Kinect sound sensor sampling audio and feeds this into the speech recognizer that has been set up.

The final thing that needs to be set up is the code that actually runs when a word is recognized. For your first program, this will just display the word on the screen.

You can connect a method to an event that is raised by the recognizer when a word is recognized. This works in exactly the same way as other Kinect sensors. To get an event produced when a word is recognized, a program can use the *SpeechRecognized* event that is provided by the *SpeechRecognizer* class.

```
recognizer.SpeechRecognized += new EventHandler<SpeechRecognizedEventArgs>();
```

When a word is recognized, the preceding code will call a method called *recognizer_SpeechRecognized*. This will display the name of the color that was detected:

```
void recognizer_SpeechRecognized(object sender, SpeechRecognizedEventArgs e)
{
    if (e.Result.Confidence > 0.9f)
        wordTextBlock.Text = e.Result.Text;
}
```

This method checks the confidence value of the returned result, and if the confidence is greater than 0.9, it displays the text result. The higher the confidence value, the more sure the framework is that the word has been recognized correctly. I've found that 0.9 (90%) seems to work well.

> **Sample Code: Word Recognition** The sample project in the "01 Kinect Speech Recognition demo" directory in the resources for this chapter (see the "Code Samples" section in the Introduction) holds a program that recognizes colors and displays them on the screen. This has been a long time coming, but it does work well, and you can use the methods in it to add audio control to any program that you like. Note that the Kinect SDK takes 4 seconds or so to begin sending audio data, so your program will take a little while to get started.

Creating a Voice-Controlled Painting Program

In Chapter 8, you saw how to create a program that draws "bones" on the screen from a skeleton that is being tracked by the Kinect. This could be used as the basis of a drawing program, but it would be hard to use because the user would have to draw the same color all the time and have no way of clearing the screen or saving a picture once it had been drawn. You can vastly improve such a program by adding some voice commands to it. These could allow the user to set the drawing color, clear the screen, and even save the drawn image to disk.

> **Sample Code: Body Drawing** The sample project in the "02 Voice Controlled Body Drawing" directory in the resources for this chapter (see the "Code Samples" section in the Introduction) holds a program that lets you draw on the screen using your right hand to paint.

To use the program, start it running and stand in front of the Kinect sensor. The sensor will display your skeleton on the screen, and you can draw with your right hand. Initially the program has the pen "up," and so drawing operations do not take place. You use the command Down to start drawing with a solid-color pen. You can also give commands to change the color being used to draw, and even select a Random pen that uses a different color for each drawing operation.

Figure 9-2 shows the program in use. The left side shows the artist and the artists' artwork, and the right side gives status information. The last spoken command that the program received was "Random," and so the program is drawing with random pen colors.

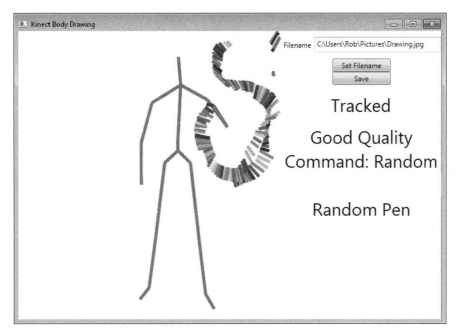

FIGURE 9-2 The Kinect gesture-controlled painting program in action.

This is the most complicated program that you have seen so far, and so it is worth spending some time looking at how it works.

Speech Commands

The program uses speech in exactly the same way as the color recognizer that you created earlier. However, this time there are 14 possible spoken commands.

```
private void buildCommands()
{
    Choices commands = new Choices();

    commands.Add("Red");    // set color to red
    commands.Add("Green");  // set color to green
```

```
commands.Add("Blue");    // set color to blue
commands.Add("Yellow");  // set color to yellow
commands.Add("Cyan");    // set color to cyan
commands.Add("Orange");  // set color to orange
commands.Add("Purple");  // set color to purple
commands.Add("Magenta"); // set color to magenta
commands.Add("Up");      // lift pen up and stop drawing
commands.Add("Down");    // put pen down and draw
commands.Add("Random");  // put draw random colors
commands.Add("Save");    // save the picture
commands.Add("Clear");   // clear the screen
commands.Add("Test");    // draw a test pattern

GrammarBuilder grammarBuilder = new GrammarBuilder();

grammarBuilder.Culture = kinectRecognizerInfo.Culture;
grammarBuilder.Append(commands);

Grammar grammar = new Grammar(grammarBuilder);

recognizer.LoadGrammar(grammar);
}
```

When the program recognizes a spoken command, it calls a method to deal with it:

```
void recognizer_SpeechRecognized(object sender, SpeechRecognizedEventArgs e)
{
    if (e.Result.Confidence > 0.9f)
  h
  {
        handleCommand(e.Result.Text);
    }
}
```

The *handleCommand* method uses a switch construction to select the required command. It also displays on the screen the command that was received:

```
void handleCommand(string command)
{
    commandTextBlock.Text = "Command: " + command;

    switch (command)
    {
        case "Red":
            setDrawingColor(Colors.Red);
            break;
```

```
// other colors are handled here
        case "Up":
            penUp();
            break;
        case "Down":
            penDown();
            break;
        case "Random":
            penRandom();
            break;
        case "Save":
            save();
            break;
        case "Clear":
            clearCanvas();
            break;
        case "Test":
            testDraw();
            break;
    }
}
```

Each of the methods performs the required task. If you want to create any kind of voice-response program, you now know how to do it; you can use exactly the same structure for your program.

Drawing a Skeleton Cursor

The program shows a "skeleton cursor" on top of the actual image being drawn. This allows the artist to see his or her location on the screen. However, the cursor is not actually part of the picture. The program does this by overlaying one canvas on top of another on the screen. Because the background of the skeleton cursor canvas is transparent, the image will show through behind the cursor.

```
<Canvas Height="480" Width="640" >
    <Canvas Name="drawCanvas" Height="480" Width="640" HorizontalAlignment="Center"
/>
    <Canvas Name="skeletonCursorCanvas" Height="480" Width="640"
HorizontalAlignment="Center" />
</Canvas>
```

The *Canvas* element in XAML allows a program to place elements onto a display at particular positions. The preceding XAML creates a canvas that contains a *drawCanvas* and a *skeletonCursorCanvas* superimposed on top of each other. The elements are drawn in the order they appear in the XAML, so the drawing canvas is drawn first and then the skeleton cursor is placed on top.

Drawing Using the Artist's Hand

The first drawing program that you created used the right arm of the artist to draw on the screen. Although this lets an artist quickly fill up the entire screen, it doesn't allow drawing with much detail. The finished drawing program contains two variables that specify the joints that are to be used to define the drawing brush:

```
JointType brushStart = JointType.WristRight;
JointType brushEnd = JointType.HandRight;
```

This drawing program uses just the right hand of the artist to perform the drawing, but you can easily change these values to allow left-handed artists to take part, or even to let an artist draw with the left leg if that is what is desired. The program performs the drawing using a slightly modified version of the *addLine* method you saw before, only this time the method specifies the brush to use and the canvas to draw on:

```
addLine(skeleton.Joints[brushStart], skeleton.Joints[brushEnd], drawingBrush,
drawCanvas);
```

This version of the method can be used to add lines to either the drawing canvas or the skeleton cursor canvas.

Saving the Drawing Canvas to a File

You have already seen some programs that have saved images from the screen into files. There are two stages to saving an image. The first stage is creating a bitmap image that can be saved to a file, and the second stage is actually saving the bitmap itself.

Rendering a Canvas to a Bitmap

Until now the items that have been saved by the programs have been bitmaps that have been created from red, green, and blue values received from the Kinect sensors. To save a Windows Presentation Foundation (WPF) element we have to convert the element into a bitmap that can be saved in a file. This process is called *rendering*. Normally the display element will render itself for display on the screen, but a program can also create a bitmap and render the control there instead.

```
BitmapSource renderCanvasToBitmap(Canvas canvas)
{
    // Create a render bitmap and push the canvas to it

    RenderTargetBitmap renderBitmap =
        new RenderTargetBitmap(
        (int)canvas.Width,
        (int)canvas.Height,
        96,                  // dots per inch
```

```
    96,                    // dots per inch
    PixelFormats.Pbgra32);

  renderBitmap.Render(canvas);

  return renderBitmap;
}
```

The *renderBitmap* method is given a canvas to render into a bitmap. It returns the bitmap that has been produced. The first thing the method does is create a bitmap that can serve as the target for the rendering. Then it renders the canvas onto this bitmap. Note that when the bitmap is created, it is given dimension settings (which are the width and the height of the canvas) and also the number of dots per inch. The format of the pixel data in the bitmap is set to *PixelFormats.Pbgra32*, which means a pixel made up of 32 bits (4 bytes) in the order blue, green, red, alpha. This is the format of the data that your program has been created. You can find out more about pixel formats here:

http://msdn.microsoft.com/en-us/library/ms635337.aspx

The number of dots per inch in an image display determines how sharp it looks to the viewer. One reason that high-definition TV looks sharper than standard definition is that the high-definition screens display more dots per inch. The standard screen resolution for Windows PCs is set at 96 dots per inch. The preceding method creates a bitmap of this resolution so that pixels in the canvas being rendered will map directly onto pixels in the bitmap that is to be produced.

Saving a Bitmap into a Named File

In Chapter 5, in the section "Triggering Pictures with Motion Capture," you saw how a program can be made to save pictures multiple times into a sequence of files. The program used a variable to count the frames as it took each one, and the user could select the initial filename that would be used for the pictures.

```
int frameNo = 0;
```

The *frameNo* variable was initially set at 0 when the program started running, as shown in the preceding statement. This worked well, but it meant that the user had to set the initial filename before pictures could be stored, and the program would overwrite existing pictures with the same starting name.

In the latest drawing program, doing this is a lot simpler. The images that the user creates are stored in the *Pictures* folder for the user, and they are numbered automatically. The program also makes sure that no pictures are overwritten. When the program starts running, it searches for the next available frame number and uses that.

```
void setupFileName()
{
    // Get the path to the users pictures directory
```

```
    string picturePath = Environment.GetFolderPath(Environment.SpecialFolder.
MyPictures);

    string fileName;
    do
    {
        fileName = picturePath + @"\Drawing" + frameNo.ToString() + ".jpg";
        if ( !File.Exists(fileName) )
            break;
        frameNo++;
    } while (true);

    fileNameTextBox.Text = picturePath + @"\Drawing" + ".jpg";
}
```

The *setupFileName* method starts by finding the path to the pictures directory for the user. This is obtained from the *Environment* settings for the user. It then repeatedly loops around creating filenames and testing whether they exist. When it has finished, it puts the default filename into the *fileNameTextBox* on the display for the user to see and change if so desired.

Tidying Up When the Program Ends

When a program finishes, it should release all the resources that it has been using. Programs that use the Kinect sensor should tell the Kinect for Windows SDK that they are no longer using the device. If the sensor is not properly released, it may not be available for the next program that wants to use it. You should therefore add behaviors to a program that will inform the Kinect SDK when the program finishes. To do this the program must get control when the program stops. It is easy to get a WPF program to generate an event that is produced when the user exits from the program. You just have to connect a method to the *Window_Closing* event.

In Chapter 3, in the section "Getting the Kinect Sensor Working," you saw how to connect a method to the event that is raised when a window is loaded. You can use exactly the same technique to connect a method to the event that is raised as a program shuts down:

```
private void Window_Closing(object sender, System.ComponentModel.CancelEventArgs e)
{
    shutdownSpeechRecognition();
    shutdownKinect();
}
```

When the window is closed, the first thing the *Window_Closing* method does is shut down the speech recognition. Then it shuts down the Kinect sensor. One thing that you must remember is that the closing methods might get called even if the system did not manage to set everything up successfully. For example, an artist might try to use the program without having a Kinect sensor plugged into the computer. This will cause the program to close down when it is unable to connect to the Kinect sensor. To address this situation, the shutdown methods must make sure that items exist before they try to shut them down.

```
private void shutdownSpeechRecognition()
{
    if (kinectSource != null)
        kinectSource.Stop();

    if (recognizer != null)
    {
        recognizer.RecognizeAsyncCancel();
        recognizer.RecognizeAsyncStop();
    }
}
bool stopCalled = false;

void shutdownKinect()
{
    stopCalled = true;
    if ( myKinect != null)
        myKinect.Stop();
}
```

The preceding are the two shutdown methods that shut down the speech recognition and the Kinect sensor. The code in the methods must also make sure that items are not null before using them.

The methods also implement a flag called *stopCalled* that indicates when the Kinect is stopping. This prevents problems in the situation where the Kinect sensor is stopped while the program is in the middle of using a skeleton value. This flag is checked in the event handler for the frame-ready event and stops the program from trying to use the sensor in a situation where it might be about to become unavailable.

```
void myKinect_SkeletonFrameReady(object sender, SkeletonFrameReadyEventArgs e)
{
    if (stopCalled) return;

    // Rest of skeleton processing here
}
```

The preceding test causes the method to ignore the skeleton event if the Kinect is being stopped.

> **Note** This illustrates a problem with multithreaded systems. You need to be mindful of the way that the two threads (in this case the one using the skeleton and the one shutting down the sensor) can interact.

Improving the Drawing Program

The program works well, and it's fun to use. It even works with two artists at the same time. However, you might like to add a number of possible improvements.

■ You could allow the user to change the color of the background rather than always clearing the screen to white each time. You could do this by adding the command word *Background,* which would tell the program that the next color command would set the background color.

■ You could add an *Undo* command so that unwanted drawing actions could be removed. This would be quite easy to do. All the lines that have been drawn in the picture are held in the drawing canvas. It would be quite simple to remove the last line that was drawn.

■ You could add a smaller drawing brush that drew a small circular dot rather than a line. WPF includes an Ellipse shape that could be used for this. You could add the commands *Dot* and *Hand* to select which drawing mode to use.

One improvement that you are going to craft next is to make the program speak responses to the commands it has been given. This is surprisingly easy to do, and really makes the program fun to use.

Adding Speech Output to Programs

You might think that you could use the Microsoft Speech Platform SDK to add voice output to your programs. However, at present the libraries that are installed with the Kinect SDK do not provide voices for spoken output. The good news is that you can use the ones that are supplied with Windows. These are in the library *System.Speech.* This can be added as any other resource, using the Add Resource dialog. However, rather than being assembly files that you have to find on the hard disk of your computer, these are available from the .NET resources on your machine.

Figure 9-3 shows you how to find the speech resources when you add a reference. The classes that perform speech synthesis are held in the *System.Speech.Synthesis* namespace, which you can add to your program along with other classes that you are using.

```
using System.Speech.Synthesis;
```

Setting up and using the speech synthesis is very easy:

```
SpeechSynthesizer speaker;

void setupSpeechOutput()
{
    speaker = new SpeechSynthesizer();

    speaker.Speak("Ready to Go");
}
```

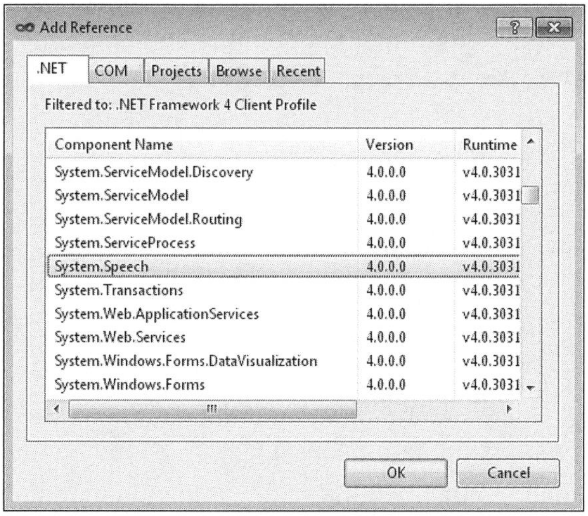

FIGURE 9-3 Finding the System.Speech resources.

The *setupSpeechOutput* method creates a new *SpeechSynthesizer* that it stores in the variable *speaker*. It then offers the message "Ready to Go." You can now add spoken messages to any part of the program. Note that this works for any Windows program that you write. You could update the alarm program you created in Chapter 5 to make it speak an alarm rather than play a sound effect.

Feedback Problems

As you have seen, it is very easy to add speech to any program. However, if you are using both speech recognition and speech synthesis in the same program, you have to be very careful to deal with any feedback that might result. I had this problem with the first version of the drawing program that I created. This version confirmed the color that had been selected by speaking it aloud. So I would say the word *Red* and the computer would respond with the word *Red*. Can you see the problem here?

It turns out that a computer is very good at recognizing computer-generated speech. So when the computer hears itself say the word *Red*, it recognizes the word and says it again to confirm, which it of course recognizes, and so the feedback repeats.

One way to address this is to stop the program from responding to messages for a short interval after it has received a valid command. This turns out to be easy to do:

```
DateTime lastCommand = DateTime.Now;
float commandDelayInSecs = 1;
```

The variable *lastCommand* holds the date and time that the last command was received. It is initially set to the time the program starts running. The variable *commandDelayInSecs* holds the number of seconds the program should wait after receiving a command before responding to them again. I have found that a 1-second delay seems to work well.

```
void handleCommand(string command)
{
    TimeSpan commandInterval = DateTime.Now.Subtract(lastCommand);

    if (commandInterval.TotalSeconds < commandDelayInSecs)
        return;

    commandTextBlock.Text = "Command: " + command;

    speaker.Speak(command);

    switch (command)
    {
            // handle commands here
    }

    lastCommand = DateTime.Now;
}
```

The preceding code shows how this works. The *handleCommand* method is called each time a word is recognized. It subtracts the time of the last command from the current time, and if the number of seconds is less than the delay that has been set (in this case, 1 second), the method returns immediately without handling the command. If a command is successfully dealt with, the method sets the time of *lastCommand* to the current data and time.

> **Sample Code: Body Drawing with Speech Output** The sample project in the "03 Voice Controlled Drawing with Speech" directory in the resources for this chapter (see the "Code Samples" section in the Introduction) holds a program that lets you draw on the screen using your right hand for painting. The program also produces voice responses that echo the commands that you enter.

Summary

In this chapter, you have learned the basis of speech recognition and how to add it to a program.

You have seen that speech recognition is not something that is specific to programs using the Kinect sensor, but it can also be used in any Windows programs that you create.

You have also learned how to create a program that produces spoken output, and you've discovered that computers are very good at recognizing their own speech.

In Chapter 10, you will learn how to use all the signals from the Kinect sensor to generate augmented-reality applications that create an artificial world for the user to work inside.

Augmented Reality with Kinect

After completing this chapter, you will:

- Understand how augmented-reality programs are created

- See how a program can display elements that are overlaid on top of a video image

- Create a game loop that allows game elements to be continuously updated

- Discover how to more accurately overlay the depth and video information from the Kinect sensor

- Create augmented-reality components that are aligned with the skeleton of the Kinect users

- Perform hit detection to allow augmented-reality components to interact

- Cut out the player display so that they can be added into digital scenes

- Use a Kinect sensor manager class that makes working with the sensor easier

An Augmented-Reality Game

AN AUGMENTED-REALITY APPLICATION STARTS with a view of a scene and then adds computer-generated elements that fit in with the scene content. The Kinect is a really good basis for an augmented-reality system. It has a video camera that provides a high-quality view of the scene and a depth sensor that allows a computer to understand the scene content so that it can add computer-drawn components to the scene as required.

You are going to create a game named BugSplat that places players in an augmented-reality environment where they must use their trusty mallet to splat bugs that fall from the sky. The bugs that are to be splatted and the mallet that the player uses will be drawn on top of the video image of the scene produced by the Kinect video camera. The game will use the depth camera and skeleton-tracking features provided by Kinect to show the player in the game and add the mallet image onto the player picture.

Creating Sprites

The first thing the game needs is some bugs that can be splatted. In computer gaming terms, this kind of game object is called a *sprite*. A sprite is an object that is defined by its texture and position. The texture gives the image to be drawn when the sprite is shown on the screen. The position determines where on the screen the sprite is drawn. By changing the position of a sprite over time, a game can give the appearance of movement. There will be two types of sprites in the game you are going to create: the mallet that the player will use to squash the bugs, and the bugs themselves. The mallet will be drawn in the player's "hand" on the screen. The bugs will move down the screen for the player to chase. The game program must detect when the player has moved a mallet over a bug and "splat" the bug.

Creating Sprite Graphics

The first thing you need is some graphics to work with. Professional game developers usually start developing their game long before the graphical artists have finished making the artwork. The programmers will start work with placeholder images and then go back and put in the final artwork later. One important point about computer game design is that great graphics do not make for great gameplay. They are a wonderful way to make a good game even better, but they do not make a great game in and of themselves. The thing to look out for is a game that is fun to play when it has really simple graphics. With this in mind, I present the design you are going to use for the bug in the BugSplat game.

Figure 10-1 shows the design for the bug that you will be using. If you want to create your own bug images, that might be fun. For best results, your bug should be created using a graphics editing program which can work with image formats that support transparency—for example, the Portable Network Graphics (PNG) type shown in Figure 10-1. The Joint Photographic Experts Group (JPEG) format that is popular for photographs does not support transparency, and so you should not use this format to hold the images of sprites that you want to use in augmented reality.

Figure 10-2 shows the importance of transparency when creating artwork for augmented-reality games. The bug image on the left is stored in a PNG file that was created using a graphical editing program that supports transparency. The bug image on the right is stored in a JPEG file that does not support transparency. If you want to make images that contain transparency, you can download the free program Paint.NET from the following address:

http://www.getpaint.net

FIGURE 10-1 A pesky bug that must be splatted.

FIGURE 10-2 Using transparency in artwork.

Adding Images to a Project

Now that you have your sprite graphic, it must be drawn on the screen. The first thing that you need to do is add the sprite to the Visual Studio 2010 solution that contains your game. The simplest way to add an image to a Visual Studio 2010 solution is just to drag the image from the folder where it is stored and drop it into the solution. This causes Visual Studio 2010 to make a copy of the image and add it to the solution. However, I prefer a bit more organization than this. If a program contains many images, it becomes difficult to find the program elements. You can organize your images by creating a folder to hold them.

Figure 10-3 shows how to create a folder in a project. Right-click on the project in Solution Explorer and select Add from the context menu. Then select New Folder from the menu that appears. The folder is initially given the name New Folder, but you can change this.

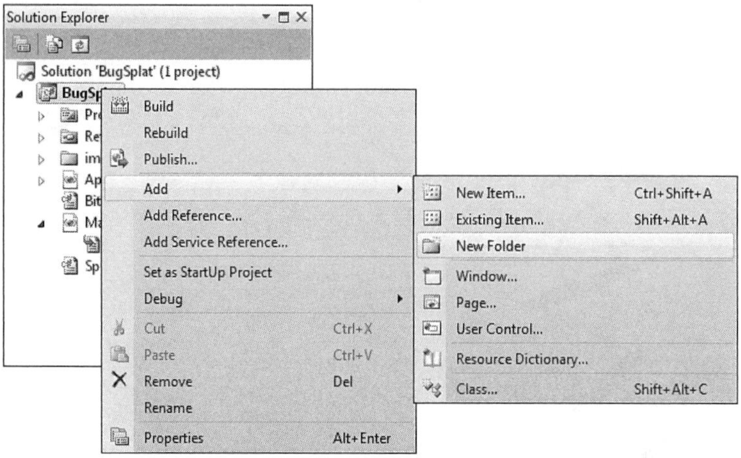

FIGURE 10-3 Creating a new folder.

Figure 10-4 shows the Images folder that I created for an advanced version of the BugSplat game. In this version there are three images: the bug, the splat image that appears when the bug is splatted, and the mallet that is used to splat the bugs. All these images are PNG files that contain transparent regions. I added them to the solution by just dragging them from my Resources folder and dropping them onto the Images folder in the Visual Studio 2010 Solution Explorer. You are going to start with a simple version of the game that just uses the bug image.

FIGURE 10-4 The Images folder in BugSplat.

An item added to a project in this way is added as a Resource to the program assembly file. You can make sure that this is the case by checking the properties.

Figure 10-5 shows the properties for the Bug image in Figure 10-2. If the Build Action for the image is set to *Resource*, a Windows Presentation Foundation (WPF) program can use the resource directly.

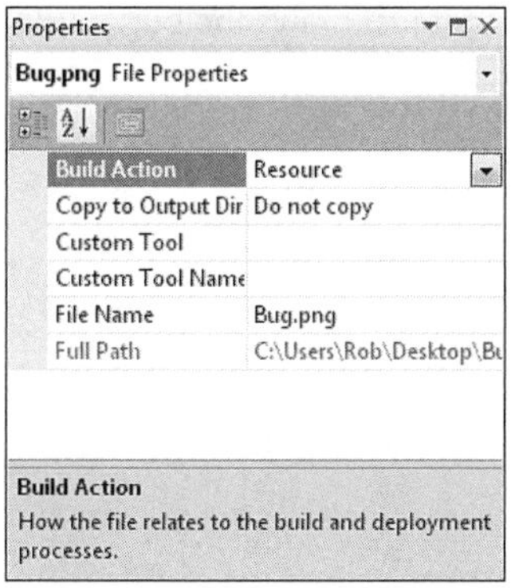

FIGURE 10-5 Properties for the Bug image Resource.

Drawing Sprite Images

Drawing images is very easy. You can create an image element in the eXtensible MArkup Language (XAML) that has the image file as its source:

```
<Image Source="images/Bug.png" Height="273" Width="220" />
```

The preceding line of XAML would draw the image of a rather large bug on the screen. The image would be loaded from the file Bug.png, which is held in the solution as a resource. The resource is actually in the Images folder, and the preceding *Source* property includes this folder in the path to it.

A WPF program uses a file of XAML to specify the items that are to be displayed on the screen. This is the complete description of the window for a program that just displays the bug.

```
<Window x:Class="BugSplat.MainWindow"
        xmlns="http://schemas.microsoft.com/winfx/2006/xaml/presentation"
        xmlns:x="http://schemas.microsoft.com/winfx/2006/xaml"
        Title="Bug Splat" Height="350" Width="525">
    <Image Source="Images/Bug.png" Height="273" Width="220" />
</Window>
```

The XAML for a window contains schema information at the top that tells the WPF system which version of XAML is being used, followed by the display elements that are to be rendered on the screen. In the case of the preceding program, this is just the single Image given right at the bottom of the XAML.

Sample Code: Bug Drawing The sample project in the "01 Bug Drawing" directory in the resources for this chapter (see the "Code Samples" section in the Introduction) holds a program that draws a large bug on the screen.

Figure 10-6 shows the display from the first BugSplat program that just draws the bug.

FIGURE 10-6 Drawing a big bug.

Setting the Sprite Position

At the moment, the bug is positioned in the top-left corner of the screen. In the finished game, the bug will move all over the screen. The WPF elements include a *Canvas* element that can contain other drawing items and position these items on the display. The following XAML creates a canvas and puts the bug image onto it:

```
<Canvas>
        <Image Name="bugImage" Source="Images/Bug.png" Height="50" Width="50" />
</Canvas>
```

I have made the bug image a bit smaller so that it will be a bit harder for the player to hit. I have also given the bug image a name, *bugImage,* so that the image can be referred to within the program.

> **Note** You don't have to give every element in an XAML file a name. You only need to give a name to those items with which you will have your program work.

A program can ask the *Canvas* container to set the position of a display element:

```
Canvas.SetLeft(bugImage, 100);
Canvas.SetTop(bugImage, 150);
```

This would place the bug image 100 pixels across the screen and 150 down it. The *SetTop* and *SetLeft* methods are given a reference to the image to be moved and the position to set.

Figure 10-7 shows how the bug would be drawn now. The bug is much smaller and is now positioned across and down the screen canvas.

FIGURE 10-7 Placing a bug on the screen.

> **Sample Code: Bug Positioning** The sample project in the "02 Bug Positioning" directory in the resources for this chapter (see the "Code Samples" section in the Introduction) holds a program that draws a smaller bug on the screen 100 pixels across the screen and 150 down it. You can change the position of the bug by adjusting the values in the calls to the *SetTop* and *SetLeft* methods.

Making a Sprite Move

At the moment, the bug just sits in one place on the screen. This would make it very easy for the player to "splat" the bug and produce a game that was not much of a challenge to play. It would greatly improve the gameplay if the game made the bug move about the screen. To do this the program needs a way to set the position of an item. A program can make an item appear to move by repeatedly using the *Canvas* to change the position of the item on the screen. There would also need to be a delay between updates; otherwise, only someone with superhuman reflexes would be able to play the game.

The *System.Threading* namespace contains classes that manage the execution of multiple threads on a system. The *Thread* class in this namespace provides a method called *Sleep* that can be called to make a thread pause for a short interval. To make your program easier to write, you can add a *using* statement at the start of the code.

```
using System.Threading;
```

The *Sleep* method is provided with the length of the required pause. The length is given in milliseconds.

```
Thread.Sleep(1000);
```

The preceding statement would cause a thread to pause for 1 second. Game developers talk about the frame rate of a game: the number of times a game updates each second. A good frame rate to aim for is 60. This means that every sixtieth of a second the screen will be updated. This is the same update rate as U.S. standard-definition TV signals. To display 60 frames a second, a program could pause for around 17 milliseconds after each update. This would not provide precise timing, as it doesn't allow any time for the updates themselves, but in practice I've found that it works well for simple games.

```
double bugY = 0;
double bugYSpeed = 1;

while (true)
{
    Canvas.SetTop(bugImage, bugY);
    bugY = bugY + bugYSpeed;
    Thread.Sleep(17);
}
```

The preceding statements would make the bug move down the screen, starting at the top and moving down 1 pixel each time it was updated. The variable *bugY* gives the Y position of the bug, and the variable *bugYSpeed* gives the speed of the bug as it moves down the screen. If you want the bug to move faster, just increase the value of *bugYSpeed*. If you want to make the bug move upward, make the value negative.

> **Note** It is very difficult when you are writing a game to know what speed values make for good gameplay. The only thing you can do is make it very easy to change the speed values in light of the experience you get from actually playing the game.

Now that you know the code that will make images move, the next thing you need to consider is how this code gets to run. When a WPF program starts running, you can arrange for a method to be called when the window is loaded.

```
<Window x:Class="BugSplat.MainWindow"
        xmlns="http://schemas.microsoft.com/winfx/2006/xaml/presentation"
        xmlns:x="http://schemas.microsoft.com/winfx/2006/xaml"
        Title="Bug Splat" Height="350" Width="525" Loaded="Window_Loaded">
<Canvas>
        <Image Name="bugImage" Source="Images/Bug.png" Height="50" Width="50" />
</Canvas>
</Window>
```

The definition of the window includes a reference to a method called *Window_Loaded*. You can see it on the fourth line of the preceding XAML. You might think that you could put the movement behavior in the *Window_Loaded* method:

```
private void Window_Loaded(object sender, RoutedEventArgs e)
{
    double bugY = 0;
    double bugYSpeed = 1;

    while (true)
    {
        Canvas.SetTop(bugImage, bugY);
        bugY = bugY + bugYSpeed;
        Thread.Sleep(17);
    }
}
```

However, this approach will not work. The *Window_Loaded* method is intended to provide a program with the opportunity to set things up, and the method must complete before the program runs. If *Window_Loaded* runs forever, the program will never get going.

You can solve this problem by creating a new *Thread* that will update the display. You saw this behavior in Chapter 5 in the section "A Complete Alarm Program." You were creating a program that needed to signal an alarm by displaying a message when movement was detected by the Kinect video camera. The program you created made use of a thread that fetched an image from the camera and then updated the display.

To get the game movement to work, you are going to create a thread of your own that will work in the background, updating the position of the bug on the screen. When a program creates a thread, it must give the method that will be executed when the thread begins running. You can put all this behavior into a method to create a thread and start it running.

```
private void startGameThread()
{
    Thread game = new Thread(gameLoop);
    game.IsBackground = true;
    game.Start();
}
```

When the *startGameThread* method is called, it creates a new *Thread* called *game*. The method marks the game thread as a background thread by setting the *IsBackground* property to *true*. This means that when the main program is stopped, this thread will be stopped as well. The *startGameThread* method then calls the *Start* method on this thread to start it running.

Last time threads were mentioned, it was in the context of trains running on tracks. The tracks were the sequences of statements in a method. The train was a thread of execution running through a method. The call of *Start* is equivalent to taking a new train and putting it on the track at the beginning of the *gameLoop* method.

```
private void gameLoop()
{
    while (true)
    {
        Dispatcher.Invoke(new Action(() => updateGame()));
        Thread.Sleep(17);
    }
}
```

The *gameLoop* method contains the loop that runs the game, but it does not contain the code that actually interacts with the elements on the display. This is because, as you saw in Chapter 5, only code running as part of the Window Manager thread is allowed to talk to display elements on the screen. The *gameLoop* method instead uses the *Dispatcher* to invoke a new *Action* that will call the *updateGame* method.

```
private void updateGame()
{
    Canvas.SetTop (bugImage, bugY);
    bugY = bugY + bugYSpeed;
}
```

It is this method that actually moves the bug down the screen.

> **Sample Code: Bug Moving** The sample project in the "03 Moving Bug" directory in the resources for this chapter (see the "Code Samples" section in the Introduction) holds a program that draws a small bug that moves down the screen and eventually disappears off the bottom.

Putting the Bug Back on the Top

The preceding program moves the bug down the screen smoothly, but once the bug has reached the bottom of the screen it disappears from view and does not return. The game needs to detect this and put the bug back on the screen at the top.

```
Random rand = new Random(1);

private void updateGame()
{
    Canvas.SetTop(bugImage, bugY);
    bugY = bugY + bugYSpeed;

    if (bugY > gameCanvas.Height)
    {
```

```
        int bugX = rand.Next(0, (int)gameCanvas.Width - (int)bugImage.Width);
        Canvas.SetLeft(bugImage, bugX );
        bugY = -bugImage.Height;
    }
}
```

The preceding version of *updateGame* detects when the bug moves off the bottom of the screen. It tests the Y position of the bug against the height of the game canvas and resets the bug when it moves off the screen. Remember that in WPF, the origin of the graphics is the top-left corner of the screen and increasing the value of Y for an object will move it down the screen.

This code makes the game more interesting by picking a random X position for the bug when it is moved back to the top, so that it appears in a different position each time. It uses the *Random* class to generate the random X position. An instance of the *Random* class provides a method called *Next,* which will produce a number in a given range. For the bug to fit across the screen, the range must be from 0 (the left edge) to the width of the canvas minus the width of the bug itself. Doing this subtraction stops the bug from hanging over the right edge of the screen:

```
int bugX = rand.Next(0, (int)gameCanvas.Width - (int)bugImage.Width);
```

The code also makes sure that replacement bugs don't pop onto the screen when they are replaced:

```
bugY = -bugImage.Height;
```

The Y position of the bug is set to just above the top of the screen so that when a bug is repositioned, it falls down onto the screen from above it.

> **Sample Code: Falling Bugs** The sample project in the "04 Raining Bug" directory in the re-sources for this chapter (see the "Code Samples" section in the Introduction) holds a program that draws a small bug that moves down the screen and reappears at the top.

Creating Augmented Reality

Augmented reality merges computer graphics with images from the real world. The program code to generate the graphics is complete; next you have to add the real-world elements and build the augmented-reality interaction, where player actions affect the computer-generated elements.

Displaying Computer Graphics on Top of the Video Image

Now that you know how to make some bugs fall from the sky, it's time to make them part of the augmented-reality scene. To do this, the program needs to display the video image of the play area with the bugs on top of this scene.

```
<Canvas Name="gameCanvas" Height="480" Width="640">
        <Image Name="kinectVideoImage" Height="480" Width="640"/>
        <Image Name="bugImage" Source="Images/Bug.png" Height="50" Width="50" />
</Canvas>
```

The preceding XAML shows the display area for the game program. The game canvas contains the bug image and also the video display. Note that the first item in the list is the video image. Because items are drawn in the same order that they are defined, the bug will be drawn on top of the background image.

The game can configure the Kinect camera in the same way as you saw in Chapter 4. When a new video frame is received, it will update the content of *kinectVideoImage*.

Sample Code: Falling Bugs on a Video Image The sample project in the "05 Augmented Reality Bugs" directory in the resources for this chapter (see the "Code Samples" section in the Introduction) holds a program that draws a small bug that moves down the screen and reappears at the top. This is drawn on top of the video image from the Kinect camera.

Adding a Mallet for the Player

The player is going to wield a mallet that will be used to splat the bugs. The mallet will be drawn on the screen and will be aligned with the right hand of the player. For this to look correct, the player must be able to "swing" the mallet around the screen. To keep things simple, we are going to draw the mallet as two lines of different thicknesses. The handle of the mallet will be a black line that is 10 pixels wide, and the head of the mallet will be a red line that is 50 pixels wide. The mallet will be drawn in the same direction as the line that joins the wrist joint with the hand.

Figure 10-8 shows how this works. You can see an image of a person with the skeleton superimposed and the mallet drawn in the correct position. As the hand and arm move, the mallet moves with them. It turns out that "waving" the mallet is actually quite fun before the game even starts running!

Matching Together Screen and Depth Coordinates

To make the mallet follow the player, a game must convert the skeleton joint position values into ones that match the coordinates in the image. The skeleton joint positions are given to the program as three values that describe the position of that joint with respect to the depth camera. The three values are x (how far to the left or right), y (how far up or down), and z (how far away). However, a program just needs the X and Y values of the pixel to draw on a screen. You have done this conversion before, when you drew your first skeleton in Chapter 8. Last time you used the method *MapSkeletonPointToColor*, which is part of the Skeleton engine provided with the SDK.

```
ColorImagePoint headPoint = myKinect.MapSkeletonPointToColor(headJoint.Position,
                            ColorImageFormat.RgbResolution640x480Fps30);
```

FIGURE 10-8 Wielding the mallet.

This method takes the position of a skeleton joint and the dimensions of the color image for which the point is being produced. The method returns a point that gives the X and Y positions of that point, relative to an image from the color camera. This means that if the program draws lines at those points, they will line up with the positions in the image. You can see this working to good effect in Figure 10-8, where the skeleton and the image are aligned with each other.

Drawing the Mallet

The game now needs a method to draw the mallet on the screen. You could call the method *drawMallet*.

```
void drawMallet(Joint j1, Joint j2)
{
    // draw the mallet here
}
```

When it is called, the method will be supplied with the two joints that give the direction of the mallet to be drawn.

```
drawMallet(skeleton.Joints[JointType.WristRight], skeleton.Joints[JointType.
HandRight]);
```

This would draw the mallet on the right hand of the skeleton. If you want to make a left-handed version of the game, you could use the joints on the other hand.

Note You could also use exactly the same technique to put a silly hat on the player, or add football boots, or even make the entire player into a mallet.

Because the mallet should align with the hand just like a real mallet would, the program will have to do some work with vectors to make everything look right.

Figure 10-9 shows what the game needs to do. The figure shows the wrist and hand of a skeleton that is holding a mallet. The *drawMallet* method must draw the mallet in the same direction as the vector that joins the hand to the wrist. The first thing the method must do is obtain the vector that describes that direction.

```
ColorImagePoint j1P = myKinect.MapSkeletonPointToColor(j1.Position,
                        ColorImageFormat.RgbResolution640x480Fps30);
ColorImagePoint j2P = myKinect.MapSkeletonPointToColor(j2.Position,
                        ColorImageFormat.RgbResolution640x480Fps30);
```

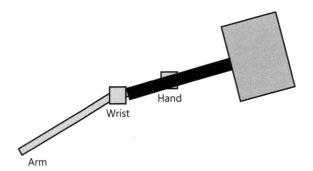

FIGURE 10-9 Drawing the mallet on the skeleton.

The preceding statements use the *MapSkeletonPointToColor* method to obtain the X and Y coordinates of the hand and the wrist on the display. These are delivered in the form of *ColorImagePoint* values that contain X and Y properties, giving the position in the color image of these two points.

Next, the method must work out the distance in the X and Y directions of a vector that joins these two points.

```
int dX = j2P.X - j1P.X;
int dY = j2P.Y - j1P.Y;
```

Figure 10-10 shows what the values *dX* and *dY* represent. They give the amount across and the amount up that you travel when moving from the wrist to the hand. The method can use these to create a Windows vector:

```
System.Windows.Vector malletDirection = new System.Windows.Vector(dX, dY);
```

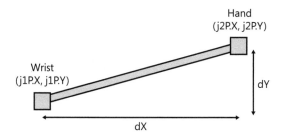

FIGURE 10-10 Getting the vector components for the hand direction.

This vector gives the direction that the hand is pointing. The program can use it to generate the lines for the mallet handle and head.

Now the method has to solve a problem that sometimes occurs during gameplay. If the player points a hand directly at the Kinect camera, the X and Y distances between the wrist and the hand of the player become very small. This is because most of the length of the hand and the arm is now pointing in the direction of Z, away from the sensor. The result is that the wrist and the hand are in the same place on the 2D image, leading to a *malletDirection* vector that does not point anywhere.

```
if (malletDirection.Length < 1) return;
```

This statement checks the *Length* property of the *malletDirection* vector. If the length is less than 1 the method returns and the mallet is not drawn on the hand.

Now the method needs to actually draw the mallet on the hand. To draw the mallet, the method must calculate the start and end positions on the screen of the mallet. The first step in calculating these positions is to normalize the *malletDirection* vector.

```
malletDirection.Normalize();
```

A normalized vector has a length of one. It is important that the mallet is the same length regardless of the size of the hand of the player. If the program normalizes the vector obtained from the skeleton, it can get a mallet of a particular length just by multiplying this vector by the mallet length required. This stops a tall player having a larger mallet than a smaller one.

```
System.Windows.Vector handleVector = malletDirection * malletHandleLength;
```

This statement creates a vector called *handleVector* that is the length of the mallet handle. The program makes the mallet length a variable so that during the game the length could change. At the start of the game, the value of *malletHandleLength* is set to 100 pixels.

```
Line handleLine = new Line();

handleLine.Stroke = malletHandleBrush;
handleLine.StrokeThickness = 10;
```

```
handleLine.X1 = j1P.X;
handleLine.Y1 = j1P.Y;

handleLine.X2 = j1P.X + handleVector.X;
handleLine.Y2 = j1P.Y + handleVector.Y;

malletCanvas.Children.Add(handleLine);
```

The preceding statements create a WPF line for the mallet handler and add the line to the canvas. The start of the handle is the wrist of the player, which is described by the values of *startX* and *startY*. The X and Y lengths of the line are obtained from the handle vector.

```
Line headLine = new Line();

headLine.Stroke = malletHeadBrush;
headLine.StrokeThickness = 50;

System.Windows.Vector headVector = malletDirection * malletHeadLength;

headLine.X1 = handleLine.X2;
headLine.Y1 = handleLine.Y2;

headLine.X2 = handleLine.X2 + headVector.X;
headLine.Y2 = handleLine.Y2 + headVector.Y;
malletCanvas.Children.Add(headLine);
```

These statements put the mallet head on the end of the handle. The head of the mallet is much thicker than the handle, so the *Thickness* property of the line is set to 50. Note that the starting position for drawing the head is the end position for the handle, so that the head of the mallet is on the end of the handle. The length of the head of the mallet is given by the variable *malletHeadLength,* which is initially set to 50 pixels.

> **Sample Code: Bugs and a Mallet** The sample project in the "06 Bugs and Mallet" directory in the resources for this chapter (see the "Code Samples" section in the Introduction) holds a program that draws a small bug that moves down the screen and reappears at the top. It also contains skeleton-tracking and mallet-drawing features.

Splatting Bugs

You now nearly have a complete game. The only thing missing is the "bug splatting" behavior. The game must detect when the player has hit a bug with the mallet and score points.

```
System.Windows.Vector malletPosition;
float malletHitRadius = 40;
bool malletValid = false;
```

The preceding three variables are those that the program will use to track the position of the mallet. The variable *malletPosition* will hold the position of the center of the mallet head. The variable *malletHitRadius* will give the radius of the "hit circle" around the mallet position. If a bug is detected in that position, it will be "splatted." The variable *malletValid* is set to *true* when the mallet position has been successfully tracked by the program. When the program has finished drawing the mallet, it will then calculate the position of the mallet "splat spot."

```
malletPosition = new System.Windows.Vector(j1P.X, j1P.Y);

malletPosition = malletPosition +
                (malletDirection * (malletHandleLength + (malletHeadLength / 2)));

malletValid = true;
```

This code sets the position of the mallet to be the center of the mallet head. The variable *j1P* is the position of the start of the mallet on the screen. To get to the head of the mallet, the program must add the length of the handle and then half the length of the head. The values *j1P.X* and *j1P.Y* give the position of the start joint for the mallet, and the code also uses the *malletDirection* and mallet length values that were calculated when the mallet was drawn.

> **Note** I put this code inside the *drawMallet* method because that is where all the vector calculations are. However, I then changed the name of the method to *updateMallet*. This is called refactoring. During coding, you will frequently change what a method actually does. When you do this, you should change the name of the method to reflect the change. Another programmer looking at my code might not expect a method called *drawMallet* to set the collision detection position as well. If the method is called *updateMallet*, chances are better that they will look there.

When the bug is updated, it must test to see if it has hit the mallet.

```
if (malletValid)
{
    double bugCenterX = bugX + (bugImage.Width / 2);
    double bugCenterY = bugY + (bugImage.Height / 2);

    System.Windows.Vector hitVector =
        new System.Windows.Vector(malletPosition.X - bugCenterX,
                                  malletPosition.Y - bugCenterY);
    if (hitVector.Length < malletHitRadius)
```

```
    {
        score++;
        ScoreTextBlock.Text = score.ToString();
        scorePlayer.Play();
        bugX = rand.Next(0, (int)gameCanvas.Width - (int)bugImage.Width);
        Canvas.SetLeft(bugImage, bugX);
        bugY = -bugImage.Height;
    }
}
```

This code runs each time the bug is updated. It checks to see if the center of the bug is close to the center of the mallet. The vector *hitVector* is set to the vector between the "splat spot" of the mallet and the center of the bug. If the length of this vector is less than the mallet hit radius, the bug has been splatted. The method also plays a sound to indicate that the bug has been hit. This is achieved by using a *SoundPlayer* object called *scorePlayer* that is loaded with a sound sample when the game starts.

> **Note** This collision detection is not perfect. The hit radius defines a circle surrounding the center point of the mallet, but the mallet head is a rectangle. The detection also assumes that the bug is circular. The good news is that the players do not tend to notice these problems when playing the game. When creating gameplay, it is best to start with something simple and easy to implement and then to add complication later if required.

If a bug has been hit, the program increases the score, updates the score display, plays a sound, and then puts the bug back on the top of the screen.

> **Sample Code: Bugs and a Mallet** The sample project in the "07 BugSplat Game" directory in the resources for this chapter (see the "Code Samples" section in the Introduction) holds a program that implements a bug-splatting game. A player can splat bugs as they fall from the sky.

Isolating the Player Image from the Background

Most action movies have a point where the hero or heroine turns to everyone and says something like "Hang on to your seats everyone—it's going to be a bumpy ride." Then everything explodes around them. You have reached that point in this chapter. The next bit is a somewhat tricky to get your head around. But don't worry—it can be done. The important thing to remember is what the program is trying to do and the information that it is using to do it.

In this section you are going to learn how you can use the depth sensor, skeleton tracking, and the video camera to isolate the image of the player from the background and put them right inside the game. Television stations do this all the time. When a presenter delivers the weather forecast, the person is standing in front of a blank wall that is colored a single bright color, usually blue or green. Video processing is used to replace the background color with images from the forecast so that the viewer sees the presenter standing in front of a moving weather map. This technique, sometimes called "green screen" or "chroma-key," involves examining the video signal and replacing the key color with parts of another video image. You could actually do it with the Kinect video camera. You have seen how a program can work with the color information from the camera.

Unfortunately you can't use this technique to isolate the image of a player of the BugSplat game because the player will not be standing in front of a colored wall (unless you are playing the game in a TV studio). However, it is possible to get a chroma-key effect by using information from the skeleton-tracking software.

Using a Display Mask

The program will get the required display by overlaying one picture on top of another. You have already seen this in action where the BugSplat game overlays the bug image on top of the background. You are going to create a mask that lets the background show through only where there is part of a skeleton in the image.

Figure 10-11 shows the video image that will be drawn first. This contains the whole picture of the scene in front of the Kinect sensor. The program will then take the "background" image and draw it on top of the video scene with holes that allow the video image to show through.

FIGURE 10-11 The background showing the video view.

Figure 10-12 shows the finished image. The holes are created by making pixels in the bitmap containing the "BUGSPLAT!!" background transparent. You have already seen the transparency or "alpha" value in pixel data; now it is time to make use of this value. Normally a program will set the alpha value of every pixel to the maximum, *255*, so that it completely obscures any image behind it. If the alpha value for a pixel is set to *0*, this allows the background to show through. In Figure 10-12 some pixels of the BUGSPLAT!! background have had their alpha value set to *0*, so my figure shows through from the video behind it. The next thing the program needs to do is find the pixels in the scene that correspond to the player. This information is available from the skeleton tracking that the Kinect SDK performs.

FIGURE 10-12 The figure on top of the background.

> **Note** The picture shows that the mask is not exactly aligned with the player. This is because of differences in the geometry and position of the depth and video cameras. Pixels in one camera do not exactly match up with those in the other, causing some of the players to be incorrectly masked and the background to show through.

Finding the Player Pixels

You saw in Chapter 6 in the section "Obtaining Depth Information from the Sensor" that the depth values received from the sensor include player information.

Figure 10-13 shows how distance information is provide to a program. You used this format in Chapter 6 when you saw that the depth information (how far an object in the scene is from the distance sensor) is given in 13 bits of data with 3 bits of "player" data at the bottom. In Chapter 6 you were only interested in the depth value, but now the program must use the player information to mask the image.

Bit 15	Bit 14	Bit 13	Bit 12	Bit 11	Bit 10	Bit 9	Bit 8	Bit 7	Bit 6	Bit 5	Bit 4	Bit 3	Bit 2	Bit 1	Bit 0
D	D	D	D	D	D	D	D	D	D	D	D	D	P	P	P
4096	2048	1024	512	256	128	64	32	16	8	4	2	0	4	2	0

16-bit depth value

FIGURE 10-13 The 13 bits of depth information.

A program can obtain the player information by doing a little manipulation of the depth data.

```
int playerNo = depthData[depthPos] & 7;
```

The *playerNo* value is obtained by using the *&* (arithmetic AND) operation to split off the bottom 3 bits of the value in the depth array. This works because the binary representation of seven is *111*.

To obtain the depth value, the original number must be shifted to the right to remove the 3 player data bits:

```
int depthValue = depthData[i] >> 3;
```

The creators of the Kinect for Windows SDK have created constants that represent the number of bits given over to player values in the depth data. Your program should use these constant values instead of the numbers three and seven:

```
int depthValue = depthData[i] >> DepthImageFrame.PlayerIndexBitmask;
int playerNo = depthData[i] & DepthImageFrame.PlayerIndexBitmaskWidth;
```

Using these constant values ensures that if, in a future version of the Kinect for Windows SDK, the number of tracked players was increased from 7 to 15, your program would still work correctly.

The program you are going to write will display a depth view of the scene in front of the camera and color blue all the pixels that are part of players that are being tracked.

```
int depthValue = depthData[i] >> DepthImageFrame.PlayerIndexBitmask;
int playerNo = depthData[i] & DepthImageFrame.PlayerIndexBitmaskWidth;

// Check for the invalid values

if (depthValue == myKinect.DepthStream.UnknownDepth ||
    depthValue == myKinect.DepthStream.TooFarDepth ||
    depthValue == myKinect.DepthStream.TooNearDepth)
{
    // show invalid values as black
    depthColorImage[depthColorImagePos++] = 0; // Blue
    depthColorImage[depthColorImagePos++] = 0; // Green
    depthColorImage[depthColorImagePos++] = 0; // Red
}
else
{
    byte depthByte = (byte)(255 - (depthValue >> 4));
    if (playerNo != 0)
    {
        // show player values as blue
        depthColorImage[depthColorImagePos++] = depthByte; // Blue
        depthColorImage[depthColorImagePos++] = 0; // Green
        depthColorImage[depthColorImagePos++] = 0; // Red
    }
    else
    {
```

```
            depthColorImage[depthColorImagePos++] = depthByte; // Blue
            depthColorImage[depthColorImagePos++] = depthByte; // Green
            depthColorImage[depthColorImagePos++] = depthByte; // Red
        }
    }
```

The preceding code is a simple modification of the depth viewer program that you saw in Chapter 6. The original program produced a grayscale visualization of the depth sensor information. It did this by setting the blue, green, and red components of a pixel to a value that represented the depth reading at that point. This version of the code sets only the amount of blue in the image if the pixel contains a player number that is not zero. This means that any depth values that contain player information will be drawn as blue pixels, as they will have no red or green components.

It is important to remember that the player number values are only added to the depth image if skeleton tracking is turned on. If skeleton tracking is turned off, the player number in every depth value is set to *0*.

Sample Code: Depth and Player Display The sample project in the "08 Depth and Player camera" directory in the resources for this chapter (see the "Code Samples" section in the Introduction) holds a program that displays the view of the depth camera and highlights any elements that contain player information by coloring them blue. If you run the program and then stand in front of the sensor, all the pixels that are parts of your body should be blue.

Using Depth Information to Make a Mask

The program is now able to tell if a reading in the depth frame is part of a player. It can work through the depth frame looking for depth readings that are part of a player and make them transparent so that the player image can show though.

```
for (int depthPos = 0; depthPos < depthFrame.PixelDataLength; depthPos++)
{
    int depthValue = depthData[depthPos] >> DepthImageFrame.PlayerIndexBitmaskWidth;
    int playerNo = depthData[depthPos] & DepthImageFrame.PlayerIndexBitmask;

    // Check for the invalid values

    if (depthValue == myKinect.DepthStream.UnknownDepth ||
        depthValue == myKinect.DepthStream.TooFarDepth ||
        depthValue == myKinect.DepthStream.TooNearDepth)
    {
        // ignore invalid values
        continue;
    }
```

```
        else
        {
            if (playerNo != 0)
            {
                // We have to make a pixel transparent
                // the pixel is at depthPos in the depth frame
            }
        }
    }
}
```

The preceding loop works through the bits in the depth image working out the depth value and the player number. The variable *depthPos* is used to count through the depth readings. If a reading has a non-zero *playerNo,* it means that the depth value is part of a player and the current value of *depthPos* gives the position in the depth frame of that reading.

The program now just has to work out which pixel in the mask this depth position represents and then make that pixel transparent to let the video image show through. Unfortunately, it's not that simple. You have already seen that the depth and video images that the Kinect sensor produces are not precisely aligned.

> **Sample Code: Player and Video Display** The sample project in the "09 Player and Video Camera" directory in the resources for this chapter (see the "Code Samples" section in the Introduction) holds a program that displays the view of the depth camera and highlights any elements that contains player information by coloring them blue. This image is overlaid on the video image. You can use this program to determine just how much of a difference there is between the two images.

The problem occurs because the depth camera and the video camera are not exactly the same devices and don't have the same view of the scene in front of them. A program cannot assume that a pixel at location (100,200) in the video frame corresponds directly to a pixel at (100,200) in the depth frame.

The Kinect SDK provides a method that you used to convert depth positions into display positions. You can use this method to align player depth positions with video coordinates. Then the program can use the video coordinate to work out which part of the image to mask. The method is called *MapDepthToColorImagePoint,* and it takes a particular position from the depth image and maps this into the color image space. The method needs to be supplied with the X and Y positions of the point in the depth image and returns a position in the color image. The program can then use this position to mask the player in the display. The first thing the program needs to do is work out the X and Y positions that correspond to the position in the depth array. It can do this by using the *DIV (/)* and *MOD (%)* operators. The *DIV* operator performs an integer division. The *MOD* operator gives the remainder after the division.

```
int x = depthPos % width;
int y = depthPos / width;
```

Figure 10-14 shows how these two statements work. It shows a screen with a width of 640 pixels that is mapped onto the one-dimensional depth array.

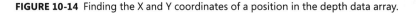

FIGURE 10-14 Finding the X and Y coordinates of a position in the depth data array.

If the value of *drawPos* is *1,480* and the depth data has a width of *640*, the distance of the pixel across the last line of the screen is 200. The first 1,280 locations in the depth array are the values for the first two rows. If we divide 1,480 by 640, we get *2* (which is the Y value) and a remainder of *200* (which is the X value). Both the X and the Y values are *0* based; in other words, the position at the start of each range has the value *0*.

The program can use these X and Y values in the call of *MapDepthToColorImagePoint* to obtain the matching position in the color image:

```
ColorImagePoint playerPoint = myKinect.MapDepthToColorImagePoint(
    DepthImageFormat.Resolution320x240Fps30,
    x, y,
    depthValues[depthPos],
    ColorImageFormat.RgbResolution640x480Fps30);
```

The mask image that I have created (the one with the word *BugSplat* on it) is made up of 240 rows of 320 pixels. This is the same resolution as the depth frame. The idea is that pixels in the mask image that are part of the player will be made transparent. However, the preceding method produces coordinates for a video image that is made up of 480 rows of 640 pixels. The next thing the program must do is convert the calculated coordinates to match the mask image coordinates.

```
playerPoint.X = playerPoint.X / 2;
playerPoint.Y = playerPoint.Y / 2;

if (playerPoint.X < 0 || playerPoint.X >= 320 || playerPoint.Y < 0 ||
playerPoint.Y >= 240)
    continue;
```

The first two of the preceding statements reduce the coordinates to the correct range. The third statement performs a range check on the values to ensure that any out-of-range readings are rejected.

At this point, the program has found a part of the depth data that is part of a player. It has worked out the X and Y positions in the depth frame of this part of the data. It has then converted the X and Y positions into positions in the video frame. The final thing it has to do is find the pixel in the background image and make it transparent.

```
gameImagePos = (playerPoint.X + (playerPoint.Y * width)) * 4;
```

The preceding statement works out the position in the image array of the required pixel. It reverses the calculation that was used to work out the X and Y positions from the *depthPos* value and then multiplies the result by four, as there are 4 bytes in the mask for each pixel. Now that the program has found the position in the mask image that is to be made transparent, it can set the color information for that pixel.

```
// Blue
maskBytes[gameImagePos] = 0;
gameImagePos++;
// Green
maskBytes[gameImagePos] = 0;
gameImagePos++;
// Red
maskBytes[gameImagePos] = 0;
gameImagePos++;
// transparency
maskBytes[gameImagePos] = 0;
gameImagePos++;
```

These statements set the color and the alpha values in the display mask to zero. You could give your players a ghostly appearance over the background by changing these values to make them a different color or slightly transparent. This is actually quite a good idea, as it makes it possible to still see things on the game image and makes it less obvious if the edges of the players do not exactly line up.

The *maskBytes* array is the display mask being used for this frame. It contains a copy of the game image. The copy is made at the start of each frame.

```
if (maskBytes == null)
{
    maskBytes = new byte[gameImageBytes.Length];
}

Buffer.BlockCopy(gameImageBytes, 0, maskBytes, 0, gameImageBytes.Length);
```

The preceding code creates a new byte array if one does not exist and then uses the *BlockCopy* method to copy the bytes from the game image into it. You used *BlockCopy* in Chapter 7, when it was used to copy camera video images.

Drawing the Mask Image

The mask image is drawn on top of the background image on the screen. You have seen how WPF allows images to be overlaid on the same part of the screen.

```
<Canvas Name="gameCanvas" Height="480" Width="640">
    <Image Name="kinectVideoImage" Height="480" Width="640"/>
    <Image Name="gameImage" Height="480" Width="640" />
    <Canvas Name="malletCanvas" Height="480" Width="640"/>
    <Image Name="bugImage" Source="Images/Bug.png" Height="50" Width="50" />
</Canvas>
```

This is the XAML that describes the screen being drawn. The first item is the video image from the frame. Next is the *gameImage,* which contains the transparent pixels that display the player. On top of these are drawn the mallet and the bug.

The drawing is performed on a *WriteableBitmap.* You saw these in Chapter 2 when creating programs that displayed camera images.

```
if (depthImage == null)
{
    depthImage = new WriteableBitmap(
        depthWidth,
        depthHeight,
        96,   // DpiX
        96,   // DpiY
        PixelFormats.Pbgra32,
        null);
    gameImage.Source = depthImage;
}

depthImage.WritePixels(
    new Int32Rect(0, 0, depthWidth, depthHeight),
    maskBytes,
    depthWidth * 4,
    0);
```

This is used in exactly the same way as previous writeable bitmaps, but it is created with the image format *PixelFormats.Pbgra32.* This causes the image to be drawn using the alpha information, letting the background show through the transparent parts.

Setting up the Game Image

The game screen was created using a drawing program, and it was saved as a PNG file with a size of 320 x 240 pixels. You can create any background image you wish to use in the same way. You can add an image resource to a Visual Studio 2010 project in exactly the same way as you add a sound. Follow the first three steps of the procedure in "Adding Sound Playback to a Project" in Chapter 5. To use the game screen image, the program needs access to the actual bitmap data so that it can set the alpha value of the pixels that have to let the background video image show through.

```
BitmapSource gameImageBitmap;
Byte[] gameImageBytes;

void setupGameImage()
{
    gameImageBitmap = new BitmapImage(new Uri("BugsplatBackground.png", UriKind.
RelativeOrAbsolute));

    gameImageBytes = new byte[gameImageBitmap.PixelWidth * gameImageBitmap.
PixelHeight * 4];

    gameImageBitmap.CopyPixels(gameImageBytes, 1280, 0);
}
```

This method creates a bitmap from the image that was added to the project. It then uses the *CopyPixels* method to get the pixels from this bitmap and into an array of bytes. The value of *1,280* in the call to *CopyPixels* is the "stride" of the source bitmap. For a PNG image that is 320 pixels across, this value is *1,280* (4 bytes per pixel and 320 pixels per line).

> **Note** If you use a game image that is not exactly 320 x 240 pixels in size, the display will not work correctly and the program may crash. The size of the game image must exactly match the resolution of the depth sensor.

Figure 10-15 shows the final display of the program. The Kinect is doing a pretty good job of isolating me from the background.

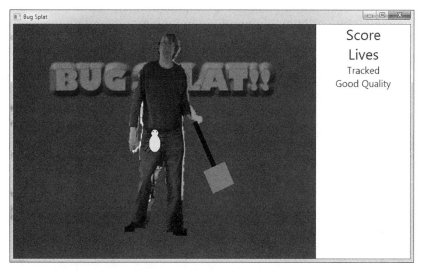

FIGURE 10-15 Final BugSplat game display.

Putting the Whole Game Together

You now have all the elements that you need to create a complete BugSplat game.

1. You have a method that will take the color video image from the Kinect camera and display it on the screen.

2. You have a method that will use the skeleton information from the Kinect to position and draw the mallet.

3. You have a method that will draw the bug moving down the screen and detect when the bug and the mallet collide.

4. You have a method that will use the depth-camera information to create a mask that isolates the player from the video image and draws them in front of a background.

Now you have to put all these elements together to make a working game. This is made slightly more complicated by the way that each element is running on a separate thread and that the threads that are running are not able to access the WPF display elements directly.

Fortunately, you can use the same pattern for each of the elements. A pattern is an arrangement of data and program code that can be reused in one or more systems. In the case of the preceding elements, the pattern contains two components:

1. A behavior that occurs when that item needs to be updated. This need for an update is either the result of time having passed (for the bug movement) or new data arriving from the Kinect sensor. The pattern uses a method called *processXX*, where *XX* is the data to be processed. There are *processDepthFrame*, *processColorFrame*, and *processSkeletonFrame* methods.

2. A behavior that occurs when the item needs to be drawn. This is triggered by a completion of an update. The pattern uses a method called *drawXX*, where *XX* is the data to be drawn. There are *drawDepthFrame*, *drawColorFrame*, and *drawSkeleton* methods.

If you look at the arrangement of the program in the following sample project, you will see how each behavior is isolated into one region of the code but that they all have the same pattern, as previously explained.

> **Sample Code: BugSplat with Player Masking** The sample project in the "10 BugSplat Game with Masking" directory in the resources for this chapter (see the "Code Samples" section in the Introduction) holds a program that implements player masking to create a bug-splatting game.

The Kinect Manager Class

If you look at the source code in the BugSplat game, you will also notice that it makes use of a class called *KinectManager* to manage the Kinect connection. I wrote this class to make it slightly easier to use the Kinect sensor. The class creates a connection to a Kinect sensor and then polls the sensor for new data. You can use it in your own Kinect programs to manage the connection to a sensor.

Creating a *KinectManager* Instance

When your program starts, it can create an instance of the *KinectManager* class to look after a Kinect sensor connection.

```
KinectManager myKinectMgr;
KinectSensor myKinect;

void setupKinect()
{
    try
    {
        myKinectMgr = new KinectManager(
            0, // Sensor number 0
            ColorImageFormat.RgbResolution640x480Fps30, // Color image needed
            DepthImageFormat.Resolution320x240Fps30,    // Depth image needed
            true);                                      // Skeleton image needed

        myKinect = myKinectMgr.Kinect;

        myKinectMgr.DoProcessVideoFrame +=
            new KinectManager.ProcessVideoFrame(processColorFrame);
        myKinectMgr.DoProcessDepthFrame +=
            new KinectManager.ProcessDepthFrame(processDepthFrame);
        myKinectMgr.DoProcessSkeletons +=
            new KinectManager.ProcessSkeletons(processSkeletonFrame);

        myKinectMgr.DoStatusChanged +=
            new KinectManager.StatusChanged(updateStatus);

        myKinectMgr.Start();
    }
    catch
    {
        MessageBox.Show("Kinect initialise failed", "Bugsplat Game");
        Application.Current.Shutdown();
    }
}
```

The preceding code shows how the *KinectManager* is used. It creates a *KinectSensor* variable called *myKinect* and a *KinectManager* variable called *myKinectMgr*. When the manager is created, it is given the data formats to use for each sensor. A program can connect handlers to events that are fired when there is new data for that particular sensor. In the preceding code, the methods *processDepthFrame*, *processColorFrame*, and *processSkeletonFrame* have been connected to these events.

Using Kinect Data

The *KinectManager* generates events in a very similar manner to the *KinectSensor* class, except that it provides the frames directly to the methods, rather than the methods having to load the data frames from the event arguments. The events are only generated if the frames are available.

```
myKinectMgr.DoProcessVideoFrame +=
            new KinectManager.ProcessVideoFrame(processColorFrame);
```

The preceding is the statement that connects the *processColorFrame* method with the event that is generated when a new frame of color video is available.

```
void processColorFrame(ColorImageFrame colorFrame)
{
    frameWidth = colorFrame.Width;
    frameHeight = colorFrame.Height;
    if (colorData == null)
        colorData = new byte[colorFrame.PixelDataLength];

    colorFrame.CopyPixelDataTo(colorData);
    Dispatcher.Invoke(new Action(() => drawColorFrame()));
}
```

The preceding specifies the method in the game that displays the player image. It is connected to the *DoProcessVideoFrame* event that is generated by the *KinectManager* each time it has fetched a new image frame from the sensor. You can see that it gets the image data from the *ColorImageFrame* and then invokes the *drawColorFrame* method to draw the image on the display. There are similar handlers for the depth and skeleton-event handlers.

Displaying the Kinect Status

A program can also connect an event handler that is fired by the *KinectManager* when the Kinect sensor status changes.

```
myKinectMgr.DoStatusChanged +=
    new KinectManager.StatusChanged(updateStatus);
```

The preceding statement is part of the *setupKinect* method you have already seen. It links the method *updateStatus* to the event that is generated by the *KinectManager* class when the status of the Kinect changes. The program can use this to update a status message on the game screen.

```
string newStatus;

void updateStatus(string status)
{
    newStatus = status;
    Dispatcher.Invoke(new Action(() => updateMessage()));
}

void updateMessage()
{
    KinectStatusTextBlock.Text = newStatus;
}
```

The preceding status display follows the same pattern as all the other elements of the program. When it is called by the *KinectManager,* it makes a copy of the new status information and then uses the *Dispatcher* to update the display on the screen.

Polling the Sensor

The *KinectManager* class does not use the events that are produced by the Kinect for Windows SDK. Instead it waits for each new frame in turn and makes sure it has been processed by loading the next one. This works better on lower-performance computers that use the Kinect sensor, as there can be a problem if a computer is not able to process an incoming frame before the next one arrives. A machine with a clock speed of 1.3 GHz (which is around half the recommended speed for the Kinect SDK) will work successfully with the sensor if the *KinectManager* is used.

Starting and Stopping the *KinectManager* Sensor

The BugSplat game starts the sensor running when the main window of the game is loaded and stops the sensor when the window is closed.

```
private void Window_Loaded(object sender, RoutedEventArgs e)
{
    // Set up rest of game here
    setupKinect();
}

private void Window_Closing(object sender, System.ComponentModel.CancelEventArgs e)
{
    // Shut down rest of game here
    if (myKinectMgr != null)
        myKinectMgr.Stop();
}
```

The *KinectManager* class provides a *Stop* method that will cleanly turn the sensor off and stop it running.

Using the *KinectManager* Class in Your Programs

To use the class, you just have to add the *KinectMgr.cs* source file into your project and then add the following using statement at the top of your program:

```
using KinectUtils;
```

You can then create your own Kinect event handler methods and use your own version of the preceding *SetupKinect* method to start them running.

Improving the Game

This version of the game is very simple. You could do lots of things to make it even better:

- You could make the player lose a life after letting a bug reach the bottom of the screen. After three lives, the game could end.

- You could make the bugs speed up after one has been splatted.

- You could make the mallet get smaller after a bug has been splatted.

- You could make the bugs move across as well as down the screen, to make them harder to hit.

- You could make the bugs "stick" to the player and slowly cover up the player.

- You could create "transparent" bugs that are much harder to see. These would have only eyes and legs. After a few ordinary bugs had been splatted, the game could switch to the transparent ones.

- You could make the game store pictures of the gameplay as it is played.

- You could add multiplayer support and give each player a separate score.

- You can use video masking to put players on top of other images.

Summary

In this chapter, you have learned a lot about augmented reality and how to add computer-drawn elements to live video from the Kinect sensor.

You have created a game loop that allows a program to produce graphical sprites that move over the screen.

You have seen that the Kinect skeleton tracking can be mapped into a video frame and how computer-drawn elements can be aligned with the human figure.

You have also discovered how a program can detect collisions between game elements and use these as the basis of game behaviors.

You have learned a lot about images and masking and how to use transparency to create masks that can be overlaid on images.

Finally, you have seen how to create software that uses the Kinect sensor and been given a manager class that will look after the sensor for you.

In Chapter 11, you will build on this to allow augmented-reality programs to make music and control external devices.

PART IV

Kinect in the Real World

You have seen how the Kinect can be used to control programs on a computer. Now it is time to learn about the sensor's ability to drive other systems, including making music and controlling robots. In this section you will discover the fundamentals of music generation and the control of other music and sampler devices, along with how to control any remote device connected to your computer through a serial port.

Chapter 11

Real-World Control with Kinect

After completing this chapter, you will:

- Understand how to add augmented reality to a real-world control

- Create a program that has a Kinect interface and a configuration console

- Use Kinect to produce outputs for a MIDI music device

- Use Kinect to produce control outputs using the serial port of a computer

Controlling MIDI Devices with Kinect

THE PROGRAMS THAT YOU HAVE created up to now have displayed messages on the screen and perhaps stored images in a file. However, it is also possible to use programs to interact with the outside world. The first program you are going to write will send MIDI commands that can be used to control a range of external digital music devices.

The MIDI Protocol

MIDI stands for Musical Instrument Digital Interface. It is a standard that was created in the 1980s to allow personal computers to interact with computer-controlled sound devices. Most electronic musical instruments, sound samplers, and even DJ equipment for sale today are fitted with a MIDI connection, which is characterized by large, round MIDI-IN and MIDI-OUT sockets (Figure 11-1).

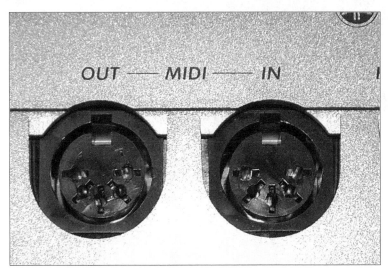

FIGURE 11-1 MIDI connectors.

MIDI connections can also be found on sound samplers and even stage lighting controllers. In a Windows PC the internal sound hardware of the computer can be controlled using a built-in MIDI connection. If you want to control external MIDI devices with your PC, you can purchase a USB-to-MIDI converter cable for a few dollars. These devices plug into a USB port on your computer and provide a MIDI in connection and a MIDI out connection.

MIDI was developed to allow keyboards to be connected to sound synthesizers. A musician playing a keyboard will want to send note information (a key has been pressed or released), requests to change to a different voice (select the trumpet sound), and "after touch" commands (make a note wobble in pitch to get a vibrato effect). The musician might also want to select various effects as they are playing (adjust the amount of echo). MIDI also provides system messages that can be used by particular hardware manufacturers. The MIDI protocol sets out the format of the messages that request these actions and also defines the electrical standards of the cables that link devices together. If your program can send MIDI messages, it can control any MIDI device. You can find out more about the MIDI protocol at the following address:

   http://www.midi.org

Although the MIDI protocol sets out the fundamentals of the message, note, and command types that make up MIDI, the actual function of a particular message on different devices might not always be the same. For example, the command to select an electric piano sound on one device might select a drum sound on another. MIDI musical instruments are supplied with documentation that gives the mapping of the various commands to different device functions. This is actually good news: it means that after a bit of research, you can write a program that will allow a Kinect user to trigger any action on any MIDI device.

Creating a Class to Manage a MIDI Connection

You are going to use a class called *MIDIControl* to represent a connection to the MIDI device the program is using. If you think about it, this is exactly like the job the Kinect for Windows SDK programmers did when they created the *Runtime* class that represents a connection to a Kinect sensor.

Figure 11-2 shows how this works. A program can create objects to represent connections to physical devices. The program in Figure 11-2 will create a *MIDIControl* instance that will communicate with the MIDI sound hardware and a *KinectSensor* instance that will use the Kinect SDK.

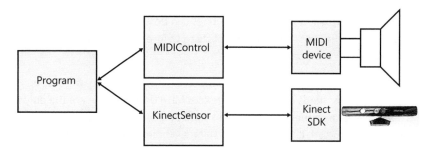

FIGURE 11-2 Using objects to represent connections to devices.

There is no reason why a single program could not connect to multiple MIDI devices. If you have a drum machine and a sound sampler, you could write a program that creates two *MIDIControl* values: one for each physical device.

Using MIDI in Windows PC Programs

The first problem that you need to solve is connecting the *MIDIControl* class to the MIDI device. The Windows operating system contains a media manager component that can set up a MIDI connection and send messages to it. The component is supplied in the form of a Dynamic Link Library (DLL) file that contains methods that you can call from your programs. These methods can be used to set up a connection to a MIDI device and send and receive MIDI messages. However, the files containing these methods are not built as .NET components, so they cannot be used directly from a C# program. Fortunately .NET is supplied with a set of services that allow a C# program to interoperate with these methods. The services are in the *InteropServices* namespace, which must be added to your program:

```
using System.Runtime.InteropServices;
```

Once these services are available your program can use them to create connections to particular methods in the library. The connections work by mapping a call to a C# method onto a method in the MIDI library. When your program uses the method, the interop services create a call to the required library function and then return the result that the function produced.

```
class MIDIControl
{
    [DllImport("winmm.dll")]
    static extern uint midiOutOpen(ref IntPtr lphMidiOut, uint uDeviceID,
IntPtr dwCallback,
                                    IntPtr dwInstance, uint dwFlags);

    [DllImport("winmm.dll")]
    static extern uint midiOutShortMsg(IntPtr hMidiOut, uint dwMsg);
}
```

In the preceding code, you can see how two MIDI routines can be added to the *MIDIControl* class. This might look a bit scary if you haven't seen this kind of thing before. The MIDI methods use the type *IntPtr* (pointer to integer) for their parameters.

The first method, *midiOutOpen,* is called to open a connection to a MIDI device for output. The second method, *midiOutShortMsg,* sends a short message to a MIDI device. These are the only two methods that you need to create a connection and send sound playback requests. When an instance of the *MIDIControl* class is constructed, it will use the *midiOutOpen* method to create a connection to a MIDI output device on the computer.

Constructing a MIDI Connection Class

A programmer can add a constructor method to a class. This method runs when a new instance of the class is created. The job of a constructor is to set up the contents of the class and make it ready for use. Many of the classes that you have used in your programs have constructor methods. The *MIDIControl* class will have a constructor method that sets up a connection to a MIDI device. The constructor for the *MIDIControl* class will be told which MIDI device to use by means of a parameter that gives the required MIDI device number. If this is zero, it means "Use the MIDI sound hardware built into the computer." If it is set to 1, it means "Use a MIDI adapter plugged into the USB port."

```
class MIDIControl
{

    // import the two MIDI methods

    // reference to the active MIDI device, initially set to zero
    private IntPtr midiDevice = IntPtr.Zero;

    /// <summary>
    /// Create a new instance to manage the MIDI connection
    /// </summary>
    /// <param name="deviceNo">0 means local midi and 1 means external interface
</param>
```

```
    public MIDIControl(uint deviceNo)
    {
        uint result =
            midiOutOpen(ref midiDevice, deviceNo, IntPtr.Zero, IntPtr.Zero, 0);
        if (result != 0) throw new Exception("MIDI error " + result.ToString());
    }
}
```

In the preceding code, you can see the constructor for the *MIDIControl* class. The variable *midiDevice* holds a reference to the MIDI device that this *MIDIControl* instance will represent. The *midiDevice* variable is of type *IntPtr*. This is a class that is used to manage a pointer to a location in memory. The *midiOutOpen* method uses this location to store a handle to the MIDI device that has been opened. If you are finding this a bit confusing, think about what happens when you ask a delivery service to deliver a package to your house when you are out. You will send an email that says, "Leave the package next door at number two, please," and the service will leave it with your neighbor. Then, when you get home, you will go next door to pick up the package.

The *midiOutOpen* method works in the same way. The *midiDevice* variable is declared as a reference (*ref*). It is like your email to the delivery man: it tells the *midiOutOpen* method where to leave the result that the method generates. When the *midiOutOpen* method has finished, the program knows that the handle to the MIDI device is on the end of the *midiDevice* pointer. In programming terms, a handle is just a value that can be used to uniquely locate something. The variable *myKinect* in the Kinect programs that you have written up to now is the handle to the active Kinect device.

The constructor method is given a *deviceNo* parameter that identifies the physical MIDI hardware to be used to produce the sound.

The preceding code checks the result returned by call to *midiOutOpen*. The convention is that if the value of this result is non-zero, something has gone wrong with the call and the result contains an error code. If the constructor receives a non-zero result, an exception is thrown that delivers the error number as part of the message. This stops a program from using a MIDI connection that has not been set up correctly.

Creating a *MIDIControl* Instance

Programs that want to use a MIDI interface create an instance of the *MIDIControl* class, specifying which device to use.

```
MIDIControl myMidi;

myMidi = new MIDIControl(0);
```

This would create an instance of the *MIDIControl* class called *myMidi,* which is connected to the internal sound hardware on your Windows PC. Now you need to find out how to use this MIDI class to send messages to external MIDI devices. You will do this by adding a method to the *MIDIControl* class.

Creating MIDI Messages

The simplest MIDI message is made up of three integer values. The first value identifies the command, and then there are two additional data items for that particular command. The *MIDIControl* class will contain a method that will accept three values, construct a MIDI command, and then send it to the MIDI device. The method will be called *SendMIDIMessage* and will be used as follows:

```
myMidi.SendMIDIMessage ( 0x90,  // midi command byte - note down on channel 0
                         60,    // note value - 60 represents middle C on the keyboard
                         100);  // note velocity - how hard the note was hit (0 to 127)
```

This shows how a program will use the method to send three command values to a MIDI device. The three preceding values make a command that would cause a MIDI device to play a note. Different command numbers will make the MIDI device do different things, and changing the other parameters will cause other notes to be played or will change the volume of the note that is played.

The preceding call would send the three bytes, *0x90, 60,* and *100,* to the MIDI port. I've expressed the first byte of this command sequence as a Hex value because it is easier for me to work with. The compiler identifies hexadecimal (base 16) values by the sequence *0x* given at the beginning of the number.

Computers do not "work" in numbers that are decimal, hexadecimal, or even binary. A computer just works on patterns of bits that we happen to find it useful to think of as numbers. The value *0x90* in the preceding call could have been written as the decimal number 144 as far as the computer is concerned, but using hexadecimal makes it easier for me to assemble the MIDI command byte elements.

The MIDI Command Byte

A MIDI command byte is made up of separate elements that are all packed together in an 8-bit value.

Figure 11-3 shows how the command byte is constructed. The left-hand four bits give the command code. The right-hand four bits give the channel that will receive this command. The *Note Down* command is the hex digit 9. The channel number is the value *0.* A MIDI system can use 16 different channels, each of which could be a different instrument. Using Hex to express this value makes it very easy to select different channels or command numbers. For example, the command code with the value *8* is *Note Up,* which is used to indicate when a key has been released. So, to tell a MIDI device on channel 3 that a note has been released, the command would be *0x83.*

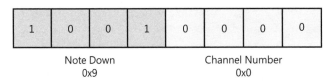

FIGURE 11-3 The MIDI *Note On* command byte.

The Note Value

The note value is in the range 0 to 127. The value *60* represents middle C, which is around the middle of the piano keyboard. The value *61* would play the note C# (which has a nice programming feel to it). Each successive note has a pitch that is one semitone higher, up to the note represented by the value *127*, which is a very high note that I can only just hear. You are going to make a "human piano" on which the player can play different notes by touching different areas of the screen. Each part of the screen will send a different note value to the piano.

The Velocity Value

Some keyboards are touch-sensitive in that they can measure the speed of the keys when they are pressed. The velocity value in the "note pressed" MIDI message tells the sound synthesizer how hard the note was struck, in the range 0 to 127. The harder the note was pressed, the louder it will play. A note produced with a velocity value of *100* was the result of quite a solid press.

Sending MIDI Messages

The *SendMIDIMessage* method accepts the three values and then builds a command for the *midiOutShortMsg* method that is the other external method imported into the class.

```
public void SendMIDIMessage (int command, int d1, int d2)
{
    byte[] data = new byte[4];

    // data [0] = command
    // data [1] = first byte of command data
    // data [2] = second byte of command data
    // data [3] = third byte of command data (not used)

    // assemble the message into the array
    data[0] = (byte)command;
    data[1] = (byte)d1;
    data[2] = (byte)d2;

    // send the message
    midiOutShortMsg(midiDevice, BitConverter.ToUInt32(data, 0));
}
```

The *midiOutShortMsg* sends a block of bytes out down the MIDI connection. The method is given a block of data that describes the MIDI message to be sent.

The message is made up of three values: the command value and then two extra bytes that give information about that particular command.

```
SendMIDIMessage ( 0x90,    // midi command - note down on channel 0
                  60,      // note value - 60 represents middle C on the keyboard
                  100);    // note velocity - how hard the note was hit (0 to 127)
```

Playing MIDI Notes

Remember that MIDI was invented to connect keyboards to sound generators. When a MIDI sound-generating device receives the preceding message, it will start to play the note it has been asked to play on the channel it has been asked to use. What happens next depends on the instrument being used on that channel. Some instruments—for example, a piano—will play the sound of the piano hammer hitting the string, making the sound that will then decay just like a real piano would. However, if the instrument being used is an organ, the note will play continuously, just like it would if you held down a key on an organ keyboard. It is important that a keyboard does not leave a note "hanging." Even if the sound of that note finished (for example, the piano has finished sounding the note), it is still important that the note be switched off properly.

Releasing MIDI Notes

The MIDI protocol contains a "note off" message to tell the instrument that the note has been released. This is command number 0x8, and the command is followed by the number of the note to release and the velocity of the release. The release velocity determines whether the key is released gradually or suddenly.

```
myMidi.SendMIDIMessage (
                  0x80, // midi command - note up on channel 0
                  60, // note value - 60 represents middle C on the keyboard
                  100); // note velocity - how "hard" the note was released (0 to 127)
```

The preceding call of *SendMIDIMessage* would turn off the note that was started earlier. Remember that command 8 means "note up."

You now know enough to get some MIDI sounds out of your PC.

Creating the MIDI Connection

The first thing that you need to do when the program starts is open up a connection to a MIDI device. This is just the same as the procedure that is required to set up a connection to a Kinect sensor, except that this time you have created both ends of the conversation: both the target device and the code that uses it.

```
MIDIControl myMidi;

private void setupMidi()
{
    try {
        myMidi = new MIDIControl(0);
```

```
    }
    catch {
        MessageBox.Show("Midi setup failed", "Midi Control");
        Application.Current.Shutdown();
    }
}
```

The variable *myMidi* holds the *MIDIControl* that is being used by the program. The method *SetupMIDI* creates a new instance of this class and selects the default MIDI device, usually the sound hardware built into the PC (that is what the parameter value *0* means in the *MIDIControl* constructor). If the constructor throws an exception, a message is displayed and the program stops.

The *Window_Loaded* method is called when the program starts running. This calls *setupMidi* to set up the MIDI connection.

```
private void Window_Loaded(object sender, RoutedEventArgs e)
{
    setupMidi();
}
```

Now that the program has a working MIDI connection, it can use it to play notes.

Sending Note Messages

The simplest program would play a note when the mouse button is pressed and stop the note playing when the mouse is released.

```
private void note_MouseDown(object sender, MouseButtonEventArgs e)
{
    myMidi.SendMIDIMessage(
                    0x90,  // midi command - note down on channel 0
                    60,    // note value - 60 represents middle C on the keyboard
                    100);  // note velocity - how hard the note was hit (0 to 127)
}
```

```
private void note_MouseUp(object sender, MouseButtonEventArgs e)
{
    myMidi.SendMIDIMessage(
                    0x80,  // midi command - note up on channel 0
                    60,    // note value - 60 represents middle C on the keyboard
                    100);  // note velocity - how "hard" the note was released (0 to 127)
}
```

The preceding two methods are connected to *MouseUp* and *MouseDown* events that are produced by a Windows Presentation Foundation (WPF) *TextBlock* on the screen.

```
<TextBlock Text="Play" FontSize="50" TextAlignment="Center" Width="250" Height="100"
           MouseDown="note_MouseDown" MouseUp="note_MouseUp" Background="Green" />
```

This *TextBlock* contains *MouseDown* and *MouseUp* events bound to the preceding handler methods. A *MouseDown* event is created on a display item when the user clicks the left mouse button when the cursor is resting on that display item on the screen. The *MouseUp* method is created when the mouse is released. The idea is that clicking on the note will start the note playing and releasing the note will cause the note to stop.

Figure 11-4 shows the display produced by the program.

FIGURE 11-4 A single-note piano.

> **Sample Code: Single-Note Piano** The sample project in the "01 Single Note Piano" directory in the resources for this chapter (see the "Code Samples" section in the Introduction) holds a program that displays a single note, as shown in Figure 11-4. You can click on the note to play a piano sound via MIDI. Note that if you release the mouse button as the note is playing, the sound is cut short by the note-released method. You can change the note value to hear different pitch notes. (Remember to change the note value in the turnoff message as well, so that all the played notes are also switched off.)

Making a Multi-Note Piano

A single-note piano is not very impressive. What you want is a screen with multiple panels, each of which can be used to trigger a different note. This could be achieved by writing a lot more XAML to design a WPF screen with lots of panels on it. However, it is much easier to create the panels within the program.

Creating the Keyboard Display Elements

A WPF program can create display elements when it runs. These can be added to the display. You have already seen this working when we create the lines during skeleton drawing. Now you are going to see how the same approach can generate some screen panels to be used as keys.

```
int noOfKeys = 13;

Brush lightKeyBrush = new SolidColorBrush(Colors.Green);
Brush darkKeyBrush = new SolidColorBrush(Colors.DarkGreen);
```

The program is going to create 13 keys and display them. It will draw alternate keys in different colors so that the player can tell each key from the next. The preceding variables set the number of keys to be drawn and the colors of the "light" and "dark" keys.

The keys will be positioned on a canvas called *KeyboardCanvas*. Each key will detect mouse events that will start and stop the MIDI note for that key. The method *createKeyboard* will be called to create the keyboard display elements and add them to the canvas. This method will be called when the program starts running. Once you have built this, you will have an input panel for any Kinect program that is to be driven by user actions.

```
private void createKeyboard( )
{
    double keyWidth = keyboardCanvas.Width / noOfKeys;
    for ( int i=0; i < noOfKeys; i++ )
    {
        // Make a new key
        TextBlock key = new TextBlock();

        // Set the key size
        key.Width = keyWidth;
        key.Height = keyWidth;

        // Make alternate keys different colors
        if (i % 2 == 0)
            key.Background = lightKeyBrush;
        else
            key.Background = darkKeyBrush;

        // Place the key on the keyboard canvas

        // tag the key with the note number

        // Connect the key to the mouse events
    }
}
```

This is the first part of the method. First the method works out the width of each key, and then it performs a loop creating the keys and adding them to the display. The keys are drawn as square areas of the screen. The program uses the % operator to work out which color to use to draw the key. The % operator gives the remainder of the value of i divided by two. This is either *1* (for an odd number) or *0* (for an even number). Even keys are drawn in the light color; odd keys are drawn in the dark color.

```
// Place the key on the keyboard canvas
keyboardCanvas.Children.Add(key);
Canvas.SetTop(key,0);
Canvas.SetLeft(key, i * keyWidth);
```

The next part of the method places the key on the display. The key is added to the canvas, and then the position on the canvas is set. The key is drawn at the very top of the display. The position across the screen is calculated by multiplying the width of the key by the loop counter for each key.

```
// tag the key with the note number - start at middle C (60) for the first note
key.Tag = 60 + i;
```

All display elements have a *Tag* property that can be used by the programmer to store information associated with that element. Each key must be associated with a particular note value. The program uses i, the loop counter, as the note value for each key. The value of i is increased by one each time around the loop to give a different note value for that key.

The final part of the setup is where the events generated by *MouseUp* and *MouseDown* events are connected to the method that will deal with them.

```
// Connect the events
key.MouseDown += new MouseButtonEventHandler(key_MouseDown);
key.MouseUp += new MouseButtonEventHandler(key_MouseUp);
```

These two statements connect the *MouseUp* and *MouseDown* events to the *EventHandler* methods.

Responding to Keyboard Events

If the player clicks on a key, the *key_MouseDown* method will run. This method must work out which note is to be played for that key.

```
void key_MouseDown(object sender, MouseButtonEventArgs e)
{
    // Conver the sender into a TextBlock
    TextBlock key = (TextBlock)sender;

    // Extract the key number from the tag
    int keyNo = (int)key.Tag;

    myMidi.SendMIDIMessage(
        0x90, // midi command - note down on channel 0
        keyNo, // note value
        100); // note velocity - how hard the note was hit (0 to 127)
}
```

When an event hander is called, it is given a parameter with the name *sender*. This is a reference to the object that has caused the event. In the case of the *key_MouseDown* method, this reference will refer to the *TextBlock* for the key that was pressed. The preceding method creates a reference of type *TextBlock* that refers to that key. It then uses the *Tag* property of that reference to obtain the key number to be played. Finally, it sends a MIDI message using the key number to select the note to be played.

This method uses quite a bit of *casting*, which is where the compiler is told that it is okay to regard a reference as being of a particular type. The *sender* parameter is supplied as an *object* reference. The program casts this into a *TextBlock* reference so that the method can use the *Tag* property that is present in a *TextBlock* but not in an object.

```
TextBlock key = (TextBlock)sender;
```

The method also uses casting to convert an object referred to by the *Tag* into an integer that can be used as a note number:

```
int keyNo = (int)key.Tag;
```

This value is used as the number of the note to be played.

Figure 11-5 shows the display produced by the program.

FIGURE 11-5 A multi-note piano.

Sample Code: Multi-Note Piano The sample project in the "02 Multi-Note Piano" directory in the resources for this chapter (see the "Code Samples" section in the Introduction) holds a program that displays a row of notes that you can press to play a piano sound via MIDI.

Playing a Proper Scale

If you have a go with the preceding sample code, you will find that the sound of the notes might not be quite what you want. Rather than playing a scale when you play each successive note, you actually get the notes increasing by a semitone at a time. This is the sequence you would get if you went up a piano keyboard and pressed each successive white or black key. It would be much nicer if the player could play a scale by pressing successive notes.

You might think that since the notes go up by a semitone each time, the program just has to play every other note. Unfortunately, because of the way that the music scale is constructed, this does not work. Some of the notes in a scale are actually just a semitone apart. If, like me, you have ever had piano lessons, then you will be used to this idea. If you are new to music theory, then don't worry about this; it is just one of the things with which the program must deal.

```
int[] cscaleNoteValues = new int[] { 0, 2, 4, 5, 7, 9, 11 };
```

The array *cscaleNoteValues* gives the "distance" in semitones down the scale of each successive note in the scale of C. The first note is C, and so that is a distance of 0 semitones. The next note is D, which is two semitones down.

```
// Find the octave which this note is part of
int octave = i / 7;
// find the note number in the octave
int note = i % 7;

// an Octave has 12 semitones in it
key.Tag = 60 + (octave*12) + cscaleNoteValues[note];
```

These statements use the *divide* and *modulus* operators to find the octave and the note that the value *i* represents. They then work out the octave and add on the offset of the note within that offset. The value of *60* is there because I want the notes to start at middle C.

> **Sample Code: Multi-Note Scale Piano** The sample project in the "03 Multi-Note Scale Piano" directory in the resources for this chapter (see the "Code Samples" section in the Introduction) holds a program that displays a row of notes that you can press to play a piano sound via MIDI. These notes play a scale.

Creating a Human MIDI Keyboard

Now that you have a scale on the screen, the next thing to do is allow the user to play the notes on it.

Figure 11-6 shows how the program will work. When the player raises the right hand into the music playback area, the keyboard plays the required note. The music program uses the skeleton drawing code that you saw in the augmented-reality game you made in Chapter 10.

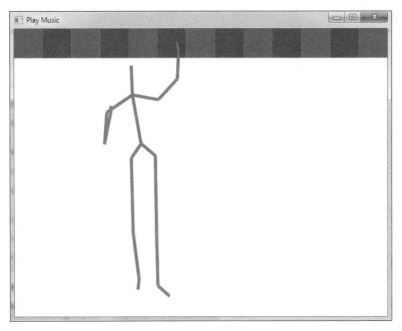

FIGURE 11-6 Playing the piano.

Creating a List of MIDI Note Keys

The program contains a list of all the keys on the screen and works through this list to find keys that the user might have selected.

```
List<TextBlock> keys = new List<TextBlock>();
```

The keys list is set up when the keyboard is created.

```
private void createKeyboard()
{
    double keyWidth = keyboardCanvas.Width / noOfKeys;

    for (int i = 0; i < noOfKeys; i++) {
        // Make a new key
        TextBlock key = new TextBlock();

        // Set the key size
        key.Width = keyWidth;
        key.Height = keyWidth;

        // Make alternate keys different colors
        if (i % 2 == 0)
            key.Background = lightKeyBrush;
```

```
    else
        key.Background = darkKeyBrush;

    // Place the key on the keyboard
    keyboardCanvas.Children.Add(key);
    Canvas.SetTop(key, 0);
    Canvas.SetBottom(key, keyWidth);
    Canvas.SetLeft(key, i * keyWidth);
    Canvas.SetRight(key, (i + 1) * keyWidth);

    // Find the octave which this note is part of
    int octave = i / 7;
    // find the note number in the octave
    int note = i % 7;

    // an Octave has 12 semitones in it
    key.Tag = 60 + (octave * 12) + cscaleNoteValues[note];

    // put the key in the list
    keys.Add(key);
    }
}
```

You have seen the *createKeyboard* method before. This one performs the same function as the previous one, but it sets up a list of keys that can be used to detect user actions. It is the code that creates the keyboard. It sets the size of the key, places it on the screen canvas, and adds it to the list of keys. The method sets the *Top, Bottom, Left,* and *Right* positions of each key area on the canvas. These are set to make it easy for the program to test if the player has touched one of the keys. The method also sets the *Tag* for each key as the note value that is to be played if that key is selected.

If you write your own program to use touch response, you could make the value of the *Tag* reflect whatever you want to use the key to do.

Controlling Note Playback

The program must check to see if the player has moved a hand inside a key area and played the appropriate note. The program must not play a note every time it finds a hand inside the play area, as this would make a note repeat if the player held a hand on the key.

```
bool notePlaying = false;
int keyNo;
```

The variable *notePlaying* is set to *true* when the music is playing. The program will not start playing a note if one is already playing. If the player moves a hand outside all the notes, the note currently playing will be switched off. The *keyNo* variable holds the note that is currently playing.

```
void updateNotes(int x, int y)
{
    foreach (TextBlock key in keys) {
        // find out if the position is in the key
        if (x < Canvas.GetLeft(key)) continue;
        if (x > Canvas.GetRight(key)) continue;
        if (y < Canvas.GetTop(key)) continue;
        if (y > Canvas.GetBottom(key)) continue;

        // if we get here the position is inside the key

        if (!notePlaying)
        {
            notePlaying = true;
            // Extract the key number from the tag
            keyNo = (int)key.Tag;
            myMidi.SendMIDIMessage(
                0x90,  // midi command - note down on channel 0
                keyNo, // note value - 60 represents middle C on the keyboard
                100);  // note velocity - how hard the note was hit (0 to 127)
        }
        return;
    }
    // if we get here the position is outside the keys
    // turn off the note
    stopNote();
}
```

The *updateNotes* method looks through all the keys for one that "contains" the location with which it was supplied. If it finds a note and the music is not playing, it constructs a MIDI message and plays it. If the position is not inside a note, the *stopNote* method is called to turn off any playing notes. The player can reach up and play the notes, and the note will play as long as the player holds a hand inside the note. When the player removes the hand from the note, it will stop playing.

The *stopNote* method stops playing the currently active note. It then clears the *notePlaying* flag so that another note can be played.

```
void stopNote()
{
    if (notePlaying)
    {
        notePlaying = false;

        myMidi.SendMIDIMessage(
            0x80,   // midi command - note up on channel 0
            keyNo,  // note value - 60 represents middle C on the keyboard
            100);   // note velocity
```

```
        }
}
```

The program uses the *stopNote* method to stop music playing. If the skeleton tracking stops working, the program will call *stopNote* to turn off the playback. This prevents the program from getting stuck playing a sound with no way to stop it.

Using the Player Position to Control Notes

The final link in the chain is to use the player position to control the music playback. When you last created the augmented-reality program, you saw that the skeleton joint positions have to be transformed to produce values that are properly aligned with the display values. The program can use the same transformation to obtain the location of the skeleton joint that will be used to control note playback.

```
void playKeyboard(Joint joint)
{
    if (joint.TrackingState != JointTrackingState.Tracked)
    {
        stopNote();
        return;
    }

    ColorImagePoint notePoint = myKinect.MapSkeletonPointToColor(
        joint.Position, ColorImageFormat.RgbResolution640x480Fps30);

    updateNotes(notePoint.X,notePoint.Y);
}
```

The *playKeyboard* method is called each time a new set of skeleton data is available. It is given the joint that is being used to "play" the keyboard. This is usually the position of the right hand, although you could create a keyboard that can be played with any part of the body. If this joint is not being tracked, the method stops the music playback and returns immediately. If the joint is being tracked, the program gets the pixel coordinate position of the joint and then calls the *updateNotes* method to update the MIDI playback based on these locations.

Sample Code: Kinect-Controlled Piano The sample project in the "04 Kinect-Controlled Piano" directory in the resources for this chapter (see the "Code Samples" section in the Introduction) holds a program that displays a row of notes that you can press by moving your right hand into the note area.

You might want to add a way for the left hand to play the lower notes. Your program could detect when the player was using the left hand to touch the note and play it an octave or two lower than the right hand. You could even make a two-player version.

Developing the MIDI Program

You can use the preceding program to make a Kinect-controlled program that can send any kind of MIDI message when the player performs a particular action. You could add keys that let the player select different MIDI voices or trigger MIDI events on connected devices.

Using the Kinect with a Serial Port

You now know how to design a display and then allow the user to interact with elements on it. The Kinect MIDI program sends MIDI messages to sound hardware, but you can also send commands to external devices such as robots by using an RS232 serial connection.

RS232 is the name given to a standard that describes how to transfer data between two computer-controlled devices. It is called a *serial protocol* because the digital bits that make up the information transferred between machines are sent one at a time down the connection that links the two devices. Before the information is sent, it is very important that the sender and the receiver agree on the format of the data and the rate at which it is transferred between them.

Older computers were fitted with RS232 serial ports. They were called COM ports on those machines as they were frequently used to connect to communication hardware such as modems. However, on more modern machines the serial ports have been replaced by Universal Serial Bus (USB) connections. These also send data serially, but they do not need to be configured in the same way as RS232 devices do. If you want to perform serial communications using RS232, you can easily obtain USB-to-serial-port adapters that plug into a USB port and provide a serial connection.

Serial Ports and Devices

Many devices can be controlled by serial ports, and lots of devices contain components that communicate using serial data. For example, the Global Positioning System (GPS) receiver in a smartphone sends location information to the phone over a serial connection that is built into the phone. The location information is sent as sequences of characters, each of which is sent along the serial data stream. Serial data was also used to connect early computers to the Internet, and the Modulator Demodulator (MODEM) that linked a computer to the phone line was controlled via a serial port.

The serial connection is usually used to implement a *protocol* between the two devices. In the case of the GPS chip inside a smartphone, the protocol sets out the format of the messages sent from the GPS receiver and how location information in each message is expressed. You are going to create a protocol that will allow a program to use a serial port to send commands to an external robot.

The protocol you are going to use will be made up of the commands *<Forward>*, *<Back>*, *<Left>*, *<Right>*, and *<Stop>*. These command messages can be used to control the movement of a robot. If you want to control a different device, you can change these commands or add new ones.

Note Each of the command messages starts with a < character and ends with a >. These are an important part of the protocol. They allow a system that is receiving commands to tell when a command message starts and ends.

The Robot Slave

The robot slave that I used is based on a platform created by GHI Electronics. You can find out more about it at the company's website:

http://www.ghielectronics.com

The robot is controlled by a FEZ Mini processor that runs the .NET Micro Framework. The sample programs are written in C# and contain customized code to drive the motors on this robot, but they can be adapted for any .NET Micro Framework–controlled robot. The robot understands the afore-mentioned commands.

FIGURE 11-7 The .NET Micro Framework robot.

The .NET Micro Framework is a platform that allows creation of C# programs that run inside small processors. The programs are written and compiled using Visual Studio 2010 and then transferred into a .NET Micro Framework device for execution. The .NET Micro Framework devices are fitted with serial ports that can receive messages from a Windows PC. The devices are also fitted with connections that allow them to transmit and receive analog and digital signals. If you wish to use your Kinect to control hardware, this would be a good way to get started.

You can find out more about the .NET Micro Framework at the following Microsoft website:

http://www.netmf.com

> **Note** If you don't wish to use the .NET Micro Framework for your robot control, you can create any device that can be connected to a serial port and made to understand the messages that the Kinect program can send out.

Linking a Kinect Program to a Serial Port

Now that you have an understanding of how data is transferred down a serial port, the basis of a command protocol, and a robot to command, you can start to write a program that allows the user to control a remote device using a Kinect.

In your programs, a serial port will be represented by a software object that exposes methods you can use to send messages to the port and read information from it. This is exactly the same mechanism that you have used with the *Kinect Runtime* class and also with the *MIDIControl* class that you have just seen. The first thing the program needs to do is create an instance of a serial port that is connected to the actual serial hardware on your PC.

> **Note** Not all computers have serial port connections. You may need to obtain a USB-to-serial-port adapter cable. These are not very expensive and do not normally require installation of any drivers on your computer. The drivers for the adapter will be installed the first time you plug it into the computer. You can find out which particular serial port the adapter provides by using Device Manager in Windows Control Panel.

Creating a Serial Port Connection

The *SerialPort* class is defined in the *System.IO.Ports* namespace. You need to add this resource to any project that uses the serial port.

```
using System.IO.Ports;
```

Once we have made the *SerialPort* class available, we can create an instance of the port. A program can call methods on this to send messages to a device on the end of the connection.

```
SerialPort robotControl;

private void setupSerial()
{
```

```
    try
    {
        robotControl = new SerialPort();
        robotControl.PortName = "COM3";
        robotControl.BaudRate = 19200;
        robotControl.StopBits = StopBits.One;
        robotControl.Parity = Parity.None;
        robotControl.DataBits = 8;
        robotControl.Open();
    }
    catch
    {
        System.Windows.MessageBox.Show("Failed to open serial port.");
        Application.Current.Shutdown();
    }
}
```

This code creates a serial port that can be used to control a .NET Micro Framework robot. The baud rate, stop bits, parity, and data bits must all be configured to match the settings of the receiving device. The PC that was running the preceding program was fitted with a serial port named COM3. You would need to find the name of the port on your machine to perform serial data transfer. A corresponding *Close* method must be used to release the hardware for use by other parts of the program.

```
private void CloseSerial()
{
    if ( robotControl != null)
        robotControl.Close();
}
```

Sending Messages to the Robot Using the Serial Port

The *SerialPort* class provides a method that will send 8-bit values (bytes) out of the serial port device. These will be received by the device on the end of the connection. The format and rate at which the data is sent are determined by the settings that were given when the port was created. The method is called *Write*, and it is supplied with a string of text to be written out of the serial port:

```
robotControl.Write("<Forward>");
```

This statement would send the message *<Forward>* to a device connected to the serial port that was just created. Of course, this would only be a sensible message to send if the device actually understood what the message meant and what to do when it was received. If you do want to use the Kinect to control devices such as these, you will have to create a protocol of your own that will allow devices to understand and act on the commands that you give them.

Creating Command Touch Areas

The MIDI music program that you created earlier mapped areas of the screen onto notes that were then played by a MIDI device. This program can be extended to create a framework for using similar gestures to send serial commands.

```
// List of the touchAreas
List<TextBlock> touchAreas = new List<TextBlock>();

void makeTouchArea(double x, double y, double width, double height,
                   Brush areaBrush, string command)
{
    // Make a new touchArea
    TextBlock touchArea = new TextBlock();

    // Set the touchArea size
    touchArea.Width = width;
    touchArea.Height = height;

    // Set the background
    touchArea.Background = areaBrush;

    // Place the touchArea on the keyboard
    touchCanvas.Children.Add(touchArea);

    // Position the touchArea
    Canvas.SetTop(touchArea, y);
    Canvas.SetBottom(touchArea, y+height);

    Canvas.SetLeft(touchArea, x);
    Canvas.SetRight(touchArea, x+width);

    // Put the command on the touchArea
    touchArea.Text = command;
    touchArea.TextAlignment = TextAlignment.Center;
    touchArea.FontSize = 15;

    // put the touchArea in the list
    touchAreas.Add(touchArea);
}
```

The preceding *makeTouchArea* method creates a touch area and displays it on a *Canvas* called *TouchCanvas*. It also adds the newly created touch area to a list of touch areas. It is supplied with the position on the screen of each area, the size of the area, the command name to be displayed on the touch area, and the brush to be used to draw the touch area.

```
Brush touchBrush = new SolidColorBrush(Colors.Green);

private void setupCommands()
{
    double keyWidth = touchCanvas.Width / 7;

    makeTouchArea((touchCanvas.Width-keyWidth)/2, 0, keyWidth, keyWidth,
                touchBrush, "Forward");
    makeTouchArea((touchCanvas.Width - keyWidth) / 2, 3*keyWidth, keyWidth,
                keyWidth, touchBrush, "Back");
    makeTouchArea(0, keyWidth, keyWidth, keyWidth, touchBrush, "Left");
    makeTouchArea(touchCanvas.Width-keyWidth, keyWidth, keyWidth, keyWidth,
                touchBrush, "Right");
    makeTouchArea((touchCanvas.Width - keyWidth) / 2, 1.5*keyWidth, keyWidth,
                keyWidth, touchBrush, "Stop");
}
```

The preceding code creates a set of touch areas on the screen containing the text of each serial command. The commands are drawn using a green brush.

Figure 11-8 shows how these touch areas will be drawn. You can change the calls of *makeTouchArea* if you want to display different commands on different parts of the screen.

FIGURE 11-8 Commands on screen.

Now that the program can draw the touch areas on the screen, the next step is to create the code that decodes the actions and sends the messages to the serial port.

```
string lastCommand = "";

void sendCommand(int x, int y)
```

```
{
    foreach (TextBlock area in touchAreas)
    {
        // find out if the position is in the touchArea
        if (x < Canvas.GetLeft(area)) continue;
        if (x > Canvas.GetRight(area)) continue;
        if (y < Canvas.GetTop(area)) continue;
        if (y > Canvas.GetBottom(area)) continue;

        // if we get here the position is inside the touchArea

        if (area.Text == lastCommand)
            // don't repeat the last command
            return;

        lastCommand = area.Text;

        sendCommand(area.Text);
    }
}
```

The *sendCommand* method is given a position on the touch canvas and looks through the list of touch areas to find one that matches. If it finds a matching area, it sends the name of that area down the serial port. The method keeps track of the previous command so that it does not repeatedly send the same command if the user keeps a hand in that area.

```
void jointCommand(Joint joint)
{
    if (joint.TrackingState != JointTrackingState.Tracked)
    {
        return;
    }

    ColorImagePoint touchPoint = myKinect.MapSkeletonPointToColor(
        joint.Position, ColorImageFormat.RgbResolution640x480Fps30);

    sendCommand(touchPoint.X, touchPoint.Y);
}
```

The *jointCommand* method determines the X and Y positions of the supplied joint and then uses *sendCommand* to check for a command at that position.

> **Sample Code: Kinect-Controlled Robot** The "05 Kinect-Controlled Robot" directory in the resources for this chapter (see the "Code Samples" section in the Introduction) holds two projects: a Kinect application that sends serial commands and a .NET Micro Framework program for a GHI robot that can respond to them. By touching the command areas on the screen, you can drive the robot around the room. It is hard work—but great fun to watch.

Receiving Messages from the Robot Using the Serial Port

A serial port can also receive messages, so it is possible for the remote robot to send status messages back to the program. A serial port can generate events when data is received from the serial port.

```
robotControl.DataReceived += new SerialDataReceivedEventHandler(robotControl_
DataReceived);
```

The preceding statement is part of the *setupSerial* method you have already seen. It connects the method *robotCotrol_DataReceived* to the event generated by the serial port when data arrives from the robot. This method takes the message and displays it on the screen.

```
void robotControl_DataReceived(object sender, SerialDataReceivedEventArgs e)
{
    Dispatcher.Invoke(new Action(() => updateResponseDisplay()));
}

private void updateResponseDisplay()
{
    string text = robotControl.ReadExisting();
    robotResponseTextBox.AppendText(text);
}
```

When the serial port receives data from the serial port, it uses the *Dispatcher* to invoke the method *updateResponseDisplay*. You have seen this technique several times now. It is how a program can run code that is able to update the screen display. In this case, the update takes the form of adding the message received from the robot to the end of the text displayed on the screen in the *robotResponseTextBox*.

If you use the program to connect to the robot-control program, you will find that the robot replies to each command with the sequence *<OK>*.

> **Note** The preceding commands can be used with the robot program, but they can also be used to control any device that responds to messages.

You might like to extend the program to allow more commands to be sent to the robot. You could also use relative joint positions, so that the robot moves when the user performs a particular action. A Windows PC can use multiple serial ports at the same time. This means that a program can control a number of different devices simultaneously.

Summary

In this chapter, you have learned a lot about data transfer and construction objects to represent connections to physical devices.

You have unpicked the MIDI protocol and seen how a program can send note messages to connected music hardware.

You have devised a mechanism that allows you to put virtual "buttons" on the screen with which a player can interact.

Finally, you have had a brief taste of serial communications and seen how a program can send commands to distant devices.

In Chapter 12, you will discover some other ways that the Kinect sensor can be used in more advanced applications.

Chapter 12

Taking Kinect Further

After completing this chapter, you will:

- Discover how a program can adjust the sensor position

- Understand how to track multiple skeletons using Kinect

- Use the Kinect microphone to locate the source of a sound

- See how Kinect can be used in robotics

- Have some ideas about what to do next

Adjusting the Sensor Angle

THE KINECT SENSOR BASE CONTAINS a small electric motor that can be used to adjust the angle of the sensor. The sensor can be adjusted up and down to allow it to have the best possible view of the scene in front of it. A program can change the angle of the sensor by altering the *ElevationAngle* property of an active Kinect sensor.

```
myKinect.ElevationAngle += 10;
```

The preceding statement would tilt the sensor up by 10 degrees.

> **Sample Code: Kinect Angle Adjust** The sample project in the "01 Kinect Angle Adjust" directory in the resources for this chapter (see the "Code Samples" section in the Introduction) holds a program that displays the view from the video camera in a sensor. The program provides Up and Down buttons that can be used to adjust the angle of the Kinect sensor.

You might like to experiment with a program that automatically aligns the sensor by using the *ClippedEdges* values described in the section "Skeleton Information Quality" in Chapter 8. If the top of the skeleton is clipped, a program could tilt the sensor up to capture more of the head.

> **Note** The Kinect SDK restricts the number of times you can adjust the elevation of the sensor bar in a particular time period. This is done to stop a program from wearing out the motor and gears in the sensor bar.

Using Kinect to Track Multiple People

Most the programs that you have written so far have had a single user. The Kinect SDK is capable of tracking two people in detail. In this section you are going to find out how a program can use the skeleton data from two people and keep track of which one is which.

When the Kinect SDK finishes analyzing a depth scene and identifying the skeletons in it, the SDK delivers a collection of skeleton data values to the program. It does this via the *SkeletonFrameReady* event. The programs that you have written until now have worked through this collection of skeleton data items looking for a set of skeleton data that is fully tracked. Until now, the programs have used the first fully tracked data that they find in the collection.

Identifying Particular People in a Scene

The Kinect can track up to six people, or "players," at the same time. Two players can be tracked in detail, with full information about the position of their skeleton joints. The Kinect will just track the position of the remaining four. When the SDK is providing this information, it is important that the program using the data can tell which skeleton belongs to which player. The Kinect software must make sure that even if the two players change their positions in front of the sensor, the program using the Kinect can still identify which player is which.

This turns out to be easy for software to do, because the Kinect SDK always puts tracking information for a particular player at the same position in the collection of skeleton data it supplies to your program. In other words, if the Kinect SDK delivers a fully tracked skeleton in location four of the skeleton collection, the information for that particular skeleton will always be in location four of the array.

```
Skeleton[] skeletons = null;

void processSkeletonFrame(SkeletonFrame frame)
{
    skeletons = new Skeleton[frame.SkeletonArrayLength];
    frame.CopySkeletonDataTo(skeletons);
    Dispatcher.Invoke(new Action(() => drawSkeletons()));
}
```

The preceding *processSkeletonFrame* method is called by a *KinectManager* instance that generates an event when new skeleton data is available. The method copies the skeleton data from the *SkeletonFrame* into the skeleton collection called skeletons and then uses the *Dispatcher* to invoke the *drawSkeletons* method to draw the contents of this collection.

```
Color[] skeletonColors = new[] { Colors.Red, Colors.Green, Colors.Blue,
                                 Colors.Yellow, Colors.Purple, Colors.Cyan};

void drawSkeletons()
{
    if (skeletons == null) return;

    skeletonCanvas.Children.Clear();

    for (int i = 0; i < 6; i++)
    {
        Skeleton skeleton = skeletons[i];

        if (skeleton.TrackingState != SkeletonTrackingState.Tracked)
            continue;
        skeletonBrush = new SolidColorBrush(skeletonColors[i]);
        drawSkeleton(skeleton);
    }
}
```

The preceding *drawSkeletons* method works through the skeleton information one element at a time using a for loop with a counter variable called *i*. Each time around the loop, the variable *skeleton* is set to the next skeleton in the collection. The Kinect SDK can track up to six skeletons and so the upper limit of the loop is set to six. In the collection of skeletons up to two of them will have the status "Tracked," and others may be "position only." The *Skeletons* collection always contains six elements, even if no skeletons are being tracked. In this situation the tracked status for every item in the array will be "NotTracked."

If the method finds a tracked skeleton at a particular position in the collection—for example, in the element with the subscript four—then this position will be used for tracking data for that player until the player moves out of the sensor range. When this happens, the data at this position will be changed to "NotTracked." If the same player walks back into the sensor range, he or she will be tracked again but might not be in the same position in the array. By storing the position where skeleton data is held for a player, a program can detect when a person walks out of the game and is replaced by someone else.

The preceding skeleton data event handler shows how a program can use the skeleton data position to select a drawing color for the skeleton. The *skeletonColors* array gives a color for each position in the array. When the event handler finds a skeleton, it draws it using the color that matches that position.

A program can't make any assumptions about the actual elements of the skeleton collection that will hold skeleton information. You might think that the first two elements in the skeleton collection would hold the two fully tracked skeletons, but this is not the case. It is perfectly possible that the fully tracked skeletons could be at the positions right at the end of the array.

> **Sample Code: Colored Skeletons** The sample project in the "02 Colored Skeletons" directory in the resources for this chapter (see the "Code Samples" section in the Introduction) holds a program that displays skeletons of tracked players in particular colors. If two people are tracked, each will be shown as a particular color, irrespective of how they move around in front of the sensor. A person who walks out of the field of view of the camera and then walks back in will probably be drawn as a different color, as that skeleton data moves to a different "slot" in the skeletons array, lining up with a different color.

Combining Skeleton and Person Depth Information

In Chapter 10, you saw how the skeleton-tracking software can tell a program which part of the depth image from the sensor corresponds to a particular player who is being tracked. You used this tracking information to mask out the image of a player from the background in the BugSplat game. Now it is time to find out how this player information is related to the "skeleton slot" information that we get for each skeleton.

Figure 12-1 shows how the player number information is combined with the depth information for each depth value. The bottom 3 bits of the value provide the number of the player corresponding to this data value. If the player number is zero, it means that this value in the depth information does not correspond to any player.

Bit 15	Bit 14	Bit 13	Bit 12	Bit 11	Bit 10	Bit 9	Bit 8	Bit 7	Bit 6	Bit 5	Bit 4	Bit 3	Bit 2	Bit 1	Bit 0
D	D	D	D	D	D	D	D	D	D	D	D	D	P	P	P
4096	2048	1024	512	256	128	64	32	16	8	4	2	0	4	2	0

16-bit depth value

FIGURE 12-1 Person information and depth values.

```
int depthValue = depthData[i] >> DepthImageFrame.PlayerIndexBitmask;
int playerNo = depthData[i] & DepthImageFrame.PlayerIndexBitmaskWidth;
```

The preceding statements will convert a depth value from the array of depth data into a player number and a depth value. The player number is split off and the depth value is shifted into position, discarding the three player number bits.

The useful thing about the player number that is obtained in this way is that it corresponds to the position in the array of the skeleton information for that player. A program can obtain the position of skeleton information for that player by subtracting one from the player number that was obtained. The subtraction is required because items in the skeleton data collection are numbered from 0 to 5, whereas player numbers in the depth data are from 1 to 6, with 0 meaning no data available. This means that a program can line up the depth data values with skeleton information.

```
if (playerNo != 0)
{
    // got a player
    // Convert to playerno in the array
    playerNo--;

    Color playerCol = skeletonColors[playerNo];
    // Blue
    depthColorImage[depthColorImagePos] = (byte)(playerCol.B / 2);
    depthColorImagePos++;
    // Green
    depthColorImage[depthColorImagePos] = (byte)(playerCol.G / 2);
    depthColorImagePos++;
    // Red
    depthColorImage[depthColorImagePos] = (byte)(playerCol.R / 2);
    depthColorImagePos++;
    // transparency
    depthColorImagePos++;
}
```

The preceding code creates a depth pixel with the same color as the skeleton that was drawn in the previous section. If the *playerNo* value is not zero, it is reduced by one and then used to index the *skeletonColors* array. The code extracts the blue, green, and red values from the selected color and then uses these to set the color of the depth pixel to that value. It divides the color values by two, so the colors will be drawn darker than the skeleton outline.

Figure 12-2 shows the effect of this code. The player has been colored using a solid color value selected from the array. The color used is green (although you probably can't tell that). This indicates that the skeleton data for this player is held in the element at the beginning of the array. The program that created the screenshot in Figure 12-2 is also drawing the skeleton on top of the image. The background color is being drawn at half the brightness of the skeleton, so that one is shown on top of the other.

Sample Code: Skeleton and Depth Data The sample project in the "03 Skeleton and Player Color" directory in the resources for this chapter (see the "Code Samples" section in the Introduction) holds a program that colors in the depth pixels and skeletons of tracked players in particular colors. The skeleton is overlaid onto darker versions of the depth pixels.

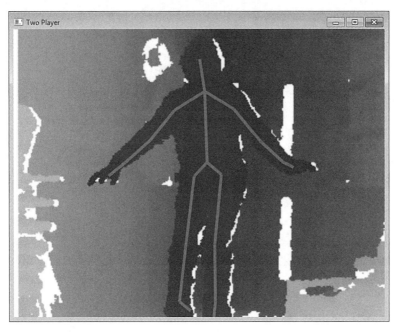

FIGURE 12-2 Coloring the active player.

Sound Location with the Kinect Microphone Array

The Kinect sensor contains four microphones arranged as a "microphone array." The signal-processing hardware in the sensor can measure the time at which parts of a sound arrive at the sensor. The sensor can use the timings to calculate the direction from which the sound is coming.

Figure 12-3 shows a drum being played in front of the Kinect sensor. The sound of the drumbeats will take longer to reach the microphones on the right side of the sensor. Signal-processing hardware in the Kinect sensor can measure this delay and then work out the angle to the sound. It can then reduce the volume of sounds that come from different directions. You used the microphone in this way in the speech recognition examples in Chapter 9. The Kinect SDK makes the angle to the sound available to your programs. The angle is provided as a value in degrees.

Figure 12-4 shows how this works. If a sound source is directly in front of the sensor, it is at an angle of 0 degrees to the sensor. If the sound moves to the left side of Figure 12-4, the angle to the sound decreases until when the sound is edge on to the sensor, at which time the angle would be –90 degrees. Moving to the right of the figure increases the angle up to a limit of 90 degrees.

FIGURE 12-3 Sound and the Kinect sensor.

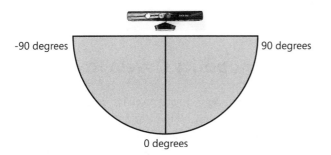

-90 degrees   90 degrees

0 degrees

FIGURE 12-4 Kinect sound angles.

When you wrote the Kinect speech recognition program, you created an instance of the *KinectAudioSource* class:

```
kinectSource = new KinectAudioSource();
```

This was used to create an audio stream that was processed by the speech recognizer. This instance can also be used to obtain the angle to the current audio source:

```
directionTextBlock.Text = kinectSource.SoundSourcePosition.ToString() + " degrees";
directionSlider.Value = kinectSource.SoundSourcePosition;
```

The two preceding statements display the sound source position. The first statement displays the text on the screen. The second uses the value to set the position of a slider control.

Figure 12-5 shows the program in action. In my experience the sensor does not return values that reflect sound source at the extremes of the range, but it is very consistent with angles that are closer to the zero position. It is certainly reliable enough to be used in a game to determine which of two players on each side of the player area is speaking.

FIGURE 12-5 Displaying the color angles.

> **Sample Code: Showing the Sound Direction of a Source** The sample project in the "04 Sound Direction" directory in the resources for this chapter (see the "Code Samples" section in the Introduction) holds a version of the speech recognition program that also displays the direction from which the speech came.

Using Kinect with the Microsoft Robotics Development Studio

The Kinect sensor is a very good way of allowing a computer to get more information about its surroundings. It can also be used to give robots a better view of the world. The Microsoft Robotics Development Studio is a complete robotic development environment. It provides all that you need to create powerful robotic systems that are made up of a large number of cooperating processes. Learning how to use it is not a trivial exercise, but it is a great way to find out about a lot of advanced computer science and robotics concepts.

Microsoft Robotics Development Studio 4.0 can be used to control a range of different robot devices, from simple ones based on LEGO Mindstorms technology to highly powerful and complex industrial devices. The software is a free download from the Microsoft Robotics website:

http://www.microsoft.com/robotics

Mobile Autonomous Reference Using Kinect

Microsoft Robotics Development Studio 4.0 also contains a specification for the **M**obile **A**utonomous **R**obot using **K**inect (MARK) platform. This is also called the Reference Platform Design. The idea is that you can create your own robot that conforms to the specification or purchase one. You can then use any software written to work on the platform.

Figure 12-6 shows what a MARK robot would look like. The design has two driving wheels at each side and castors front and rear. The robot can be made to spin on its axis or turn, depending on how the motors are driven. In addition to the Kinect sensor on top, the platform also has infrared and ultrasonic sensors along the front of the robot that can detect obstacles a short distance from the platform. The robot itself is controlled by software running in the laptop sitting on the platform. The motors and the Kinect are powered by large batteries underneath the platform.

FIGURE 12-6 A MARK robot.

Emulating a Robot Environment

Microsoft Robotics Development Studio 4.0 provides a simulated environment that allows robot builders to test their programs without doing any damage or hurting themselves. The environment includes simulation of physics, so if a robot collides with any items in the environment, it will respond in an appropriate way. You also may design or model your own environments.

Figure 12-7 shows a simulated robot in an apartment. The robot is being drawn as a 3D image that is based on the MARK design. The great thing about the robot simulator is that it can also show the view from the robot.

FIGURE 12-7 A robot in a simulated environment.

Figure 12-8 shows the view of the apartment from the Kinect sensor mounted on top of the robot. This image is provided to the robot software in exactly the same form that you have been working with, so all your Kinect programming experience can be used to process image data from the robot.

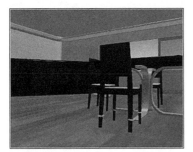

FIGURE 12-8 Kinect video camera view.

Figure 12-9 shows the view that the depth sensor has of the same scene. This makes it possible to write and test Kinect software running on the robot in the simulated environment. You can try different ideas and test the effects of different program techniques without needing any robot hardware at all. The Kinect skeleton tracking can also be used in the robot, so it could be made to recognize and follow people.

FIGURE 12-9 The Kinect depth sensor view from the robot.

Robots and Kinect in the Future

One of the big ongoing problems facing robot creators has been the difficulty of making the robot able to "see" objects around it. The Kinect depth sensor makes it possible for a robot to be much more aware of its surroundings. The Microsoft Robotics Developer Studio 4.0 platform gives a set of powerful and free tools that you can use to take ideas for Kinect-enabled robots and turn them loose. The book *Programming Microsoft Robotics Studio Developer Reference* by Sara Morgan (Microsoft Press, ISBN 9780735624320), gives a good introduction to robot programming.

Taking Kinect Further

I hope that this book has shown you how to make your Kinect work for you and how your programs can get access to the sensors and signals that the Kinect produces. The great thing about Kinect is that it provides computers with a genuinely new way to view their environment. This provides a lot of opportunity for you to come up with situations where this exciting new technology can be used. The following are a few ideas that you might like to try.

Mount the Sensor in Different Orientations

Rather than having the sensor look across a room, how about making it look down on people? You could use it to count the number of heads in a room, perhaps to stop a lift from being overloaded. You could use it to track dancers on the dance floor, causing a DJ program to try different sounds when the dance floor goes quiet, or to award the dancers prizes when they move into different patterns. You also could use it to detect when a queue is forming and perhaps call for help.

Use Multiple Sensors

The Kinect for Windows SDK can connect up to four sensors to a single PC, and a program can use all the sensors at the same time. You can use this ability in two ways. For one, you can give the computer a wider view of the area in front of it, by directing the sensors in different directions. Alternatively you could use multiple sensors to view the same scene from different angles, and so attempt to build up a 3D view of a scene. You might have to position the sensors carefully to keep the infrared projectors from different devices from interfering with each other, but this can be done.

Move the Sensor Around

You have seen that the sensor can be mounted on a mobile robot, but you could also put it on a rotating mount that could be motorized. This would allow the sensor to be scanned over an area, and perhaps generate a depth map of the space around the sensor.

Use Skeleton Tracking to Measure Things

You could use tracking information to watch people grow up. As they grow, the distance between the joints that are tracked will increase. You could use this over time to produce a profile of which bones in the body are growing fastest. You also could use skeleton tracking to measure the distance between the hands of the skeleton, so that a user could indicate required sizes just by hand spacing.

Investigate *TransformSmoothParameters*

You can configure the skeleton tracking in the Kinect SDK to perform extra processing of the skeleton data. The aim of this processing is to remove noise from the data values that will show up as jitter in the position of the skeleton joints. This will make it easier for a program to detect gestures and work out the position of a person, at the expense of extra processing that may reduce responsiveness. A program can configure the amount of smoothing and noise reduction by creating a value of type *TransferSmoothParameters* and then using this to set up the skeleton data stream. You might like to investigate the effect of various values on the behavior of the sample programs.

Use Voice Response to Do Anything

It would be very easy to make a program that simply adds up numbers that you say out loud. You could create all kinds of password programs using voice response. You could even use the directional microphone so that the password only works when you say it in one part of the room, or you could have different passwords for different parts of the room.

Have Fun Playing with Video

You have seen how much fun you can have with the Kinect camera when you average video images together. You have also seen how easy it is for a program to capture and work with sound from the Kinect microphone. You could create a program that responds to sound and changes the way that images are processed. You could make a "time lapse" camera that records an image every minute for a day.

Make More of MIDI

By adding a MIDI interface to your computer, you can enable it to control external MIDI devices. You can use this ability to trigger videos, cue music, and make yourself into a human drum kit if you like.

Good Luck and Have Fun!

I've had a lot of fun writing this book. I've had more wow moments with this little sensor bar than I've had with much more expensive toys that I've played with over time. I hope you have fun, too. Please let me know if you make anything you reckon is impressive. I'd love to hear from you!

Summary

In this chapter, you learned how to manage multiple players in a Kinect game and combine their depth image and skeleton data.

You discovered how a program can use the Kinect microphone array to track the source sound in front of the sensor.

You have also seen how Kinect is making an impact in the field of robotics, and how you can get involved.

Finally, you acquired numerous ideas that you can use to take your own Kinect experience forward.

Index

Symbols

.NET Input/Output library
    Stream class, 107
.NET Micro Framework, 220–221

A

actions, triggering with gestures, 140–143
Action type, 64
AdditionalInfo property (RecognizerInfo class), 149
Adjustable Sound Alarm sample, 119
Allow Unsafe Code checkbox (Microsoft Visual Studio), 52
alpha value of pixel data, 183
application(s), 25–40
    camera images, displaying, 35–38
    error handling, 38–39
    sensor bar, connecting to, 28–33
    sensor initialization in, 31
    sound, adding to, 72–73
    speech recognition, required libraries for, 147
    video frame, displaying, 33–38
    Visual Studio Project, creating, 25–28
    WPF image display elements, creating, 33–34
Audacity, 72
audioCaptureActive flag, 116, 117
audio data vs. video or depth data, 106
AudioSource property (KinectAudioSource type), 106–107
augmented reality, 165–198
    Bug Drawing sample, 169
    Bug Moving sample, 174
    Bug Positioning sample, 171
    Bugs and a Mallet sample, 180, 182
    BugSplat with Player Masking sample, 192
    Depth and Player Display sample, 186

    depth information and, 186–189
    display masks, using, 183–184
    Falling Bugs on a Video Image sample, 176
    Falling Bugs sample, 175
    frame rates for, 172
    game image, setting up, 190–191
    human MIDI keyboard, creating, 214–218
    Kinect-Controlled Piano sample, 218
    MapDepthToColorImagePoint method (KinectSensor class), 187–188
    player image, isolating from background, 182–191
    player pixels, finding, 184–186
    player position, using to control applications, 218
    screen/depth coordinates, matching, 176–177
    sprites. *See* sprites
averaging of images, 59–61

B

background threads, stopping, 65–66
BeamAngleMode values (Microsoft Speech Platform), 153
BGR32 (data format), 47
biometric recognition, 141
bitmap element (WPF)
    creating, 36
    rendering from canvas element, 158–159
    saving to a file, 159–160
BitmapSource object
    memory usage of, 45
    when to use, 46
Black and White Motion Detector sample, 78
BlockCopy method, 69
Body Drawing sample, 154
Body Drawing with Speech Output sample, 164
body tracking. *See* skeleton tracking
Bug Drawing sample, 169

S

About the Author

Rob Miles wrote his first computer game on the original Commodore PET in Microsoft Basic, after learning to program some time before that at school, where he began by writing his first programs on cards using a hand punch, posting them off to a distant mainframe and getting a message back two weeks later that he'd omitted a semicolon. A good many years have gone by since then. He's still omitting semicolons, but the turnaround has improved quite a bit.

Rob has been at the University of Hull in the United Kingdom for over 30 years now, moving from the Computer Center to Electronic Engineering to Computer Science, where he teaches programming (in C# of course) and software engineering, among other things. He also had a hand in quite a few industrial projects, and considers it a matter of great personal pride to be the man who wrote the software that puts the date stamps on Budweiser beer cans, as well as many other products. Rob has also been known to turn out bad verse, the highlight of this being a whole page of poetry for The Independent (a British newspaper). He is a Microsoft Most Valuable Professional (MVP) for Windows Phone and has been a judge and competition captain for the Imagine Cup Software Design Challenge for a few years.

Rob lives happily in East Yorkshire in the United Kingdom with number one wife Mary (she calls him "husband zero") and a pinball machine. His kids, David and Jenny, return every now and then so that they can play happy families properly. You can find out more about Rob's interesting times at *www.robmiles.com*.

What do you think of this book?

We want to hear from you!
To participate in a brief online survey, please visit:

microsoft.com/learning/booksurvey

Tell us how well this book meets your needs—what works effectively, and what we can do better. Your feedback will help us continually improve our books and learning resources for you.

Thank you in advance for your input!